The Selected Letters of
William Carlos Williams

By William Carlos Williams

The Autobiography of William Carlos Williams
The Build-up
Collected Earlier Poems
Collected Later Poems
The Doctor Stories
The Embodiment of Knowledge
The Farmers' Daughters
Imaginations
Interviews with William Carlos Williams
In the American Grain
In the Money
I Wanted to Write a Poem
Many Loves and Other Plays
Paterson
Pictures from Brueghel and Other Poems
A Recognizable Image: WCW on Art and Artists
Selected Essays
Selected Letters
Selected Poems
A Voyage to Pagany
White Mule
The William Carlos Williams Reader
Yes, Mrs. Williams

The Selected Letters of William Carlos Williams

Edited by John C. Thirlwall

A NEW DIRECTIONS BOOK

Copyright © 1957 by William Carlos Williams

Manufactured in the United States of America
Originally published clothbound in 1957 by McDowell, Obolensky, Inc.; first published as New Directions Paperbook 589 in 1984
Published simultaneously in Canada by Penguin Books Canada Limited

Library of Congress Cataloging in Publication Data

Williams, William Carlos, 1883–1963.
  The selected letters of William Carlos Williams.
  (A New Directions Book)
  Reprint. Originally published: New York: McDowell, Obolensky, 1957.
  1. Williams, William Carlos, 1883–1963—Correspondence.
  2. Poets, American—20th century—Correspondence.
I. Thirlwall, John C. II. Title.
PS3545.I544Z48 1984   811'.52   84-20550
ISBN 0-8112-0934-2 (pbk.)

New Directions Books are published for James Laughlin
by New Directions Publishing Corporation,
80 Eighth Avenue, New York 10011

Acknowledgments

First of all, to Florence Herman Williams, who sat with us day after day, offering pertinent and helpful information about friends and letters—and then brewed tea for us.

Secondly, to Fuji Thirlwall, who typed most of the letters and made her own canny comments thereon.

Third, to the entire world of literature and scholarship, without whose aid and encouragement such an undertaking would be impossible. Specifically to: The Lockwood Memorial Library, the University of Buffalo, Mr. Charles Abbott, Librarian, and Gene Magner, sometime Curator of Poetry. The Sterling Library of Yale University, Mr. Donald Gallup, Curator of the American Collection and to Professor Norman Holmes Pearson, who encouraged us at every step. The Houghton Library of Harvard University, William A. Jackson and Carolyn E. Jakeman. The Princeton University Library, manuscript division. The University of Chicago Library, The Harriet Monroe Modern Poetry Collection, Judith Bond, Curator. The New York Public Library, particularly the page boys who brought material to the typing room. The Library of the City College of New York, Jerome Wilcox, Librarian, and to the entire staff of the Circulation, Reference, Periodical, Accessions and Cataloguing Divisions. No librarians have been more cooperative than they. The Library of New York University, University Heights. *Golden Goose*, Sausalito, California, Richard Wirtz Emerson, editor, in which seven of these letters were first published. And to the following individuals, not all of whose letters have been used but who have cooperated wholeheartedly:

To Kenneth and Libby Burke, who lent to this task not only their letters but also their kindly wit and hospitality. To Margaret Anderson, Mary Barnard, Robert Beum, Robert Carlton Brown, Harvey Breit, E. E. Cummings, Edward and R'lene Dahlberg, Babette Deutsch, Vivienne Koch Day, Richard Eberhart, Rolf Fjelde, Charles Henri Ford, Horace and Marya Gregory, John Holmes, Josephine Herbst, Milton Hindus, Kathleen

Acknowledgments

Hoagland, David Ignatow, Viola Baxter Jordan, Matthew Josephson, Alfred Kreymborg, James Laughlin, Oswald Le Winter, Robert Lowell, David McDowell, Norman MacLeod, Louis Martz, Marianne Moore, Frank L. Moore, Merrill Moore, Gorham Munson, Ralph Nash, Dorothy Norman, Harold Norse, Georgia O'Keefe, D. D. Paige, Ezra and Dorothy Pound, Sr. Bernetta Quinn, John Crowe Ransom, Selden Rodman, Helen Russell, Srinivas Rayaprol, Robert Stallman, Charles and Musya Sheeler, the late Wallace Stevens, Dr. William Sullivan, Alva Turner, Parker Tyler, Jean Starr Untermeyer, Peter Viereck, José Garcia Villa, Henry Wells, Robert L. Wetterau, Edgar Williams, William Eric Williams, Louis and Celia Zukofsky.

And to my friends, Arthur Waldhorn and Arthur Zeiger, who read proof and gave encouragement.

To Floss and Fuji

1902

[The earliest surviving letters of WCW were written to his mother, Mrs. William George (Raquel Hélène Rose Hoheb) Williams, of whom WCW has written at length in the introduction to their translation of Quevedo's The Dog and the Fever. *After her husband's death in 1918, Mrs. Williams lived with her son until her death in 1949, at the age of 102.]*

1: TO HIS MOTHER

University of Pennsylvania
[ca. Oct., 1902]

My dear Mother: Today, Sunday, it has rained continuously. I went to church today for the first time at the Y.M.C.A., here in the college.

My first acquaintance is a young fellow about my age from Buffalo, a freshman but not in my department. He takes his meals with me and is, as far as I know, a gentleman of high morals—his name is Van Winkle and he comes here on a scholarship. Therefore, as you can judge, he is not one of the fast crowd, which is very easily distinguished by its speech as well as by its looks. Through him I met another young fellow who is a junior in the college. This last one is a very popular man here, not in athletics but in social life. He sings very well. He is also writing a book on "The famous graduates of Pennsylvania." He is a prominent figure in the Y.M.C.A. and is in every way a gentleman. Of course I don't have anything to do with him, as he is quite a big man here, but I expect through him to get into the Mask and Wig Club.

With love to you and Ed and Mrs. Dodd, I remain your loving son.

WILLIE C. WILLIAMS

2: To His Mother

My dear Mother: We have been having awful weather here. . . .
I went to the dance . . . and I certainly was glad I had a dress
suit, for every other fellow there had one. . . . I went downstairs
and was introduced to about fifteen young ladies. Of course I
asked each one for a dance and trusted to luck to determine
whether they knew how or not. . . . I had the first dance with
Miss Ecob. It was a two-step, and I got along all right but next
came a waltz. Oh, boy! I don't know who my partner was but
I do know that she can't dance the waltz. We started. At the first
step I knew something was wrong; about halfway round the
room I started to walk up the front of her dress. I descended
hurriedly and excused myself as best I could. We started again.
Pretty soon she started on a journey up my leg. This was too
much for me and I backed out. As I went upstairs for repairs I
saw her comtemplating me with a sad, disgusted look on her
face. After this I sat out all the waltzes. Not a single person there
knew how to dance a waltz. . . . After a while I began to get acquainted and just then everybody went home. My only regret is
that now I have started I may be invited to more dances and it
is either a case of refusing or finding a gold mine somewhere. I
don't like these kind of dances much, because they are too formal. The people I met are too sporty for me.

Love and kisses to you, papa, and Ed from your loving son.

WILLIE

1904

3: To His Mother

University of Pennsylvania Dormitories
Feb. 12, 1904

Dear Mama: I have head nothing about my exams as yet, but will probably hear tomorrow morning. However I have heard from the Mask and Wig. They have chosen me to try for a part in the big performance. . . .

Last night I went down in the slums of Phil. to a settlement club, as they call them, where college fellows devote their spare time to helping the little bums to learn something. I went down to fence an exhibition with the captain of last year's fencing team. I pity and admire those poor little kids. Some of them are mighty bright and quick and they know what is good and what isn't. One thing I am convinced more and more is true and that is this: the only way to be truly happy is to make others happy. When you realize that and take advantage of the fact, everything is made perfect. . . .

Demuth, that fellow who is studying art here, has invited me to a dance at his school[1] on Saturday evening. I am to take a girl whom I have never seen, but who is very nice nevertheless. . . .

As to muscular exercise, I have an exercising machine in my room and I use it every night before going to bed. Dancing is all the exercise my legs need, to say nothing of fencing. . . .

Au revoir, with lots of love and kisses to you all.

Your loving son,
WILLIE

---

[1] Drexel Institute.

4: To His Mother

U. of P. Dorms
3/30/04

Dear Mama: The reason I didn't write last Sunday was because I was out of town. My friend Pound invited me to spend Saturday and Sunday with him, so on Friday I wrote to you and then set off on my trip. . . . His parents are very nice people and have always been exceptionally kind to me. Mrs. Pound had prepared a fine meal. . . . After supper Pound and I went to his room where we had a long talk on subjects that I love yet have not time to study and which he is making a life work of. That is literature, and the drama and the classics, also a little philosophy. He, Pound, is a fine fellow; he is the essence of optimism and has a cast-iron faith that is something to admire. If he ever does get blue nobody knows it, so he is just the man for me. But not one person in a thousand likes him, and a great many people detest him and why? Because he is so darned full of conceits and affectation. He is really a brilliant talker and thinker but delights in making himself just exactly what he is not: a laughing boor. His friends must be all patience in order to find him out and even then you must not let him know it, for he will immediately put on some artificial mood and be really unbearable. It is too bad, for he loves to be liked, yet there is some quality in him which makes him too proud to try to please people. I am sure his only fault is an exaggeration of a trait that in itself is good and in every way admirable. He is afraid of being taken in if he trusts his really tender heart to mercies of a cruel crowd and so keeps it hidden and trusts no one. Oh, what a common fault it is—this false pride. True faith is that which dares all and gains love in the daring but there is much truth in his position after all.

Well, that is about the tone of our conversation. At twelve we went to bed where I slept, oh so well. The bed was big and soft and warm . . . next morning we arose at our leisure and then talked, ate, read, sang, walked in the country, but principally rested with our feet before a big fire or rather a little one.

WILLIE

5: To His Mother

U. of P. Dorms
Nov. 8, 1904

My dear Mother: It seems to me that you and Papa need advice, not me. This sounds funny but still judge it coldly. You have told me lots of things that made me feel awfully bad and taken lots of things for granted that I never dreamed of till you spoke to me of them. . . . I know I am almost always wrong, but still, Mama, give me credit for just a little judgment. You and Papa seem to think that I am always doing just what I shouldn't do. . . . When I am most happy to think I am doing right I am probably doing the worst thing possible. Why, I begin to believe I have no power to reason at all, for as soon as I arrive at a conclusion I am advised to do the opposite and what can I do?

Still I want you to believe these few statements once for all; although I have made them time and time again, you don't seem to believe them or you forget them or something.

First, that I never did and never will do a premeditated bad deed in my life. Also that I never have had and never will have anything but the purest and highest and best thoughts about you and Papa, and that if anybody ever says a word contrary to your wishes or high ideals I never fail to fight them to a standstill. . . . I have always tried to do all that you and Papa wished me to do and many times I have done things against my own feelings and convictions because you wanted me to. . . . Still, Mama dear, I know you are right and I am wrong. Don't think I blame you, for a second; I don't, but feelings will come.

This may sound harsh but I do not mean it to be so. I try to do right and then I am blamed for doing wrong and really it is hard to be happy then. . . .

Well, love to you all; good-bye till Thanksgiving.

Your loving son,
WILLIE

1905

[*Edgar I. Williams, junior by one year to his brother, was very close to all the members·of the family. His bent, it turned out, was architecture; and after graduating from M.I.T., he studied in Europe under a Prix de Rome. He still lives in the house in Rutherford in which he was born.*]

6: To Edgar I. Williams

University of Pennsylvania Dormitories
318 Joseph Leidy
Wednesday, April 12, '05

Dear Ed: I haven't written sooner simply because life has been too strenuous for me to find time for it. Say, Bo, talk about Phila. being slow, well I can't see it.

Last Monday night I was invited out to take supper with a fellow who used to be at Penn but now goes to a little college way up in New York State.[1] We were good friends and he certainly treats me great whenever he is at home. He had five fellows to supper and five girls and at last I have met some dandy ladies. They're a deuced of an intellectual bunch, daughters of professors, doctors, etc., but they are fine. Not one is good looking, I mean pretty, but they are all pleasant to look upon because they are so nice. One in particular struck me. She is tall, about as tall as I am, young, about eighteen and, well, not round and willowy, but rather bony, no that doesn't express it, just a little clumsy but all to the mustard. She is a girl that's full of fun, bright, but never telling you all she knows, doesn't care if her hair is a little mussed, and wears good solid shoes. She is frank and loves music and flowers and I got along with her pretty well. Now can you see what she's like? Anyway, she is the daughter

---

[1] Ezra Pound; the college is Hamilton.

8

of the professor of astronomy at U. of P. and lives out in the country on the grounds where the observatory is.[2]

After the party I was invited to go to her house on the following Saturday, and of course I accepted, not knowing what to expect. I went with the fellow that introduced me to her and— well judge for yourself whether I had a good time or not by the following.

We got to her house at three o'clock and found a party, we included, of eight girls and eight fellows all in their old clothes; these people never dress up, which is slick, I mean hardly ever.

Then I learned we were going for a walk. The day was perfect, the girls had on short skirts, to their ankles I mean, and sweaters and no hats and most of the fellows left their hats behind also.

Away we went, despising road and paths, right across fields on the run just like a game of hare & hounds. It was great. We went over fields, through woods, climbed fences, jumped streams, and laughed and talked till everyone simply had to get into the game. Well, this lasted hours, then Miss Doolittle, that's her name, found some flowers and sat down beside them to protect them from the rest of the party. I sat down beside her and the rest passed on. We began talking of flowers, when she said she knew a place where hepaticas grew so thick the ground was blue with them. I said I would like to see it, and we being at the tail end of the crowd turned aside and went into the woods. Needless to say we lost the crowd and had a great two hours walk by ourselves. Oh, Ed, but she is a fine girl, no simple nonsense about her, no false modesty and all that, she is absolutely free and innocent. We talked of the finest things: of Shakespeare, of flowers, trees, books, & pictures and meanwhile climbed fences and walked through woods and climbed little hills till it began to grow just dusky when we arrived at our destination. We had by this time, as you imagine, gotten pretty well acquainted. She said I was Rosalind in *As You Like It* and she was Celia, so I called her that, although her real name is Hilda.

The evening was spent at the house of another of the girls who lives out in the country also. We had a great time singing

---

[2] H. D.

and dancing and, by the way, I have a reputation as a songster which is spreading rapidly. I got home at twelve, covered with some mud, a little glory and oceans of a fine comfortable happy feeling inside of me somewhere. I am going to call some day, perhaps.

Now for other news. The Mask and Wig performance is well on its way to a successful season, I think. The songs and dances are at last down to the queen's taste, and I think the show will be good. As you will see by a paper I am sending you, I am still in it. Of course you will be on the team this summer if you want to, why, gee whiz, you are the main gazabo. I may not get on, but as to you there is no doubt about it—but you will be on. I have had a great picture taken of myself which I will send to you as soon as I get it. Go in for the "Tech show," it's fun.

Lots of love from

Your only brother,

BILL

1906

U. of P. Dorms
Jan. 14, 1906

Dear Ed: Don't think I am a mucker when I don't write to you for a long time, the simple reason for it is that I have so much to do that really I cannot find an opportunity in which to sit down and wield my pen. The work, while it is not getting any harder, is getting intensely interesting as we near the finish, and I tell you a fellow just can't help studying as long as he can keep his eyes open.

However I have dissipated a little on several occasions and last Friday night was one of them. I went out to call on Miss Doolittle and then took her to the preliminary performance given by the Mask and Wig Club for the fellows who are trying for the big production. The show was great, but the best part of it all was that I met one of the most sensible and generally likable, beautiful girls I have seen in a long time. She is of French descent and a college graduate, which is a combination hard to beat. She has learned to moderate her natural French vivacity, while that same vivacity has kept her from being dull and pedantic. She is the first girl into whose eyes I have looked and forgotten everything around me. My, but she has fine eyes. I came home feeling sort of funny, so I sat down and wrote a sonnet to her brown eyes. Isn't that fierce? I guess you think I'm pretty badly off, but I'm not. Just the same, Ed, she is a beautiful girl and no mistake. Here is the gem she inspired. How do you like it?

> Last night I sat within a blazing hall
> And drank of bliss from out a maiden's eyes.
> The jeweled guests passed by as forms that rise
> The charm in dreams the sleepy night for all
> Sped nameless on, no face can I recall.

Those eyes, those eyes, my love entombed lies
In their deep depths beyond recalling cries,
As lost as rings adown a well that fall
What wondrous phantoms there I saw asleep
Of joyful springs and prophecies untold
Laugh-filled tomorrows which some lover bold
Shall free from magic and their slumber deep.
'Twas o'er too soon, she fled with sudden sweep,
Or has she waked? The next look shall unfold

Is it any good? I like it very well, but of course that may be the
false pride of a father in his sickly baby.

Well, Ed, I am going to church, so I will say ta ta. Don't think
that I'm in love or anything foolish; the truth is I am working
like a blooming truckhorse. My *Carthaginia est delenda* shall be
"Get that prize."

Your loving brother,
BILL

8: TO EDGAR WILLIAMS

*Univ. of Penn. Dorms
March 11, 1906*

Dear Ed: Your last is what I call a letter. That is something like.
I am mighty glad you had such a fine old time out at Wellesley,
but it certainly is a shame that such distressing formality must
still be gone through with at what may be called a very center
of polite learning.

As to the criticisms of "Arlo,"[1] I appreciate it. In so far as he
agrees with me do I consider him a very just and learned man;
when he disagrees, why, of course one of us must be wrong and
I being right he is "it," therefore neither just nor learned. But
Ed, that is written allegretto tempo di Mazurka, so don't let your
thoughts run to largo.

---

[1] Prof. Bates of M.I.T. had read and disapproved of some poetic
effusions of WCW.

Last Saturday afternoon, the day being glorious though the
ground was soggy, I hied me away to the abode of Miss Hilda
Doolittle, bent upon taking a walk through the country. She
was at home, as luck would have it, and besides, for luck was
with me again, was anxious for a walk. Just as we were about
to start I saw someone go into the observatory. This reminded
me that of all the many times I had been out to see Miss Doolittle I had never seen the inside of the place. I mentioned the
fact to Hilda, I call her Hilda now, and she replied, "Gather ye
rosebuds while ye may." So accordingly we went on a tour of
inspection. I tell you that those great instruments are truly
wonderful. From one marvel I went to another with open mouth
and never before have I been so conscious of my own appalling
ignorance. There were clocks that never varied more than an
eighth of a second in a hundred years, instruments with dials,
instruments with levers and other instruments nameless to me,
but each a paragon of accuracy. After this tour of inspection we
set out for a walk, and finally ending up at Miss Sniveleys, spent
the evening much as we did the time you were here. By the way,
I have invited Miss S. to our big senior dance at the end of the
year, so be ready to ship me five bones if necessary. Today I have
heard that the exams for the French Hospital are to be held on
April 20, so I'm off at last with the finish in sight. I hope I make
good.

With lots of love,
BROTHER BILL

9: TO EDGAR I. WILLIAMS

French Hospital
450 West 34th St.
New York City
Nov. 12, 1906

Dear Ed: You wonder why all this is so. Perhaps I do not know
myself, but here at least you find a partial answer. I am not even
remotely cynical. The truth is I am troubled with dreams, dreams

that merely to mention is too daring, yet I'll tell you that any man can do anything he will if he persists in daring to follow his dreams. To do what I mean to do and to be what I must be in order to satisfy my own self I must discipline my affections, and until a fit opportunity affords, like no one in particular except you, Ed, and my nearest family. From nature, Ed, I have a weakness wherever passion is concerned. No matter how well I may reason and no matter how clearly I can see the terrible results of yielding up to desire, if certain conditions are present I might as well never have arrived at a consecutive conclusion for good in all my life, for I cannot control myself. As a result, in order to preserve myself as I must, girls cannot be my friends. If I am foolish to aspire above my ability why let me be disappointed, but till now nothing has frightened me. I have seen men failing because they began poorly; I will not begin so. If a man fail in attempts too great for him he is a better man than the whimpering weakling who is frightened away by obstacles. At home the people are in general small; they see their little neighborhood. I have seen that, I have seen the world and love to contemplate and, in all humbleness of mind, wonder at even greater things. For that reason I have little interest in the people I have known. Pardon me, Ed, if you think I am a boaster.

Lots of love from,

BILL

1909

Promenadin Str. #431, Leipzig
Aug. 11, 1909

Dear Ed: You are four kinds of a lobster not to have written me
ages ago so that I would have received your letter on arriving at
Leipzig. You can also give my compliments to the Hermans in
general and to Florence in particular and tell them and her that
if they are or she, in particular, is ever in a foreign country alone
without knowing the language or without having a soul to talk
to, I say that if ever they are or she is overtaken by such a ca-
tastrophe I hope that they or she may find many letters from
home awaiting their arrival so that no feelings such as I have
experienced may have occasion to arise. As for you, I will take
revenge merely by using some of this bum writing paper on you
which I have just gotten stuck on. . . .

Now into the fray! I have sent a couple of letters to Mamma
and Pop giving certain details of my trip and I will send others
to complete the tale in time. I will not go into a further account
with you. Instead I'm just going to rattle off a few odd pictures
and impressions to you more or less at random.

Of England naturally I saw little, but as luck would have it we
had wonderful weather on the Channel with most wonderful
J. M. W. Turner skies—you know the kind with little white frost-
like fingers pointing at all angles for a background and then a few
heavy flocculent masses like big ships floating slowly over them.
Around the horizon was a transparent sunny-looking mist through
which the shore shone almost fairy-like, it was so silent, so dim and
yet so green and white and beautiful. Around us the water had
changed from blue to a pale opaque green and it was quite still.
There were fishing boats all about with sienna-colored sails, some
flying the French flag, which looked strange and very beautiful
also. It is peculiar to see so many boats of so many nations all

15

jumbled into one body of water. Then there were British men-of-war everywhere; we seemed to be running past them continually. At first I was surprised at this but later I heard that there had just been a big review at Cowes, I think, which explained the incident.

On arriving at Antwerp, of course, French is spoken, so I had little trouble but I made one mistake and that was to go to a cheap hotel. The only reason I did it was because the cattle men who had been to Antwerp before recommended it. However I am glad now I went, for I would not have missed the experience for the world.

There were in all twelve of us, I think, not more at any rate. The hotel is in an old part of the town and as we sat around the long table with the ancient cathedral showing through the window the effect was odd, to say the least.

At first the whole conversation hinged on how cheap everything is in Europe and this is very true, but later on it struck the usual "stag" tone when the topic of street closets came up. It was the funniest thing in the world to hear these fellows talk of these places and without a doubt there are so many of these little conveniences about that no fellow could help noticing it and they are so open—*ach Gott es ist frecklich!* Two of the bright remarks made were: "These people only wear clothes to keep themselves warm," and on account of the frequency of the above-mentioned places and salons or cafés: "They seem to do nothing but drink," which is true. In the midst of all our hilarity there entered an old or rather middle-aged man with a peculiar perforated tin horn which he held up in front of his mouth and then he began to sing. Once he must have had a voice but now, as one of the fellows said, he was all "shot to pieces." Still he could sing. It was a remarkable sight. Here he was, the very essence of the old world spirit, run down, the wreck of the artistic spirit, one might say the refuse of art, failure written all over him and sadness and even desperation in every line of his face, a figure absolutely not to be understood by our Americans and here he had come, Lord knows from where, in the midst of this young, ignorant but enterprising New World spirit full of the strength of abundant resource and opportunity not unmixed with contempt for old forms and the unpractical in art. The effect was dramatic in the extreme and a truly remarkable incident. It was absolutely fascinating for me to watch the play of feelings and forces and to read the contempt on both sides. There stood the old man, dirty, baggy at the knees, with his horn to his mouth and his hat held I don't know how, his eyes staring down sad and far away and singing the old, old songs of the Italian operas with such feeling that sometimes I even thought his color changed. He sang with all the consummacy of an artist, but his voice— Then around the table were the Americans, flunks from colleges, educated bums, football players, at least one famous athlete, three men who are going to teach in Constantinople, and myself.

There we sat around the table, smoking, laughing, talking while the old fellow sang. The effect was absolutely to be predicted. Most of the fellows yelled "Rotten, Rotten! Take it away!" or "Beat it!" Finally someone threw an empty match box and hit the old fellow. This made him mad and he yelled in French *"Pas de blague, eh!"* or "I'll take this knife (pointing to one on the table) and cut your throat!" No one understood him but I, so they only laughed. Then he passed around his hat cursing them all under his breath, but oh that miserable money! I could see how he needed it and how he hated those who gave it. How easily one can be debased and how futile is pride and how low one can humble oneself for money, money, money—it is the crying need here. I tried to thank the old fellow as he passed me, but he went out. I have dwelt on this a long time and perhaps tired you but it was such an odd scene it will not leave my mind.

In Leipzig I have had a funny time. The men dress like hell, the women worse. The men are all narrow in the shoulders, wear derbies, or straw hats with narrow brims and high crowns, carry canes, wear shoes two feet long, narrow trousers and, as I said, look fierce. The women have feet proportionate with the men and as to style, well, I haven't seen many yet but their bodies look like their clothes—they certainly must be wonders when they are naked. They seem made to be mothers, strong, able to work, broad in the hips—this particularly—and they have kind intelligent faces. I tell you this is the country for "doing not seeming." It is a woman's business here to keep house and be a mother and they show it to beat the band, but I must say I don't like to see a girl eighteen years old with a "corporation" big enough for a baby to sit on.

The houses are well built but poorer than New York houses. In fact everything is cheaper looking in every way than in New York. This fact bothered me a lot at first. In New York the rich people own the place, that is, all the best things are for the rich, but here the middle class runs things. That is, suppose all the people of about our means in New York were to get together and say we are going to have theaters in which we can afford to buy orchestra seats twice a week, etc. The same with restaurants and, in fact, all public establishments—then you would have about the "speed" of Leipzig. It bothered me because I thought I was "getting in wrong," but this is not the case or it doesn't seem so as yet.

Next come the beer gardens. These are everywhere, in every corner and at every corner and mostly out of doors. Go to Karlstadt and you will get the true spirit. It is absolutely misunderstood in U. S., and I myself never understood it, but I see now how identical is the East Rutherford spirit with the sub-middle-class German spirit. These beer gardens are the center of every activity and festivity. The German art is quite ponderous but it is founded on German thought and independence. It is solid and good but often there comes out a monstrosity.

The whole life here is a picture of economy, specialization, long hard systematized work and a quiet perseverence. I do not admire the types I have seen so far and I do not think the people as a nation are gifted with inspiration. They are plodders and home lovers and beer lovers. Also they are thinkers and I may on this account like them better later, but oh, they lack spontaneity or something akin to innocence and joyousness. Their delight is to sit in a restaurant, under the trees, perhaps but nevertheless to sit and drink beer; they seem material to me. The young men are one lump of vanity. They make me sick. The girls are better in the eyes but worse in the waists and their feet—Bo, this country is worn out. It is hedged in by enemies, you can feel it in your bones. They fear France and England, and how do they hope to overcome this fear? By faith in the ultimate brotherhood of man which will break down all barriers and countries? No, but by an army to crush and kill. This is Germany in my inexperienced eyes.

Give me my country where there is water to drink and freedom such as they only dream of here. You can say what you want about rotten politics but it's rotten because I want it rotten but when I want it clean it will be clean, but here only bloodshed can wipe out tyranny. There is all the difference in the world between the two.

Good-bye, Bo, I hope this stuff is legible and interests you.

Your loving brother,
BILLIE

Please tell Pop to send me a few copies of my verses, *bitte*.

1910

[Viola Baxter (later Mrs. Virgil Jordan) was young, beautiful and witty when Ezra Pound suggested that Williams make her acquaintance in New York, where he was interning at the French Hospital in 1907. He did call, under rather distressing circumstances, but retrieved the situation by asking her to the Columbia-Pennsylvania basketball game. Fifty years later, like Ezra Pound, Mrs. Jordan is still a good friend of Williams.]

11: To Viola Baxter Jordan

Leipzig of course! Naturally.
Emilienstr. 34
Jan. 23, 1910

Dear Viola: There is something magical about you and yet not entirely fairy-like. It riles me and, frankly, makes me think more of imps than angels, but even here you have no exact counterpart.

First, though, I should humbly beg once again for forgiveness. My recent behavior was gross ungentlemanliness and only thru your kindness and consideration have I any right to address you at all. I once again acknowledge my fault and in again seeking your friendship I am forced to say that this little affair has all come about thru my own vanity, which you, dear lady, burst as neatly as ever child did soap bubble.

From henceforth let the dead past bury its dead. I am in Germany; "how peculiar," you say, and trying to study, again you remark, this time, "how unusual," but it remains a fact, even if you don't agree with Darwin's *Descent of Man*. Wasn't that the book?

You see, I have always thought the Germans were on a totally false path and so I have come over here to prove it to myself and, remarkable to relate, I have succeeded.

There is no more purity of inspiration in this land than there are milk teeth in the jaws of a white-haired coon. These people have the spontaneity of a freight train, and although much that they accomplish is altogether necessary and worthwhile, the greater part of their beauty is of the theoretically correct variety which is bred only by a crass, unsympathetic egotism.

You see, I do not like the Germans and yet I must admire them, and this is the burden of my song which here comes to an end.

If you care to write me before Feb. 16 do so, I leave here in March.

Sincerely yours,

BILLIE

1912

12: To Viola Baxter Jordan

131 W. Passaic Ave., Rutherford, N. J.
May! May! May! [*1912*]

Viola, the dearest: And nothing else or I refuse to jump—hem or no hem to kiss.

I once told "the beloved likeness" that I would lose my soul to marry you. She remarked that it would be a calamity. I wonder which she meant? Jealous of course.

My sympathy for movers, but the blue-bogged cat is good.

The violin is more than a relic to me, it is a warning, therefore I keep it. With grovellings,

WILLIAM

Erminie is not yet but will be soon. I will have the *Times* flashlight turned to the north if it is a success.

Let me be serious.

> Belovéd you are
> Caviar of Caviar
> Of all I love you best
> O my Japanese bird nest
>
> No herring from Norway
> Can touch you for flavor. Nay
> Pimento itself
> Is flat as an empty shelf
> When compared to your piquancy
>   O quince of my despondency.

WILLIAM

1913

[Harriet Monroe, a leading figure in the Chicago literary renascence, launched Poetry: A Magazine of Verse *in 1912, with a subsidy from one hundred patrons. Conservative herself in poetry, under the goadings of Pound, her European correspondent, and Williams, she opened the pages of her magazine to much new and experimental talent. She acknowledged Williams' influence by including one of his letters in* A Poet's Life, *her autobiography.]*

13: To Harriet Monroe

131 W. Passaic Ave., Rutherford, N. J.
March 5, 1913

My dear Miss Monroe: Your courteous letter startles me—not merely because you return with it two of my poems, truly. I shall take up the suggestions it contains, but I cannot resist the pleasure first of expostulating with you a moment.

I had looked upon *Poetry* as a forum wherein competent poets might speak freely, uncensored by any standard of rules. *Poetry* seemed to me a protest against the attitude of every other periodical American publication in this respect.

I am startled to see that you are fast gravitating to the usual editorial position, and I am startled to feel that perhaps this is inevitable: that as soon as one says, "I am an editor!" he, having been in the march of the poets, faces about upon them.

I mean that perhaps it is a law that between the producer and the exposer of verse there must inevitably exist a contest. The poet comes forward assailing the trite and the established, while the editor is to shear off all roughness and extravagance. It startled me when I realized that this is perhaps inevitable.

Now, that was not my view of the function of *Poetry* at all. My notion was dependent on this: most current verse is dead from the point of view of art (I enclose some doggerel showing one of the reasons why). Now life is above all things else at any moment

subversive of life as it was the moment before—always new, irregular. Verse to be alive must have infused into it something of
the same order, some tincture of disestablishment, something in
the nature of an impalpable revolution, an ethereal reversal, let
me say. I am speaking of modern verse.

Poetry I saw accepting verse of this kind: that is, verse with perhaps nothing else in it but life—this alone, regardless of possible
imperfections, for no new thing comes through perfect. In the
same way the Impressionists had to be accepted for the sake of
art's very life—in spite of bad drawing.

I do not assail you because you fail to praise my exquisite productions but—in perfect good humor—I find fault with your expressed attitude toward my exquisite productions.

Perhaps I am more than ever obscure.

Why doubt that the reader will see the stars in "Peace on
Earth," when you saw them? Yet to capitalize as you suggest is
good: please do so. Isn't the art of writing titles, as all art is, a
matter of concrete indirections made as they are in order to leave
the way clear for a distinct imaginative picture? To directly de-
note the content of a piece is, to my mind, to put an obstacle of
words in the way of the picture. Isn't it better in imaginative work
to imply war in heaven, for instance, by saying, "Peace on Earth,"
than it would be to say it flat out, "War in Heaven"?

Your suggestion: "The Immortal," is better than simply "Ignorance"; it is also permissible in the place of "Proof of Immortal-
ity," but not so amusing. Do as you please in this case.

As to the meter in the above-named piece, if you wish to judge it
as a fixed iambic measure you are dogmatically right as to the disturbing fourth and sixth lines; but why not call it some other kind
of a measure?

Surely if Yeats teaches anything that can be learnt—that is, anything that it would not be copying to take to one's self—he teaches
what can be done with the three-syllable foot by dropping the last
syllable in the foot every time but once or twice in the entire poem.
Witness "The Mountain Tomb" in your own *Poetry*.

As to "Postlude," it is perhaps hyper-digested to the point of
unintelligibility, but to me it seems that there is so much of an
escape from the tiresome rehashings of optimism and its equiv-

alent in rhythmics that from pure love of humanity it might have
been forgiven its few bumps and bruises.

I'm afraid I am open to the accusation of being out of touch
with my public—that's isolation—I know my trend—but if *Poetry*
does not open freely to me, in my absolute egoism, how am I to
grow?

It's the new seed, the one little new seed that counts in the end:
that will ultimately cover fields with vigorous growth. My idea of
Poetry was that it must find this new seed, just as Burbank seeks
and finds the new seed that is to grow his thornless cactus—pardon
the moral.

Anyhow, I'm a great poet, and you don't think so, and there we
are, and so allow me to send you a revised "Postlude" (when it is
done), hoping to gain your good favor in that way—for I must
succeed you know.

> Faithfully yours,
> WILLIAM C. WILLIAMS

I must not forget to thank you for the acceptance of the three
poems which you have accepted; I do so now and hope to have
the pleasure of pleasing you again as soon as possible.

> W. WILLIAMS

14: To HARRIET MONROE

> *9 Ridge Road, Rutherford, N. J.*
> *Oct. 10, 1913*

My dear Miss Monroe: How a thing can be hammered out until it
is first perceived is beyond me—but if your editorial judgment is
correct—patience.

To me, what is woefully lacking in our verse and in our criticism is not hammered-out stuff but stuff to be hammered out. A
free forum, there is the need, which asks only, "Is it new, interesting?" I should think, even, that at times you would be concerned
lest you get nothing but that which is hammered and worked out
—except when the divine Ezra bludgeons you into it.

France is France; we are not France. Would you not rather have anticipated a Lincoln than acclaimed a McMahon?

Figure me, of course, the Lincoln.

Sincerely yours,
W. WILLIAMS

15: TO HARRIET MONROE

Oct. 14, 1913

My dear Miss Monroe: To tell the truth, I myself never quite feel that I know what I am talking about—if I did, and when I do, the thing written seems nothing to me. However, what I do write and allow to survive I always feel is mighty worth while and that nobody else has ever come as near as I have to the thing I have intimated if not expressed. To me it's a matter of first understanding that which may not yet be put to words. I might add more but to no purpose. In a sense, I must express myself, you're right, but always completely incomplete if that means anything.

But—by the gods of exchange—"the divine"[1]—shall be greeted and the words presented to him for the acid test.

I'll surely let you know what he writes—that is, provided he writes anything.

I once sent him one other epoch-making article; this, in sum, was his answer: "It has arrived! Here and there I *do* get a glimpse of a meaning, you do seem to have something to say, Bill, even if you don't say it."

Whether it bears you out or whether it bears me out I don't know.

May enlightenment come upon both of us in the days hereafter.

Sincerely yours,
W. C. WILLIAMS

---

[1] Ezra Pound.

1914

16: To Viola Baxter Jordan

Jan. 1, 1914

Liebes Veilchen: A letter from Ezra—he tells of a sojourn in Sussex with W. B. Yeats—praises me—tells me I am a Catullus—tells me to subscribe to *The New Freewoman,* the organ of his "gang"—says Gwen should be in London—says he has discovered *the* coming sculptor, a Russian, Gaudier-Brzeska. It is a male. Tells me of a publisher who should do my American edishun—*Tempers* plus new masterpieces, better & fuller—this same pub. is doing Ezra's anthology of *Les Jeunes*[1]—I am in it—Wants me to go to England in the spring—perhaps. À la steerage!!!

Thanks for—but my wife has you down for a note.

No, the baby has not appeared. Flossie is more or less disgusted and more than less uncomfortable. It really is quite hard on her, poor kid.

Well, the top o' the season to you all—may the Gods carry you lightly.

Yours,
Billie[2]

17: To Harriet Monroe

May 22, 1914

My dear Miss Monroe: Certainly I can work for any imaginable period at the work I choose without the encouragement of recognition—but actually to have work of mine prove valuable to your purposes or to another's—doubles all my brilliances.

Not that alone—good, bad or stupid, what I have done clings

---

[1] *Des Imagistes.*
[2] This is the first but not the last letter to mirror Pound's eccentric spelling and punctuation.

to me horribly until someone relieves me by ridicule, praise or any positive action. *Poetry* cuts the rope between the ox and his dung. Pardon the coarse allusion.

As my brother once told me of Rembrandt: a saying of his I believe: "It takes two men to paint a picture: one to put on the paint and one to cut off the other's hands when it (the picture) is finished." *Poetry* accomplishes the equivalent of this when it rescues a verse from me, or better—me from my verse, etc.

I respect your choice of the 3 out of 6 & listen with attention to your remarks. In "The Shadow"—line 3 "so soft, so smooth &
"so soft, etc.——& so *cool*"
so as to avoid repetition of "dark" which occurs again in the last line.

In "Sub Terra"—line 8
"Subtly as *upon* a bush in May"
is better thus:
"Subtly as *on* a bush," etc.
Many thanks.

Yours,
W. C. WILLIAMS

1915

May 8, 1915

Dear Miss Monroe: The check for 35 dollars rec'd and spent—.
. . . but isn't there 10 dollars coming to me or have you reduced
your rates?

It's not the money—oh, of course not!—only, you see, I was
thinking of endowing some young poet.

Will you kindly explain my mistake to me.

You know, there are people who find E. P. chiefly notable as a
target—and yet they cannot perceive his greatness. Take, for instance, Mr. Peoria Oshkosh, or whatever his name was, who
claimed to be so astounded at dear Ezra's unversial knowledge.[1]
Is it any more wonderful, this knowledge of our Ezrie's, than that
of any 1,000 passable students of chemistry picked out at random
over the earth's surface—you cannot make fools of these men in
their line by quoting some chemist who happens not to be a near
neighbor. The minds of men in any profession, including poetry,
meet at a certain plane, above which the greatest have not advanced. Here knowledge knows neither place, time nor nationality.

"Damn"—is it a crime to know anything!

I perceive, however, that it is knowledge and not E. P. that is so
hated—the confusion is, of course, inevitable under the circumstances.

Would it make any difference to a geologist—or to the world
either—whether or not it was China, Oklahoma, Yucatan or
Chile in which he had found the sapphire? These students—these
students get so picky about their knowledge that sometimes one
despairs of satisfying them!

KINDLY INFORM OUR FRIEND THAT I DO NOT—AS HE DOES—BELIEVE
THAT POUND KNOWS EVERYTHING.

And as to this matter of what shall and what shall not go into

---

[1] In a letter to *Poetry*.

a line, let him try to line off some of his work according to the sense of the meter—for you have misrepresented the Imagists: meter is the essential and not merely cadence—let him try! Ha! he will fail! Ha! Ha! he will fail, he will fail!

W. WILLIAMS

[The Egoist, *the London monthly which succeeded* The New Freewoman, *was edited by Harriet Shaw Weaver, assisted by T. S. Eliot, Dora Marsden, and of course by Ezra Pound, who got Williams to contribute regularly.*]

19: TO THE EDITOR OF *The Egoist*

Vol. 3, No. 9, p. 137: 1915

The Great Opportunity—New York Letter

In New York in the spring of 1915, one was feeling a strange quickening of artistic life. It seems that due to the preoccupation of Paris and London in cruder affairs, New York has taken over those spiritual controls for which no one had any time in the war-swept countries. Here was a chance to assert oneself magnificently.

The weekly papers began to notice that Duchamp was with us—and Gleizes, and Croty. There were even productions of photographs and paragraphs speaking of "New York's gain due to its little progressive colony of artists forced out of France and England."

There was an exhibition of Cézanne at Knoedler's and one of young Americans, the Forum Exhibit, from which such a good man as [Charles] Demuth was excluded.

But in poetry the fiercest twitchings appeared. Two hundred and fifty dollars were put forward by a man, himself a poet. Kreymborg was employed to carry out his idea of a magazine free for the new in poetry. He gave up his newspaper writing, came out of his garret, married!, and in a little hut to which water had to be carried for washing, he started his magazine, *Others.*

There was, I think, wild enthusiasm among free verse writers, slightly less enthusiasm among Sunday Magazine Section reporters, and really quite a stir in the country at large.

Kreymborg was awakened at midnight once for an interview. That was years ago.

Actually it seemed that the weight of centuries was about to be lifted. One could actually get a poem published without having to think of anything except that it be good artistically. Kreymborg was the hero.

Every Sunday afternoon there were meetings at Grantwood. We sat on the floor, brought our own lunches, played ball in the yard and struggled to converse with one another. For the most part one looked and wondered but continued to be optimistic.

Good verse was coming in from San Francisco, from Louisville, Kentucky, from Chicago, from 63rd Street, from Staten Island, from Boston, from Oklahoma City. At least it was verse one could print.

Newcomers to the city if they were alive to artistic interests in their own parts naturally drifted into the crowd.

Others was commented on in the *New Republic, The Boston Transcript, The Literary Digest, Life,* and who knows what other magazines of importance. This little magazine was said to be the sun of a new dawn—in its little yellow paper cover! America had at last found a democratic means of expression! It was free verse! Even the papers went so far as to make extensive mockery of the men and movement in their funny columns. We were elated at our success!

And Kreymborg was receiving the lion's share of the praise. Though he insistently spoke, alas, not for the poems, but for *Others.*

Surely the present was the opening of a new era. New free verse was commented on everywhere. "The ——," with a progressive board of editors, began to accept and pay for free verse! This went on. Then the editors had a change of conscience: "We are afraid. We are at sea. We don't know what we are accepting; we have no criteria! Is this going to be thought well of tomorrow, or is it merely a whim?" So all at once, "The ——" refused even to consider new verse. But that comes later.

The weekly meeting went on. A stock company was proposed. *Others* was to be managed by a committee. We were to have a clubhouse—above 42nd Street, oh yes, it had to be above 42nd Street, that much was certain. We could have a large room for exhibits of pictures, silk goods, sculpture, etc. Here we could have our social meetings—Stevens would like that—with a little dance afterwards. Then again we could use the room for plays and readings. In the same building would be rooms for rent and at least two apartments where you and I and our families could live and edit *Others* and keep a bookstore and—that was a fine dream!

It seemed that the painters and the poets didn't get along very well together, perhaps that was why we couldn't get the things said which we were all aching to say.

Well, let's meet without the painters.

Next time it was the women who interfered. The women agreed to stay at home. Six men met one evening and had a bully time discussing the news and affairs in general in a reasonably intelligent way. This was the high-water mark.

It was midwinter by now. *Others* was wobbling badly. Subscriptions came in slowly. Kreymborg had to move to the city. A few poems of doubtful moral tone made enemies. Kreymborg insisted on keeping his hand on the tiller and anyway it began to be doubtful if there was going to be much gain, either financially or artistically, connected with the enterprise. One began to hear obscure murmurs. Fine! Now, at last, we were to get down to real values!

Unfortunately a saviour appeared in the person of a young Scotchman named Marshall, who was to take the whole burden on his own shoulders. We were all to have personal books published. There was to be a yearly anthology, etc.

In the 300 or so best poems for the year picked out by Mr. Braithwaite, *Others* had had one or two among the leaders.

One began to think of writing plays and getting them on the stage. Verse does not pay.

And then the MSS of our native artists beginning to fail to ap-appear, Marshall having failed to gauge matters rightly (being no native), financial ruin staring *Others* through, no more meetings with strange cousins of Isadora Duncan, etc., strange French

"Artists," no stir in the papers, no verse but the worst being accepted by the magazines, the anthology having failed to sell well because of one silly poem—not by Cannell—our minds began to go to sleep. One picked among the bones of the stew for a little nourishment.

At last the movement is dead. Now for the advance.

For me it comes in the form of Kreymborg's book *Mushrooms*. It consists in the skillful use of small words, the artistic effect depending on the musical design and not on the values noted and connoted by the words themselves.

One turns at last to one's desk drawer and thumbs over one's own verses with something of the feelings of a miser.

America has triumphed!

WILLIAM CARLOS WILLIAMS

1916

[*In 1913 WCW became a member of that informal poetic group
under the leadership of Walter Arensberg and Alfred Kreymborg,
meeting first at Grantwood, N. J., and then in Greenwich Village,
which published* Glebe, *in which* Des Imagistes *appeared, and
then* Others, *one of the first of the little magazines. From the first,
WCW was active in the inner councils of the group, with Max-
well Bodenheim, Robert Carlton Brown, Orrick Johns, Malcolm
Cowley, Marcel Duchamp, and Man Ray. The editorship of*
Others *was revolved from poet to poet, and WCW edited what
he described as the ultimate issue. In the course of his editorial
work he made contacts with several poets, some of whom were to
become his permanent friends: among these contributors to* Others
*were Kenneth Burke, Marianne Moore, Wallace Stevens, Conrad
Aiken, John Gould Fletcher, Richard Aldington, Mina Loy, and
other older friends, like Pound, Amy Lowell, and H. D.*

*Marianne Moore needs no introduction in these pages. The
relationship between her and WCW begun in the pages of* Others
continued personally and literally when she edited The Dial. *She
respects WCW as poet, but she deplores his poetic investigation of
the frank and sometimes vulgar.*

20: To Marianne Moore

May 9, 1916

Marianne Moore: I want something of yours for the August issue
of *Others*. I want something that you are willing to see stand
alone—some one thing—new.

Kreymborg is trying the experiment—God bless him—of letting
a few of us who are near at hand take an issue and see what we
can do with it. My idea is this: to put into the thing what I think
is the best work. I am not philanthropic. One piece by each person—some one thing that he or she is willing to stand to. Jam

34

these various units together and forget the "ensemble"—that will take care of itself.

I hope to know you some day. You met my brother in Rome, I think.

Sincerely yours,

W. C. WILLIAMS

21: To MARIANNE MOORE

May 18, 1916

Dear Miss Moore: You will realize why I welcomed the work you sent me when you read into the prose bit at the end of that August issue which I am taking so seriously.

It is odd that this poem should fit the very purpose I would wish it to serve so perfectly: to plead for careful thought, for a precise technique—the better to ensnare the intangible—or something of that sort.

You are about the only one who sees any use in using his brain.

I think you met my brother in Rome; he was then a member of the American Academy there.

Alfred still talks of your red hair.

Yours,

W. C. WILLIAMS

[*Everyone knows how Amy Lowell took over Imagism from Ezra Pound (Amygism he called it) and developed an almost completely new group of Imagists. WCW resented this for his own sake as for the sake of his old friend Pound. Refusing at first even to meet her, he weakened under her gentle (for her) prodding, and their relationship grew as close as it could become between a penurious physician-poet and an aristocratic female Maecenas.*]

22: To Amy Lowell

9 Ridge Road, Rutherford, N. J.
June 28, 1916

Dear Miss Lowell: I will be extremely glad to have your poem, for inasmuch as Fletcher has sent me a thing of his from England I do not think you will any longer feel bound to refrain from appearing with the rest of us.

Hoping for your cooperation in the making of *Others* for the coming year a success, I am sincerely yours

W. C. Williams

P.S. If you decide to send the poem you speak of, please send it at once, as my issue has been pushed ahead to July, which makes it imperative that the printer have all MSS not later than Monday if possible.

W. Williams

23: To Amy Lowell

Oct. 4, 1916

Dear Miss Lowell: Accept my homage—much as I dislike you: "The Cross Roads" is good.

W. C. Williams

10:30 P.M.
Perhaps I won't like it so much tomorrow.
Send me some money for *Others*.

24: To Amy Lowell

October 12, 1916

Dear Miss Lowell, poet: Yes, you gathered together a few rather well advertised people from both sides of the Atlantic and together with your own unquestioned prestige and a little stolen notoriety from the omission of Pound. Your commercial sense led you into making a sellable book—of some slight importance.— And yes, I referred to the *Others* movement, I am sad to say, which is definitely ended. Your sure instinct led you aright again, but there is no reason to despair of some American with farsightedness enough to go beyond the immediate past and enough generosity of spirit to play the loser's end of a fine venture.

Aside from what you stole from Pound, your venture is worthless. Aside from its failure, the *Others* movement held the future of such a man as Bodenheim in its palms, even if only for a short while.

I cannot see the slightest reason why we should meet. I have nothing to talk over with you. I admire some of your work and it is a pity that it is not put out to higher interest. To me it is a lamentable stinginess of spirit that permits you to hold your present well-known attitude toward unknown and young American writers.

I have nothing to sell.

Yours,
W. C. Williams

25: To Amy Lowell

Oct. 16, 1916

Dear Miss Lowell: I thank you for your very reserved letter in which you make all the conventional and obvious mistakes in attempting to apprehend my feelings concerning the demise of *Others*.

I am really surprised that your letter made so faint an impression on me. I fully expected to be enlightened on two or three points in which I confess I am not yet perfect.

Others did not attempt to sit in judgment over American letters.

What is the use of talk? You have your fixed ideas and I perhaps have mine. It seems to me as unlikely that we shall ever agree as that the sky will meet the earth.

To you, one who is helplessly unhappy will be always "pathetic," and one who thoroughly believes in another must be of course a "henchman." How then can you have had the vaguest notion of what *Others* meant to me?

There are undoubtedly numberless matters that would make good food for conversation should we ever meet, but I cannot see their importance.

Yes, you seem to have done something for Stevens and Bodenheim. Very good. But how does it happen that Braithwaite chose as the best poem of the year that piece of yours which I quite sincerely believe to be twaddle and which I have never yet heard any one admire? Of course it is my opinion against Braithwaite's and supposedly yours. You are an American. But I acknowledge that I am again falling into nonsense. Not that it makes much difference.

I really thank you, however, for the spirit in which you took my letter.

I thank you again for your suggestion of a meeting but finding myself totally opposed to the spirit of what appears to be your whole purpose of life toward art I must tell you the truth: I'm not interested.

Yours,
W. C. WILLIAMS

26: TO HARRIET MONROE

Oct. 26, 1916

Dear Miss Monroe: What's the good of trembling when the damage is done? Anyhow, thanks for eliminating that other thing.

I cannot understand the feeling that wants to change and rearrange according to some yardstick which has not the slightest application to the work of some person who has spent time and attention and even more important substances to bring that piece of work into the exact mould in which it is presented. What can it matter to you what my theory of line construction happens to be? In any case, it has nothing to do with articles, nouns, verbs or adjectives.

It would be far more to the point to question why your own theory of line construction happens to be as it is.

As long as the poem in question is read aloud as intended, it makes no difference how it is written, but it will be physically impossible for anyone to guess how I intended it to be read the way you have rearranged matters.

Let it go. No one will notice anything wrong, and as long as nothing is noted to disturb the gently flowing accord of the magazine from Vol. 1, number 1, until the year of Grace which is to see its end, I suppose the major part of its mission is accomplished.

I sincerely regret giving that ten dollars to *Poetry*, for I believe with my whole soul that the policy you have evidenced even in such a slight matter as the elimination of my small letters at the beginning of lines and this last matter also is of the stuff that more than anything eats the heart out of honest expression.

God help me! I seem destined to offend you, a thing which is as far from my heart as anything I can imagine, for I wish you well in your work but I heartily object to your old-fashioned and therefore vicious methods.

Sincerely yours,
W. C. WILLIAMS

1917

Feb. 21, 1917

Dear Marianne Moore: I'm in trouble over a little fussy matter of no consequence, that you can probably settle for me in two winks. So I'm—as you see—writing to you.

I'm going to have a book, as I told you. It is a fine book, naturally—or will be. But the title bothers me.

You see, I am a mixture of two bloods, neither of them particularly pure. Yet there is always in me a harking back to some sort of an aristocracy—probably of the gallows, or worse—that will have a hand in all my democratic impulses. Then again there is a certain broad-fingered strain in me that will always be handling an axe for budding King Charles Firsts. So I torture myself through life. But there are acute moments that seem distillations of agony and this is one of them.

I want to call my book:
A Book of Poems:
AL QUE QUIERE!
—which means: To him who wants it—but I like the Spanish just as I like a Chinese image cut out of stone: it is decorative and has a certain integral charm. But such a title is not democratic—does not truly represent the contents of the book, so I have added:
A Book of Poems:
AL QUE QUIERE!
or
THE PLEASURES OF DEMOCRACY.

Now I like this conglomerate title! It is nearly a perfect image of my own grinning mug (seen from the inside), but my publisher objects—and I shake and wobble.[1] Help me, O leading light of the Sex of the Future.

Yours,
W. C. WILLIAMS

---

[1] It was published as *Al Que Quiere!*

28: To Harriet Monroe

July 17, 1917

Dear Miss Monroe: You fail to grasp the point: to confess that the check you sent me strains your treasury and at the same time to insist—in effect—on paying me that check in full is evidence of wrongheadedness run to pure whimsicality. No poet expects to earn money by his verse. If he does he is a fool and had better be disillusioned at the start. To compare him, the poet, to the painter is idle, for the painter produces a single piece incapable of reproduction, whereas the poet produces nothing more tangible than the paper which anyone can purchase for a cent and a few dabs of ink which cost still less.

What you are doing by paying what you do for poems is this: you are jeopardizing the existence of your magazine in the mistaken notion that what poets want is money, when in reality—though money is sorely needed also—they need space, an opportunity to gain print often and at will. This lack of space, this lack of opportunity to appear is the hell. And you will add to this by going bankrupt!

To put you to the test. Print within the next three months another piece of mine—provided of course that I am able to please you—and you can have it for nothing, or, if you prefer, I will turn the check over to you without seeing it.

Before you go out of business, please cut your rates in half, and I venture to say you will print better stuff within the month.

Sandburg's "In the Cool Tombs" is a splendid thing. I hope with all my power to hope that I may meet Sandburg soon. He is, if I am not mistaken, really studying his form. Few men are making any progress in their art. They are adding new decoration or repeating the old stuff, but Sandburg is really thinking like an artist. He seems to me to know his America and to be getting it in. Give him my best wishes.

Sincerely yours,
W. C. Williams

If we were all great artists you might try to pay us well, but we are mainly clodhoppers in verse.

1918

29: To Marianne Moore

March 23, 1918

Dear Marianne Moore: If the book I am now sending you has already been purchased by you—send that latter copy to a soldier or some other fighter.

I presume you have read what Ezra has to say of you in the March *Little Review*. If there is one thing that stands out clearly above Ezra's other perfections, it is his unswerving intelligence in the detection of literary quality. There is one phrase in that note, about some men carrying around a whole phantasmagoria of landscape, etc.—that is magnificent. I send you my book,[1] fearing your friendship as much as anything else. It is so easy to speak well of a work—so hard to say anything of clear enough outline for an author—lost as he is in his own crooked roads—to grasp with good effect.

I have admired your mother's sole comment anent my world.

This spring Mrs. Williams and I wish to pay that long deferred visit. We will ask you to drop us a line as to when.

Sincerely yours,
W. C. Williams

30: To Amy Lowell

August 7, 1918

Dear Amy Lowell: "Appuldurcombe Park" is a fine piece of work. Accept my praise. Lines 18 to 30 are full of your best touches—a luxuriant perfection of mood set in a broken, almost sobbing rhythm.

Perhaps I would not have written this letter had I not a knife

---

[1] *Al Que Quiere!*

in my hand. I wish timorously to call to your notice that in moonlight a red coat—even a red coat—does not "crash" against anything. I have no suggestions to offer except that in reading the poem at that place one goes from moonlight into full sunlight and then is bewildered at the reappearance of the moon. *Too* violent. I realize of course that you want violence.

In any case this is the best poem of yours I have seen in some time.

Yours, with perhaps a few minor reservations—

W. C. Williams

1919

[*Alva N. Turner of Ina, Illinois, sent an unsolicited manuscript to* Others *which Williams liked so well that he encouraged Mr. Turner. Alva Turner thus became one of the first of the many amateur poets whom WCW encouraged, aided, and championed with the magazines which he knew. Typically, Mr. Turner is still corresponding today with WCW, even though they have never met in person.*]

31: To Alva N. Turner

June 25, 1919

Dear Sir: Don't you know that you cannot possibly interest me—Who am I?—by anything along unexplored lines, except it be along the line of artistic form and NEVER along the line of mere cerebral content. What the hell do I or does any artist care for the moralizings of a EUNUCH or a Fred Douglas, UNLESS the stuff be used as a PRETEXT for the REAL thing which is a new artistic form. THE FORM of your three poems that I accepted was what pleased me. You used certain semitechnical terms such as "crus" and "flavicomous" in a fascinating way. You have invented there a new COLOR. Do you get me?

The three poems I selected were charming. Full of reserve energy. The two you think I will like in this batch are ROTTEN. Now don't get mad! I'm right and you're wrong and you'll probably smile and agree with me. In fact, any man who could do as good work as you did in the first three poems cannot fail to see the truth (which he already must know) when his mind is refreshed by the pointed finger.

Others has been in existence 4 years. I am not the editor except for this issue. I'll send you a copy. . . . My dear man, God bless you, you are a wonder! Never have I seen such ROTTEN work which gives such hope—such failure mixed with

44

such an intangible something that is down in the ROCKS at the center of the world. Keep it up. You have a flavor that is unapproachable. BUT, Jesus Christ, how rottenly you can write. I read and say to myself "This man is hopeless" then a flood of feeling goes over me and I say "This man is a genius." You are a genius. BUT you don't know yet how to write. If you are not too old to learn you can take my word for it (which you don't give a damn for, of course) you have the goods.

I simply cannot afford to bring out another issue of *Others*. The magazine leads a very precarious existence. It may never appear again, I don't know, but if you ever go to Chicago look up Helen Hoyt and ask her to introduce you to some of the *Others* bunch. Wait till the issue comes out about July 1 then take a trip up there and meet some of the fellows. It'll do you good. Take this letter as an introduction: Any of them know me I think. Mitchell Dawson. Emanuel Carnevali. Carl Sandburg.

Good luck—it's a hell of a life but keep it up. You are far ahead of the game in some respects: I mean you are using a personal language, you are careless of effect and YOU HAVE SOME-THING TO SAY. AND you are full of nuts—. Don't get mad. Forget morals and long stories and write some POEMS.

Yours,
W. C. WILLIAMS

1920

Oct. 27, 1920

Dear Turner: I am always glad to receive your letters. Your criticisms of my book are just and refreshing. I like especially your revised rendering of the first improvisation. I see your point about fools having no wombs, it is well taken. Yet I am right.

You are a wonderful man. You count yourself one of the most unhappy of mortals and you are so. But you do not seem to realize why this is so. It is so because you are wise, because you are not satisfied to look only up but also down. And this knocks you out of alignment with your environment. You are so far beyond your environment by sheer instinct that the community you live in would be destroyed by your mere presence did it not make an example of you, keep you subdued. These are the fools and their breed is unnumbered. Yet you love them. You can afford to love them because you can understand what they are, the good that they generate among them. Were you a trifle more conscious of yourself, did you more thoroughly understand your relation to your environment, which would give you more repose if not more comfort, you would be great.

Disgust is my most moving emotion. Sometimes I wish it were otherwise, but it is not, so an end of it.

Particularly this morning I feel that the best thing that could happen to me would be for me to drown myself. Stupidity is powerful here as elsewhere. It is my own fault. I will not concede anything to anyone. I will not even work. I do what there is to do without imagination. Why work for the sake of work? I hate work. I want to have leisure not when I am fifty but now. And the hell of it is there is no way to have leisure save by effort. Leisure is no more free than potatoes. I am drowned in triviality, stupidity, my own heaviness, everything. It is raining. And what of it?

I have just thrashed my youngest son for spitting in his nurse's

46

lap. What in God's name is one to do? Better run out into the rain as Lear did. I wish I had the inspiration for it.

And to cap it all I am thinking of fathering a magazine. A plain damned, restless fool.

I have a friend who is trying to get out of an insane asylum.[1] His hearing is on Friday. What chance has he? Yet you say fools have no wombs. Mister Preacher, do not forget that you are a poet too. Look down. I am always, unhappily, knee deep in blue mud.

Yours,
WILLIAMS

------

[1] See "An Early Martyr," C.E.P.

1921

[*Kenneth Burke was a contributor to* Others, *an editor of* The Dial, *a founder of* Secession, *has written and received perhaps more letters to and from WCW than anyone living. In 1921 WCW was editing* Contact I *and importuning his* Others *friends for contributions.*]

33: TO KENNETH BURKE

Jan. 26, 1921

Dear Burke: God bless your bloody American heart, I want to print all you have sent—and shall sooner or later in some way or other. The Laforgue article pleases me. I object to appreciative articles on foreigners being written for us from Europe. The environment gets into the writing every time and it is inimical to me. I resent the feel I get from the composition and so I am led to antagonism against the appreciated. Criticism must originate in the environment that it is intended for. Laforgue is a new Laforgue in America. Our appreciation of him creates him for us and this I feel in your work. You have taken what you want from the master in order to satisfy your needs and your needs are the product of your environment. (I wish to God I dared print this note somewhere in the next issue where your paper will be used. What do you say?)

You fairly illustrate what Bob [McAlmon] and I mean by Contact. Why, the last paragraph, the quotation, is a perfect exemplar of our attitude. Laforgue takes what he has and makes it THE THING. That is what we must do. It is not even a matter of will. It is fate. We are here under one—Hell, you know all that as well as I.

The stuff, apart from the Laforgue thing, I have not yet read, though the story where I have dipped into it seems to be full of well-formed blocks rich with good words. I want to look it over

48

more carefully with a view to bringing it out in instalments. We'll see.

Damn it man, you encourage me. I want to go on and on with this damned magazine as long as men like you can be doubtingly approached and dragged forward against their wills. It is the way it must be done. Bob and I thought that geniuses would rush forward and fling masterpieces at us.

We will be the greatest gainers by this venture if we learn what CONTACT with the Americans we want to meet means. It's a hell of a job meeting each other. It's a battle . . .

If you see Bob tell him what I have said here. Oh, of course you won't. You're an American. Never mind. . . .

THERE IS HOPE! It's a damned lie. There is BURKE.

Yours,

WILLIAMS

[*Written down left margin in longhand*] Don't mind this God damned letter. I really mean something or other—as you shall see.

W.

34: To Alva N. Turner

Feb. 27, 1921

Dear Turner: Driven to distraction by the circumstances of my life, I have not been able to say anything to you for these many months. Time is my most precious possession, when I have it; but when I have time at my disposal there are so many things pressing to be done that I have let much of my correspondence fall away, simply because I could not bring myself to think of it.

I have been much interested in your approaches to the crowd in Chicago. I read all you send me and enjoy what you say. Carl Sandburg has never been one of my close friends. I met him one night when I was in Chicago, but that is all. Apparently you have taken a fancy to him and he to you. I think that in all probability you two are closer to being of a type than you and I. If I had any advice to give you it would be: Meet the men in Chicago as often as you can.

I cannot say that I always approve of the poems you send me. There are flashes of excellent feeling and vision in them, but the good is generally mixed with what seem to me very empty lines. You must know by this time that my liking is for an unimpeded thrust right through a poem from the beginning to the end, without regard to formal arrangements. You seem to get lost in the middle of things, to repeat for the sake of the sound. Your words are not as obscure as they used to be, but you occasionally flounder into some strange perversion of language, and sometimes your phrases are inverted and forced.

I have had no opportunity to print anything of late. But I am glad at your improved physical condition, and your satyr-eyed glances at the hospital nurses amuse me greatly. If only you would forget yourself in a wild burst of composition, building up a structure without any thought but for the development of what you see and feel when a girl of the type you praise passes you—it would be worth something. Build it up like a pleasure house—.

Maybe someday we shall meet—

Yours,
WILLIAMS

35: To Amy Lowell

March 6, 1921

Dear Miss Lowell: It was thoughtful of you to send me the ticket for your lecture last Tuesday, but it was impossible for me to attend. I would like very much to be present at the Author's Reading on April 20th.

H. D. told me nothing of your operation but then she never communicates anything to me of general information. I hope you are thoroughly well now. Personally I have had pinkeye for the past ten days, coupled with which has been a quota of hard work in my profession that incapacitated me finally for anything but drowsiness.

Bryher's sudden wedding must have surprised you. I say nothing of McAlmon. I wish I had the boy back with me and not lost there abroad, to no good purpose I feel sure. My God, have we not had enough Pounds and Eliots? *The Sacred Wood* is full of them and their air rifles. But perhaps Bob will do better. He will do better only on condition that he comes back to America soon.

I must confess that I am heartbroken.

Yours,
W. C. WILLIAMS

36: TO KENNETH BURKE

March 22, 1921

Dear Burke: Want you and your wife and baby to come out to spend the afternoon with us a week from this coming Sunday. Arrive here sometime about noon. We'll have dinner then, after which we can disport ourselves as may best suit our fancy. And want you *solus* to lift yourself to this province of darkness and cellars and four-months-old puppies that are mistaken for senile hounds sometime earlier. Come out Friday late in the afternoon if you like, this Friday, and stay for supper. Let me hear from you.

We shall hear from each other this summer. It would be a pity not to have some traffic between the poles. I have long wanted to have a correspondence with someone very dissimilar to myself, the thing to be planned as a dialogue criticizing the universe (literature), which might be published later. Procrus *vs.* Aprocrus. In any case, I should like very much to write, though I feel, without meaning to spoof, that I'll be the gainer rather than you.

As a rule I detest argument—no one is ever convinced by it, since it is nearly always a mere confusion of terms, like a football game. But your objections to McAlmon on the score of his general ignorance of French literature and Remy de Gourmont's 1890 satires in particular almost stirs me to reply. But after all it would be no use. We are too far apart yet to indulge in talk profitably. Perhaps someday we'll get some sense out of each other.

I like your ill-natured jabs at myself, so come on out and let's

play around for a couple of hours and see if we can't amuse
each other—perhaps even complement each other in something
serious.

I received word from Bob in London. He's having a noble time
of it. My word what a chance! . . .

Don't forget to let me hear from you, Mr. Whitman.

Yours,

(*signed*) Oscar

37: TO MARIANNE MOORE

March 23, 1921

Dear Marianne: You make the blood to flow in my smallest capil-
laries again by what you say of my book.[1] I feel even that my brain,
somewhat dull of late, is getting fed quite as amply as my skin.
Such is the miracle of a friend's good words.

But how can I use this writing? I'll keep it, hoping that you
have a copy which you will send perhaps to *The Bookman* or
the—what? Or, best of all, send it to no one else.

Your gentleness makes me stop and think. Perhaps you are
right in your adverse view of my sometimes obstreperous objections to decorum. I must think more of that. But each must free
himself from the bonds of banality as best he can; you or another
may turn into a lively field of intelligent activity quite easily,
but I, being perhaps more timid or unstable at heart, must free
myself by more violent methods. I cannot object to rhetoric, as
you point out, but I must object to the academic associations with
which rhetoric is hung and which vitiate all its significance by
making the piece of work to which it is applied a dried bone.
And so I have made the mistake of abusing the very thing I most
use.

The same with rhyme: who can object to rhyme except in the
sense of the pendulum's swing against it brought about by stupid
usage? I thank you for calling my attention to these inaccuracies
of approach.

---

[1] *Kora in Hell: Improvisations.*

But you startle me by your praise of the piece in *Contact*. Yet you quite convince me that you are speaking accurately and with enlightened judgment. You can imagine how hard it is for me to believe that!

Florence sends her love to you in return and seems happy that you have liked what her husband has performed. Sometimes marriage is gay! It is nearly always so when a wife can flatter her husband's vanity.

In any case you have made me feel again as if I wanted to put some words on paper. I feel much stronger than I ever did toward this work. Let us see what comes of it. Surely there is no greater excitement than that of composition. I am dead when I cannot write and when I am at it I burn with a fever till one would think me mad.

It should be *tough cords* not *touch cords*. It is one of the few errata in the book but doesn't make much difference. Of course, it makes a little difference—not so "poetic" but—

Yours,
WILLIAM

38: To Kenneth Burke

October 21, 1921

Dear Ken: Congratulations on the sale to *The Dial*. May the God of all good men shine in the minds of that editorial staff until you get tired of writing essays—which I hope will be never. I enjoy your essays.

As soon as *Sour Grapes* appears you shall have a copy. It should be out at any moment—but it may not be out for a month. It would be fine to have you do it. Of the few books I have spewed, this is the one in which I have been least interested. For this reason, perhaps, it will turn out to be one of the best, though I think not. It has been more "composed" than any so far, which, if it is discoverable, should please you. The fact of its appearance is due more to the pressure of ordinary circumstances, such as having a lot of stuff lying around, than to anything else. Yet, one hopes—proof that I am not yet an artist. An artist is always beyond hope—please do not remind me of it.

You "haystackers" are the naive children of genius. Yes, medicine pays. Bless your heart, it is easy for me to admire you, surrounded as I am with paying dirt in the form of grippe, tonsillitis. Each to his own filth.

I'll see you someday—I expect soon.

Do you want to come out for a rest and a meal some day?

Yours,

BILL

39: To KENNETH BURKE

Nov. 19, 1921

Dear Ken: I accept your apology.

English being, as you imagined, the lousiest language on earth, you thought to write well by writing lousily. You wrote better than you imagined. If I could tell you why, I would, flower from the crannied wall, tell you all you don't know.

Besides, didn't you once tell somebody that the only reason my own work was readable was that it was so damned mediocre—in tone, that is, with itself and its natural circumstances of being?

I suppose I am at heart a mystic. But who isn't until he clarifies his meaning or dies trying to? Even the Arabs or the Phoenicians, or whoever it was that invented the rule of three, were mystics until they found out pretty damned clearly that they were fooling themselves and so had to invent the science of mathematics to save their faces. Contemplate that last sentence a while and you'll know a hell of a lot more than I knew—once.

I like your theories—they're so puerile that they don't count, so you have plenty of opportunity to write and save your face. Kiss me again Merdito. Because you CAN write.

I'll do all you ask concerning Bob.[1] In fact I have sent your stuff on already.

---

[1] Robert McAlmon.

No, I have not contributed to Alfred's[2] *Broom.* I may someday soon. I haven't much to send.

Crazy about your Matthew Arnold tidbit. You really delight my heart. Do you think me a fool if I say that at present I find you to be the only interesting character writing in America today? Paul Rosenfeld seems good in his way but he has no flare or flaire or insanity to temper his bricklaying. Yes, writing is bricklaying.

L'architecture c'est poser un cailloux sur un autre. You like that? My brother handed it to me. I wish he really knew what it means.

Up Irland! You knife.

Yours,
BILL

---

[2] Alfred Kreymborg.

1923

[*Robert McAlmon, a young man from the wind-swept prairies, drifted to New York in the late teens. There at a Greenwich Village party, he met WCW, whom he literally challenged to a friendship. WCW took him up on this, in a sort of father-son relationship, which proliferated into poetry. They shared the editorship of* Contact I *(1920-23) in New York and of* Contact II *(1932-33). For thirty years WCW and McAlmon maintained the closest literary-personal relationship possible.*]

40: To Robert McAlmon

[*1923*]

Dear Bob: It's a damned good book;[1] I have just finished reading it this minute—I'm sending it off to the literary agent at once with a brief letter asking them to write to me if they have anything to say. This will obviate the two weeks delay that would be necessary if you had to be communicated with on the other side. I like the book immensely and have made up my mind to go to some trouble about getting it printed, god damn them all, the asses of publishers, for not being up to anything with a rare merit in it.

I suppose you'll have a hell of a time getting this printed. The thing is that what you have to say is too important, too finely grained—in its adjustments, while it is at the same time too casual and unlettered in surface appearance for anyone but a most unusual person to penetrate it for its real value. What in hell is it? It is a criticism of literature itself and of life. You have to know all the crap that your writing has come gradually to shed to know what it's all about. The way of the telling is a great improvement on anything you have done before. The mud-blocks fit together, no cement. It ain't marble either. I dunno,

---

[1] *The Hasty Bunch.*

the thing seems about the cleanest tasting bit of presentation I've read, clean, that is, from the point of view of experiences set down with no more art than that necessary to make the whole a sound functioning body.

Yours,
BILL

41: TO MARIANNE MOORE

Monroe, N. Y.
Dec. 27, 1923

Dear Marianne Moore: We are here in Monroe on the farm with the children: Billie has a chemical set for Christmas. I expect to see him professor of electro-chemistry at Boston Tech in a year or two. Bobby has a cold, perhaps he'll turn out to be a doctor. Dear little mites, it seems impossible to leave them, even for a moment, and we are going to Europe. Perhaps though one might have been shot by an Indian a few years ago leaving the children to starve in an isolated cabin.

But the real theme of this letter is the review of Wallace Stevens' book by John Gould Fletcher in the Dec. 19 *Freeman*. Please read it and then please write me. Fletcher seems to me somewhat misanthropic toward that class of individuals, the younger American poets. It looks to me as though he has tried and failed, or failed according to his standard and now steps down among the populace for mud to fling.

This is what I want to think. Perhaps my nerves are ragged over leaving the children, but Fletcher has touched a sensitive spot in my consciousness for all that. You know I began with portraits of old women in bed and the rest of it, and it all seemed very important. Now there has been a quieter, more deliberate composition. This lays me bare.

Eliot's *Waste Land* (apart from the languages he uses, which I do not understand) seems to me to justify Fletcher's diatribe against the lot of those who seem "disillusioned."

You see I am troubled. I do not believe in Fletcher and came across his notes only by chance, but it is even more important that it came about in that way. Here is an outsider quietly saying: No.

Is it a tormented Fletcher who says willfully the wrong thing, or have we really been bluffed out of existence by our difficulties? Isn't it good though to be so disturbed? Of course one may shrug one's shoulders and say, Oh who is Fletcher? but once a fool stumbled and fell with his hand on a gold piece in the dust.

Heaven's, but forty is a terrible age at which to take a year's leave of absence. I feel that a vacuum cleaner in under my hair would be a great boon. So he put to sea.

Yours,
BILLIE

1924

42: To Marianne Moore

c/o Credit Commercial de France
103 Ave. des Champs Elysées
Paris, France
Feb. 10, 1924

R. S. V. P.

Dear Marianne: Florence, Bob McAlmon and I are here at a quiet pension-with-a-garden-overlooking-the-sea for perhaps a month. We came down from Paris last week where the Europe virus was injected into Floss and me, and are now, each in his own way, working.

Bob wants to have you assemble a book of your poems for us. It would be published by the Contact Press and would have my appreciation of you as a preface. We would want it to include *everything* of yours that you find good from the beginning up to the present.

Bob has hesitated to ask you about this, seeming to find you a difficult person to get at, so he waited for me to come over and embrace the job, imagining that I could find a way through your defenses more readily. Let's hope so. (I am trying to use a French typewriter.)

Oranges, mandarins, lemons and tasty little ground cherries in their flimsy shells are all in our yard, while a man that dresses and looks like Geo. B. Shaw throws feed to the chickens next door every morning.

WILLIAM

43: To Marianne Moore

Paris, Feb. 21, 1924

Dear Marianne: Your two letters arrived today—together. I was interested in your criticism of the Raleigh piece—perhaps I'll change that passage.

I've been working on "The Voyage of the *Mayflower*," which is now finished at last. I wonder if you'll like it.

It was splendid of you to answer my Monroe letter as you did. I felt pretty low that day.

Florence and I are going on now to Italy, leaving Bob and Bryher to their own resources—or rather we are the ones that will be so left, since we are the greenhorns when it comes to travel. I like Bob more and more. I have written a critique of his three prose books which I hope some day you will see.

We met Joyce, Ford and a host of other writers in Paris. I had a fine afternoon alone with Valery Larbaud, who talked to me of Spanish literature, giving me ten names (enclosed) of the newer men. We also talked of Bolivar and the grand manner in which Spain undertook its new world colonization as contrasted with England's niggardliness. We spoke also of Cotton Mather!![1] I have not yet seen Pound. He is in Italy.

Please, if you will undertake a commission for me, do what I asked you to in my last letter: get up a book of your own.

All values have grown simpler for me since I have hit Paris. America gives too much violence in exchange for her mutilations (judge that as you please—it's too long).

Yours,
BILLIE

44: TO KENNETH BURKE

Rome, March 26, 1924

Dear Ken: Leaving this ripe center of everything in a couple of days, to my sorrow, but I think I'm carrying away half of antiquity with me. The other half is what we have left today. I never so fully realized, as in the smell of these relics of the old battle, how maimed we are—and how needlessly we are crippling ourselves. Frascati in full "wildflower" yesterday won me again, just as I have been won over and over here by the bits of wisdom that I've

---

[1] This conversation is reproduced in "Père Sebastian Rasles," *In The American Grain.*

seen even in museums—the statues, the whole colossal record of their oldtime fullness and our unnecessary subservience to our crippledom. We love it. That's the hell of it. We eat it, lie in it. Sing about it and build our monuments on it. . . .

Well, so here we are again, back where I started.

One night, you are right, I let loose and said what I have said before: "To hell with Ken Burke. I can't see what it's all about (his short story theory). If he'd write and to hell with his mechanics, etc., etc." I said what was uppermost in my mind at the time. But Caracalla built great baths to wash himself in.

Good God, you are curiously a whole man to not mind the crap you hear—. What to hell?

Your letter was really in a fine climbing mood. I'm thrilled when I think of you planning your house in the mountains. *That* is you for me. Someday you'll write twenty words with *that* in it and I'll say you are Prince of Cranberry Lake and ask you to meet me in Paris for a good bottle of Pommard (Vieux) 1883.

You have the right idea about a magazine. The print shop in the cellar is the only way. And what will come off that press will be food for delight.

In fact, Ken, your letter was the perfect answer to my present need. Everything I am doing now is unprintable. To hell with printing and selling work. McAlmon is with us on that, or we with him. There is a perfect unanimity on all sides; no use to quarrel, nor can there be offense to fastidious preferences of humor. Print and distribute here and there until we all land in a (patriot's) jail—it will come to that in the end, you wait and see. That or Paris for us all—but *never* silence.

That sounds heavily serious but it isn't, don't give it a thought.

The print shop must be forwarded. And it amounts to this: how much?

I think you must have received my last letter by this time so I shall not attempt to remember it. The point was only that your story (January *Broom*) seemed to rise up out of the dead wood of your theories, so I wrote the letter.

Yes, my *Great American Novel* never found a beginning. It was that I must have wanted to say. And that's how you get me, one of the ones with *that* in him that I am after. It's got to be said to be read. I *am* trying to *speak,* to tell *it* in the only way possible—but I do want to *say* what there is. It is not for me merely to arrange things prettily. Oh, purple anemonies! You get what I mean? . . .

Write again. I'm delighted that you are south and that *Dial* will give you money. It's its only use now, as far as I see.

We go to Vienna in 2 days.

Yours,
BILL

45: TO MARIANNE MOORE

Vienna, Austria
April 14, 1924

Dear Marianne: I meant to begin "dear Dopple" but forgot. It must be hard to stand and see the beautiful birds of paradise (like me) winging southward each year over your ploughed and reploughed ten acre lot. But then, there are the rabbits who are really never seen till nearly winter. You always see them too.

So did I, in coming into Vienna. We had crossed rather high and very cold mountains during the night. After Venice this was a sad experience, but in the early spring fields, as we came over the great flat expanse south of the capital, I began to notice great jack rabbits—sometimes two or three together—who would leap off as the train approached. There wasn't a bit of cover as far as the eye could see. I wondered why these cabbage devouring beasts were allowed to go about that way—but apparently it is the custom here.

Then there are the blackbirds; they too stay all winter in the north. The curious thing here is that they are perfect American robins—except that they are black. Their whole build, their walk, and the way they stand looking sidelong in one direction and then leap in the other at the worm is perfect robin. The song too is very robin like. Of course they are both thrushes.

St. Mark's Cathedral in Venice—have you ever seen it?—is my rich ideal of pelt and plumage—and you really should let us publish your book.

Valery Larbaud spoke only of Bolivar's sweep of imagination. The English came to America on a 3% basis, but Bolivar saw another Spain in America. He liked the way the Spaniards "moved in" to the new world, bringing *lares, penates* and Olympus too with them. I could say little at the sight of the six two-inch-thick volumes on Bolivar which Larbaud threw before me, like pomegranates, on the table. Perhaps I stammered a word about admiring something of the Maya culture.

I have just met a Hungarian modernist painter, Kassak. He seems Russian in his beady-eyed, white-browed seriousness about things political. He and his friend take me for a boy—and I suppose I am. It is hard to talk American politics to a serious Hungarian through a translator who speaks poor English—especially if one has long since forgotten that laws are made and kill people and that the Great United States is a democracy.

Kassak frowned, and I just caught the word—"passivist."

Good heavens, I suppose I am just that. It all seems so odd to an American that anybody takes these things seriously.

And there is another anthology edited by L. A. G. Strong—author of *Dublin Days*. I am in it and you are *not*. You can guess the rest.

Florence is trying to go to sleep under a great feather bolster and the Spaniard in the next room is puffing like a cow or a horse—so good night—*gutter nacht*, as the Spaniard says to the maid, and I hear him through the double door with the clothes press in front of it—*gutter nacht*.

Yours,
"WILLIAM"

46: TO KENNETH BURKE

Vienna, Austria
April 14, 1924

Dear Ken: *Secession* No. 7 was handed to me here the other day by one Gaspar, coeditor (apparently) with Kassak of *MA*—or *AM* or whatever it is. My excuse for this ignorance is that they had never heard of James Joyce.

Anyhow I was astounded to find your story, "A Progression," so thoroughly enjoyable and so—able. Please pardon my astonishment. In this piece you have done a fine thing in retaining a classic (or Gothic or Persian) hold on the material·of composition, on each word, I mean, and on ideas—but, at the same time, you use the latest way of composition—. I begin to see a little light.

I don't know whether it is that I have gained better insight into writing and things by my present experiences or whether you have improved. Perhaps it is something of both. The *MA* people speak very highly of your work. I had only a glimpse of them and their wives in a café. I'll see them again in a few days.

To my further astonishment I was completely captivated by Munson's work also. I think he has a blind spot toward Waldo Frank—but it may be that he knows it—(judging by the scientific trochee he hands us on the back cover).

These people are totally ignorant of things American—barring the names of you newer writers: yourself, Munson, Cowley, Josephson and E. E. Cummings. Yes, they had heard of me. Of everything else American they live in an ideally black ignorance. They want reproductions of our paintings. They asked me if any of our men admired the newer Frenchmen, if there had been any exhibits in America! I didn't believe such questions possible.

They are trying to get hold of "Our America."

It is very nice over here, as I said before. Oh well, why not? I'll be glad to get back—in spite of it. The only sensible thing to do over here would be to go mad and kill yourself. At least that is the way I feel about it. I have heavy bones, I am afraid—there's little here for me—gravity must drag me down—over the horizon—I'm too slippery—and it doesn't matter—but so it seems.

Paris would be wonderful if I could be French and *Vieux*; it would be still more wonderful if I could only want to forget everything on earth. Since I can't do that, only America remains where at least I was born.

Yours,
BILL

47: TO KENNETH BURKE

9 Ridge Road, Rutherford, N. J.
Sept. 6, 1924

Dear Ken: My one object has been accomplished, it was just to show you that I was alive; the manuscript had no other value; if it is lost so much the better; I have received from you neither the manuscript nor any other communications save this note today. . . .

Let me make myself clear as to my present attitude toward the enemy. It is indifferentism. You are perfectly right in saying, that or a million. Within that indifferentism, however, I live at the hot center. That is my theory. Indifferentism as far as present attack is concerned but no indifference inside. Inside I want it hotter than ever before. We must weed and sharpen our weapons, with malice.

Indifference that sits back and becomes "aesthetic" doesn't appeal, but indifference from practical wisdom that is sensible of difficulties too great to be overcome at the moment has a hot center.

Yours,
BILL

P.S. We must all grow clearer, we must work in, together—not for comfort but for training and by bunching our candles to get more light. Join to gain head. I don't mean for consolation, no sect! No creed but clarity. Work in, in, in—by bringing in all we can gather—trying, testing, scrapping together—with an eye open for an opportunity to use our stuff in the open when we can.

If we practice on each other, trying to knock each other's blocks off, we'll be ready one day to knock a few real blocks into the discard.

W.

[*WCW met Ezra Pound at the U. of P. in 1903, when they were undergraduates. Recognizing one of the few intellectuals at the college, Pound encouraged WCW in his poetic endeavors, helped him to find publishers, scolded him for his backward economic notions, and is still corresponding with him.*]

48: To Ezra Pound

Dec. 23, 1924

Dear Ezra: The extracts from your notes upon music have just reached my eye via the recent *1-9-2-4*.[1] I have culled a great pleasure from them. It is the sense of form which you have so skillfully presented by what you say. I await the book with a great interest. You too have changed.

Bill Bird tells me in a recent letter of his struggles to complete the printing of your *Cantos*. It is all so slow that at times it drives me to despair. I do not wish to become Hinduistic and wait for all completions to take place in another life—or is that American Indian lore?—the Am-Indians were strayed Asiatics.

Europe seems closer since we have been there but—again—it seems infinitely further off: so great has my wish to be there become intensified by the recent trip. Paris seems just [drawing of a boat] there! Either I must be a tragic ass, or nothing—or an American. I scarcely know which is the worst.

Hoping to see you again soon

BILL

Answer by a card or as you will (to give me your true *new* address). I may want to send you some recent prose of mine to read: your "notes" have greatly encouraged me to trust my studies.

BILL

---

[1] A little magazine of that year.

1925

Columbus Day! [*1925*]

Dear Marianne: Gertrude Boyle is a woman of about our age, I imagine, who has wanted to be a sculptor about as we have wanted to be poets. She has made innumerable sketches—crayon sketches, wash drawings, water colors, etc., but has never had cash enough in hand to command the leisure necessary to complete her work in stone or metal; it may even be that she has not the ability to work in the heavy material of sculpture. Her sketches, however, have aesthetic interest.

Last night I spent an hour fingering over about a hundred of these drawings. Some of them are just good, some are strained without distinction, but a few are first rate in design—catching the modern note exceedingly well. I want to interest you and through you *The Dial* in these pieces. I want you to see the lady or have her come to see you, though it would be better (and not dangerous, I am told) for you to drop in at her studio, where I have never been. It might be that *The Dial* would reproduce a batch of her best line drawings with a note by yourself or by me or anybody else who might have the interest to do it.

If you look at her things at any time, you will come across several two-figure groups that have a distinctive mass about them. Then there are bowed female figures where the ovals and loosely related commas and crescents of the bones and flesh are capably related in the design.

I saw two or three small pieces in the plaster but they were unconvincing, too much dead weight, pulp, plaster left in, especially about the bases. But if the woman could get some of the sketches into the three-dimensional medium as they appear on the paper she would have great stuff to show.

Go for her, bite her ear off and see how she is stuffed. Do this, will you? Or ask her to visit you at the office—I think she is unusually worth *The Dial's* attention.

Hart Crane has been nibbling at her for Daniel, but he seems too timid.

And Wallace Gould[1] wants to write a cook book of regional American dishes; he is a heavenly cook, you know.

Yours,
BILL

How about a page or two of recipes for *The Dial?* Angel cake. Brunswick stew.

---

[1] See *Autobiography*, pp. 180-83.

1926

Spring [1926]

Dear Ezra: . . . Rebels to your point of view—Hell, what is the number of your patent? And if I ever tried to make anybody think anything at all—all I ever asked, even of you, is that you SEE me and not through glasses guaranteed and specially fabricated to miscolor and distort everything they come against. I do object to that. Look—if you have any eyes at all—and forget for a moment what happens to be itching you at the time. It may for a moment permit you to get a little pleasure without aching to make me something that I ain't.

You talk like a crow with a cleft palate when you repeat your old gag of heredity, where you come from or where I come from. Do you really agree that place matters? Or time either?

Hell,—somedays I can write what I want to and some days I write *In The Am. Grain*—and when I'm very low I can write a letter.

The Masses—starting again, minus Floyd Dell, Eastman, etc.— they have got hold of some cash. I don't know any of them. They have Boni's old place: 39 W. 8th. . . .

I have plans for doing something like a small bookshop in N. Y., special agent, just the books you can't get elsewhere. Trying to fix it up with a machine for getting out a monthly bundle of stuff, anything we want to get out—I don't quite see way clear yet. Maybe nothing will happen. Let you know how it progresses. Maybe continue *Contact.*

Things in general are picking up here, interest, painters, etc. Lots of loose talk, but it looks a little as if there may be something of interest going soon—always looks that way here, perhaps. Anyhow, thought you might be interested.

(To go on—several hours later)

The *New English Review* has offered space to those who speak well of you, meaning, I presume, precisely nothing.

It seemed to me there were other things to say, but apparently I was mistaken.

Yours,
BILL

51: TO MARIANNE MOORE

November 29, 1926

Dear Marianne: Surprise and delight have so upset me after the unexpected announcement[1] in your letter just received that I really do not know how to frame a letter that would properly convey to you my feelings and thoughts at this time and it would be too childish even for your friendly eyes, and there would be too much to say and no satisfaction, were it not all said, so please accept this note of thanks as an Esquimo might perhaps out of gratitude present his friend with a bone fishhook or the like.

All you have said and intimated, the need for a little haste, etc., has been noted. In another twenty-four hours I'll write again and more fully.

Had such news come from anyone else than you the pleasure of it could not have been so complete.

Sincerely yours,
WILLIAM

---

[1] That he was to receive *The Dial* award for 1926.

1927

Florence Herman Williams is Mrs. WCW, the Floss *of the dedication. In 1927 Dr. and Mrs. Williams took their two sons to Europe. Mrs. Williams remained in Europe with the boys, who went to a Swiss school for a year, while WCW returned to his practice.*

52: To Florence Herman Williams

On Board S.S. Pennland
9 P.M. *Saturday, Sept. 24, 1927*

Dearest Floss: Sylvia Beach came all the way to Cherbourg with her sister and even out to the steamer in the tender. We had a fine sunny ride down through Normandy. The fields were green and flooded, small hard-looking red apples on the trees and all that. We had a two-hour wait on the tender in Cherbourg harbor. It was cold. I did not want to walk so I stood around and watched a big clock get its hands set for 6 P.M. Then I knew you must be near Geneva. At 7 I knew you must be in the hotel.

The sunset over the gray cold houses and the square of Cherbourg was a tumble of great buff clouds. In the outer harbor there were three ships, the *Aquitania, Harding* and *Pennland.* We were last to steam out, just at dark.

The crowd is not too bad but anyhow they are as they are. My room is clean looking and I seem actually to have it alone.

By the way, all the steamers were anchored inside the big breakwater and not outside.

This is a bigger ship than the *Arabic* and quite different from it in general design. It is stiffly, coldly decorated. The dining room is large. I think I shall eat with Sylvia's sister, though I don't much feel like talking to anyone just now. If we stop at Plymouth tomorrow morning I'll mail this there.

Sylvia was very curious about what Bob had told me about his divorce and especially about what he had said about her, Sylvia.

She said she had spoken to him seriously as a friend because she had it on her mind and it is her habit to speak, and if it costs a friendship it will have to do so. She said she told Bob his writings were beginning to show the influence of alcohol. He was furious. . . .

Sylvia wanted to tell me all this as she believes Bob and I are real friends and she wanted me to know the truth as far as she could make it plain to me.

After I left you at the station I wandered out into the street and had my shoes shined by a fine old gray-haired guy who took about a quarter of an hour to do it. Then I taxied to the hotel, saw Bob for a minute, taxied to the Gare St. Lazare feeling very gaunt and now I'm at sea.

Sylvia seems to like the extracts of my novel in *transition*.

I hope you had a comfortable journey, Snooky, and found my postal cards waiting as a reception committee when you arrived in Geneva.

I received a letter from Ed here on the boat. He is staying over to come on with his family on the 8th.

Goodnight sweetheart. I'm soon going to bed. I love and think of you all the time.

Your husband,
Bill

53: To Florence Herman Williams

On Board S.S. Pennland
Sunday a.m., [*Sept. 25, 1927*]

Dearest Monkey: It's a fine Sunday morning. The weather is just about as it was on the way over, the sea is fairly smooth and the air cold.

Just before breakfast I was surprised to see land, a tall lighthouse off to the north and a row of cliffs east of it. I don't know which light it was.

The crowd on board is not bad, plenty of room for everyone. I am sitting between Miss Beach and a woman from the Canal

Zone but originally from Kentucky, a woman of about my own age.

Most of the crowd seems Southern.

The old ship is pitching a bit but it rolls almost not at all—not yet at any rate.

I slept like a log from 9:30 last evening until 7 A.M. I was tired but today things have quieted down inside me and tho I think of my Bunny in Geneva it is not with that feeling of loss within me that we knew in Paris. I am eager to be on my way to be doing work and to be getting forward with the time when I shall see you again. Everything is forward now. The thought that I am leaving you physically behind has lost its force. Next summer will come faster only by my going west now.

There is a very cute little bellboy on this ship. He is English and about Paul's age. He has the sunniest face and the quickest, readiest smile you ever saw. He seems just busting with pride at his brass buttons. Gosh! I didn't think they let them out of school that young. It seems very sensible in a way. He looks so business-like and happy. I liked your hat. I wish I could have seen the dress. Take pictures as you promised and send them to me.

The boat did not stop at Plymouth as it had already been to Southampton before reaching Cherbourg. So we headed at once into "ye ocean" and my letter of yesterday will have to be mailed from New York.

There is something else I wanted to tell you but it's gone.

I'm crazy, more or less, to get at my writing again. This year I'm going at it differently than usual. I'll write something every day but I'll keep five or six things going at once. I'll use carbon paper more than formerly and send you everything.

Oh yes, please write to Elliot Paul or Sylvia in about two weeks, or when this letter reaches you, and tell whichever one you write to that you want to get hold of my novel as soon as they are through with it. It isn't so very important even if it is lost but we might as well not be careless about the MSS.

You can picture me at table facing the very same menus we had coming over. I'm eating lightly though this time and watching my digestion. I weigh 165 lbs., a little heavy but not too heavy after all.

There is a gym on this boat.

My cabin is small and an inside one but the bed is comfortable, that's all I care.

I have enough reading matter to last me for a trip around the world.

Now my mind is beginning to turn back to my practice a little. I begin to wonder if I'll remember how to feed the little brats and what trouble has piled up for me.

I'm down to my last twenty dollars.

It was very thoughtful of you to make out my bills before leaving.

I forgot to buy a beret. Get me one. I wear a 7⅛ hat.

Well, the old ocean trip has started anyway.

I think of you all the time and see you in definite scenes walking about the hotel, going out to Coppet and sitting on the benches on the Isle Rousseau. Isn't the lake water marvellous.

An ocean of love

Yours,
BILL

54: TO FLORENCE HERMAN WILLIAMS

On Board S.S. Pennland
2 P.M., Sunday [Sept. 25, 1927]

Dearest Bunny: I probably shan't keep up this pace of writing but I feel like it now, so I'm just going to give in.

It's a glorious day outside. We're south of Ireland and running into the face of a strong blow, but the sun is brilliant and the spray from the small waves is like a shower of white flowers. That sounds poetic and so the sea is always to me.

I've been out to the stern watching the rise and fall of the ship. She is a slow old tub, heavier than the *Arabic* in all her motions. But sometimes we like 'em a little bit slow don't we?

As I stood out there I was thinking and wanted to talk to you. Therefore this letter.

I was thinking that we are doing just what we want to do. And so it is good. We have broken up that staleness of schooling and experience which the boys had gotten into. It is a bad thing. We recognized it as bad, for them and for us, and so we did what we did. I am glad. It gives me a right feeling. The risks had to be faced or we should all have been less than we are.

Doing what we know we should do for the boys, who depend wholly on us to have a fair beginning to their young lives, we get some of the good we give them shed back on us.

We've got to go on of course and so this year we'll be thinking what to do next. Whether to keep the boys in Europe another year, whether to keep them next summer at a French camp in summer and then come home—or whatever it may be.

The thing is that we have ended a period as you say and now we are going on. It is good, I add. That's what I was thinking and that it must make us happy and thoughtful. You can do as much as I. Though I'll be in America, I'll be leaning on you for this and you on me—so we will be together in that, bless you.

Now I'm going to read some more.

Quite a few people are ill in spite of the weather.

Miss Beach took her cats into her cabin before dinner. The biggest one got scared and somehow got under her bunk and up between the woodwork and the walls. He wouldn't come down, so they had to call the butcher, who has charge of such things, to go after him. They finally succeeded after much effort. She told me a good little story at lunch about an Englishman who upon seeing the Statue of Liberty on leaving New York: "Yes, in England we too raise monuments to our distinguished dead!"—Not bad, is it?

In spite of my resolve not to drink wine I have had to do so, since Miss Beach loves her's and insists on my joining her.

Maybe in another hour I'll write again.

Goodbye,
BILL

55: To Florence Herman Williams

On Board S.S. Pennland
Monday, A.M., *Sept. 26, 1927*

Dearest Floss: When you receive these letters I shall have been at
home for a week or more, so that I don't mind telling you that
yesterday was a rotten one on this ship: cold, draughty and uncomfortable. Toward the afternoon especially, when we were
south of Ireland and the sea was very choppy, few people aboard
looked cheerful. I went to bed at 8:30 and stayed there till my
baaath this A.M. Now the sea is quieter and the air is warmer and
all is well. Part of my trouble was my solitary mind. I am a poor
mixer, though I wish people well and like them.

Trying to escape the cold wind yesterday, I went behind some
bits of the superstructure on the top deck and there I found a
steamer chair in which I sat. Soon Mrs. Ship Kitty, all white
except for a brown nose and some spots on her back, came and
climbed into my lap. She was a lady and as ladies usually seem
to be she was hot and kept shoving her little arse under my nose.
Especially she seemed to like the top button of my overcoat which
she licked and licked while her front paws pumped up and down
against my chest in the usual way.

As she was doing this a couple of ex-soldier boys came by and
began to stroke her. I told them that she was looking for a man.
"A what?" says one of the ex-soldiers. "A man, a tom-cat, that is,"
I replied. "Well, kitty," said one of the fellows, "I'm no good to
you. I've been to Paris, I'm all worn out."

That's the way they all look on this ship.

There's an article in the *transition* which you have which
mentions my chapter (in *In The Am. Grain*) on Poe, to attack
it rather violently. It is worth looking at, especially as there is
some truth in what the woman says and since I am going to write
an answer to her statements. I'll send it to you, the answer I
mean, and ask you to send it to Elliot Paul.

My old bean is going around inside like a windmill. I am half nervous about my practice in the usual way and crazy to begin at my dutiful typewriter, writing I know not what.

Today it is raining but the sea is quieter.

The meals here are not nearly so good as on the *Arabic*—or maybe it is our lovely little table and the company that I miss.

"Nevada" is aboard. He is a remarkable type. Very childlike but wonderfully able to take care of himself and with eyes that see everything. He is terse in his statements and has a way of laughing silently at his own mental pictures that he raises for you with a faraway look in his serious and intense blue eyes that is like the loneliness of the prairies itself. He was most amused at the way they mixed up the people on this boat, put a woman in with two strange men, and a man in with two women: the man got mad but the woman took it as a joke. So "Nevada" smiles and ponders.

Anyhow it's Monday. I saw a big star over you in the east last eve.

Love,
BILL

56: To FLORENCE HERMAN WILLIAMS

On Board S.S. Pennland
[*1927*]

Dearest Floss: I've been absolutely heartbroken this afternoon for lack of you. Just sick with it.

I feel a little better now, so that's that. It doesn't seem right for you to be there.

BILL

If we cannot be happy I will not be separated from you. Tell me how you feel.

57: To Florence Herman Williams

On Board S.S. Pennland
Tuesday, Sept. 27, 1927

Dearest Snookie: You must get the boys to show you my letters, I have to smile at them myself sometimes.

That was a lovely dinner you gave me on my birthday, Sweetheart, I was tasting it all over again this morning. Especially delicious were the chicken and the wine.

Mornings before breakfast are my hardest hours on this ship. They push the clock back an hour or less and then keep us waiting till 8:30 for breakfast. As it is impossible for me to sleep much after 6 A.M. I scarcely know what to do with myself during those hours, since I am afraid to read because of my eyes—which are in perfect condition by the way.

The general mood on this ship is far from pleasant anyway. The boat is very poorly designed for comfort and the Legion is raising hell generally, much to the irritation of some of the cabin passengers. Not to Miss Beach and to me, however, for as she says, "And they yell, this is *their* holiday and *their* ship for this trip—and they did, many of them, go through bloody hell for us ten years ago."

But last night after and before a dance on deck they *did* cut loose, with a drum, a bass drum and six trumpets plus raucous voices of the usual manly power. Someone had told them earlier in the day to keep out of the 1st Cabin Lounge.

That proved a red rag in their faces so they paraded up and down every corridor of the ship until midnight singing "Mademoiselle of gay Paree, parley-vous!" until everyone was crazy.

One woman from Chicago near my cabin went after them and tried to lay them out. She spoke very well too, but they merely offered her cigarettes and invited her to join the parade. Even she had to laugh after they had gone.

They're a good bunch, not at all vicious and many of them on this ship carry wounds.

Miss Beach is very tolerant. She was with the Roosevelt Hosp.

Unit under Dr. Peck all through the war. She loved Peck as we did. She knew Skip Cannell but never realized that he was Kitty's husband till I told her. She said he was the worst cook in the world.

Dr. Carlisle of Passaic was in the same unit. She knew him well. Isn't that odd.

Sylvia and her sister were brought up in Lausanne and Paris. None of them has married. She and Sylvia served as nurses in Serbia for two years after the war in helping to rehabilitate that country. She says a woman is safer traveling anywhere in Europe alone day or night, than in America, and California especially.

On board ship she takes care of her four cats almost all day long, but last night we danced together and drank a beer each while we watched the mob there and especially a bunch playing crap.

I have also picked up a fellow from New Jersey who is traveling with his wife. They know many people in Rutherford and are related in some way by marriage to the Grays on Home Ave. (Last night there were five separate rain storms, blue hanging curtains, off on the horizon around us while we were in sunlight as the sun went down.) Do you remember the baby that Ogden was taking care of and which had scurvy? That's the one. They had heard of me in that way.

The sea is smoother now. The wind has switched to the south, so that I expect we shall have warmer weather soon.

Yesterday I finished my philosophy. The last chapters are easy and very fine. They deal with art and manners. If you ever get hold of the book, *Science and the Modern World* (Whitehead) you should read the final chapters. I'll send the book if you want it. Perhaps it's not worth that much trouble though.

This morning I'm going down to see the cats. It is nice to have Miss Beach on board. She is a very intelligent, modern type, not physically attractive but very tolerant, likes her gin and can hear everything that can be said very clearly. She knows Nancy Cunard and that crowd.

I will say she is a talker but—if I get a pain in my neck listening on one side I can always change my seat.

X 1 kiss. I kissed it there for you.
I was thinking of you in bed this morning.

Love from your husband,
BILL

58: TO FLORENCE HERMAN WILLIAMS

On Board S.S. Pennland
Wednesday, Sept. 28, 1927, 7:45 A.M.

Dearest Flossie: This is mid-ocean. The wind has shifted again to the north where there is a small freighter on the horizon steaming in the same direction as ourselves. It is a gray threatening sort of day but not too cold. The sea is fairly quiet. I have slept well, thank you, and my bath was splendid.

This simple life on the ocean, without close companions, without work to do and without temptation or irritation of any sort about me—unless there be a temptation to read too much—has put me in a thoughtful mood—full of love for you and of interest in that America ahead of me where the gay hell will be lit for me pretty soon.

I was really an unhappy, disappointed child—in general—during my early years. It was due to the mood of our home and to my eager desires, which no world, and certainly not the Rutherford of those days, could satisfy. I do not say it was not good for me but I never could do what I really and violently wanted to—either in athletics, studies or amorous friendships—so I was gnawing my insides all day long.

And yet underneath it all there was an enormous faith and solidity. Inside me I was like iron and with a love for the world and a determination to do good in the world that was like the ocean itself. I had a mountainous self pride and a conviction that I could afford to adventure and decide for myself.

But if, one way and another, I was a disappointed and unhappy —lit by wild flashes—boy, though this is true I am a most happy man. And the greatest thing which has caused that has been yourself.

I don't need to discuss our history. For some uncanny reason you saw through me and you saw me good. I in my turn recognized in a flash of intuition that you were the queen of the world for me at that moment. I tell you now that that feeling went through my whole body like sweetest nectar and that I knew it would last forever. And I mean just exactly forever. There was the eternal in that and I knew it at once.

I was wild then, hurt and crazy, but that tremendous reserve of strength in me was touched and it responded. No one else had seen that as you had. For me that was a stroke of genius on your part.

What "love" is I don't know if it is not the response of our deepest natures to one another. I went direct to you through my own personal hell of doubt and hesitation and I have never changed the millionth part of one inch since that first decision.

You know and I do not deny my irrational—and I still believe necessary faults—but the result of whatever I have done to lessen myself in your eyes has merely brought me back to you the stronger. All my life I have grown from that moment when I asked you to marry me, always into a clearer and more satisfying realization of what really took place at that time. I love you and you love me and so only at the end will I know what love is—and that is my answer to the world and to you.

It is wise that we have adventured once again, this time on a separation. You are a corker in your power to think and decide over emotional and other situations and wring the good out of them. You are the one to have made this "necessary evil" of separation possible. I am sure it is good. I feel it all over me in many ways not yet fully come to light: in power to work, in clarity of conception of some of my emotional difficulties, in firmness within myself and in decision and fuller realization concerning my love for you.

But you too are alone and you too are thinking. It is certain that I do not know everything in your mind. All I ask is, Isn't it good? Tell me.

I believe that with love—(how I hate the word, mistrust it I mean) with love we can dare to understand each other.

There, I'm written out on that topic. I wanted so much to say it, but it is so hard to say well. The damned words keep jumping and slipping, until before long we've said just the opposite of what was intended. But a strong emotional bias keeps the words straight—pretty well. And that's what they mean when they say that in spite of faults the truth shines through.

Money, my dear! You must write at once, for I rely on you absolutely in this, to tell me what of our funds you want me to send you. Figure out about what you'll need and figure it *large* and thus I'll be able to keep my plans clear. Of course sometimes you'll get five cents extra for candy, but do figure it so that you will be *easy*. I shall be disappointed and angry at you if you try to skimp. Now do what I tell you. If we are going broke I'll tell you in plenty of time, so while you are abroad do what you please to do and do not consider twice an expenditure of two or three or even more hundreds here and there extra if you want to. Mind me now, I am your husband.

If the boys need small extra things buy them if necessary or tell Mr. Schwarts to buy them—but in either case let *me* have the bill. It is not to come out of your money.

The Legion is still going strong. It seems some woman called them "cattle." Well, I am still fearful that something may happen.

One man was criticizing them to another fellow whom he did not know was the leader of the Legionnaires on this ship. The man spoken to said to the other: "What port did *you* sail from ten years ago?" The other fellow said, "I worked in a shipyard."

Biff! he got it between the eyes.

On the way over to Europe on the *Celtic* one ex-gob, dead drunk, climbed to the very tip of the aftermast. They had a hell of a job to get him down.

Sweetheart, do have a fine time in Europe. Do, do, do it for me. We are not separate, we are one. I am the half that is home working (and having fun too, of course) but you must not be sulky. Go on out and *see*!

Breakfast.

Love,
BILL

59: To Florence Herman Williams

On Board S.S. Pennland, *Smoking Room*
Thursday, 12:30 A.M. [*Sept. 29, 1927*]

Dearest Flossie: I don't know whether you are sick and tired of these letters or not, but it's a pastime and a pleasure for me to write them, so here goes another.

I'm in the smoking room this time in the midst of all the good beer and tobacco smells which are really very agreeable to me now, the guffaws of laughter, the miscellaneous tales of conversation, "What did you do with that jack now?" and all that. I find I like it more and more now that you are not here. I see the little round silken legs as always and I know what they mean but the silver tinkle of the dimes and quarters and halves going into the poker pots are equally lovely: "Whoo!" sings out one guy, etc., "Let's get out in the air," etc.

It's a hot muggy day today, misty and wet everywhere. We're in the Gulf Stream. I almost passed out in my cabin last night from the heat. But that's nothing, I feel fine now.

There are two or three bugle and drum corps on the ship. They practice on C Deck near the stern. I went to listen to them today. They sure can play. Paul would be delighted.

Last evening at or near sundown we passed, in mid-ocean, a French fishing schooner returning to France from the Banks. It was a blackish color all over, sails and all, a three master "morphodite" rigged as one ex-sailor said. The sense of seriousness and imagination used in that vessel was like meat and drink to me. We passed quite close up. Two or three dorys were lashed to the deck and the helmsman waved to us. Great! We miss this in our lives. We miss it to our loss. Let's see if I can draw the picture from memory:

[Drawing of a sailing vessel]

Imagine the seriousness of those lives! I am beginning to pick up stories of what happened in Paris. One fellow, a Harvard College and Law School grad, told me of the little girl he had to bed with him the last three nights in his hotel. He has the finest, kindest and most loving and respectful memories of her whenever he speaks. . . .

Tata sweetheart. I feel very close to you when I write, almost as if I were beside you talking.

Love,
BILL

60: TO FLORENCE HERMAN WILLIAMS

On board S. S. Pennland
Friday, Sept. 30, 1927

Dearest Bunny: Friday! Yea bo, no office hours today. And the last day of this eventful September. It has been a telling month for us all, crammed to the lid.

This has been a stormy, unsettled trip all the way. Today is no exception. There has always been a high quartering head-wind and it has almost always been wet. The sea has not been very bad except the second day off Ireland, and yesterday toward evening when we began to pitch heavily but, to my taste, magnificently. They say that the ships ahead of us have been in a storm.

All day yesterday we were in the Gulf Stream. It was stuffy everywhere with a southwest wind constantly blowing, bringing mist and showers. Today we are out of the Gulf Stream. There is a marked difference in sea and air. A young gale is coming down on us from the northwest. The sea is beginning to rise (I think) and we should have some fun before long. I do not speak much in my letters of you and the boys, for I can only guess and feel things about you. It has seemed best to me to write to you about what is going on about me, trusting to your coming letters to tell me what other things I want to know. I think of you always.

I have written constantly on this trip, that is, as I write, in mad spurts. I have written the reply to Miss Riding which you have, a ten-page thing called *"Philosophy as Literature,*[1] rel-

---

[1] Unpublished but existing in typescript.

ative to a subject brought up in the concluding chapter of Whitehead and which I shall have to finish at home before sending
it to you. Then I have decided on the title and general contents
of a book, my next book of poems and written the first two poems
which I'll send also later. The title is *Sacred and Profane*.[2] They
are to be all love poems such as you shall see. Speak of this only
to your own lovely little ears. Then I have written a poem to my
friend McAlmon enclosed in this letter. Do not show it to Bob.
Send it direct to *transition* for them to publish. I'd like for him
not to see it till it is in print.

Miss "Holly" Beach (we have come to first names) is a most
interesting talker and an able little slat of a person. She sure has
traveled and seen things in Europe. By the way, she says it is all a
lie about Wilson's immorality as far as she knows. She knows all
the principals intimately who were concerned in the "Scandals,"
and she says it's nothing but a lot of silly bungling that has given
weight to the charges. She lays them all to the Dean of Princeton
who hated Wilson. The Rev. Beach, Miss Beach's father, was with
Mrs. Wilson when she was on her deathbed and she told him,
among other things, that her husband had never in his life caused
her an unhappy moment. Well, there it is as I heard it yesterday.
Knowing a few men, as you do, you can take it or leave it, and
what of it?

The other story I heard yesterday was of a little model whom
Miss Beach knows well. This girl was an orphan, very beautiful
in body and face. She was brought up in a convent. Very early in
her teens she got away somehow and joined Barnum and Bailey's
Circus where she did trapeze work, horseback tumbling and some
other stunt. It was about this time that the man, the artist, painted
her picture. During the next two or three years, when she was
still in her teens, she had two children, fell from the trapeze and
broke her back. This was cured after a year in the hospital. From
there she went to Morocco where she lived with all sorts of men
and incidentally broke in horses for the French during the war.
She was too good for this, so they put her doing spy work, lying
out on the beach in Boulogne where she picked up so much stuff
that they gave her a more difficult job, in a whorehouse some-

---

[2] Published as *The Descent of Winter*—but *not* all love poems.

where, where she did excellent work getting information from all sorts of men, but contracted syphilis which seems to have been neglected. After the war she met an American. He fell in love with her and they are married. He too has syphilis, but he is crazy about her and her children whom he is bringing up with the utmost devotion. (Some storm is getting up, believe me.) This man had to do some photography, and Miss Beach was detailed off to travel with him and show him what was wanted. As soon as the little model heard of *that* she came down from Paris instanter and raised purple hell all over the place until she too had to be included in the official itinerary and had to be taken along. Interesting, isn't it?

Dear Monkey, tell me what you are thinking and doing.

This is a sore bunch on this boat. Half the Southerners have heavy colds. Many of them are down on H. Deck, imagine! And they hope to die. Really, some are desperately sick.

Love,
BILL

61: To Florence Herman Williams

On Board S.S. Pennland
Friday, 10 A.M. [*Sept. 30, 1927*]

Dearest Floss: I have been out astern watching the lash and slash of the waves for the past hour. It is wonderful, wonderful, wonderful. Nothing else is like it in this world—unless it be an enraged woman! But today the sea is particularly entrancing. The sky is luminously cloudy, so that everything is dove gray with a cold metallic sheen to the waves in the misty sunlight southward.

But to the north the waves come in racing crests which rise and as they thin out so that you can see that cold but glorious blue; through them the wind catches the crests and tears them apart right and left in great showers of pure white spray like driven snow.

The wind in the rigging is whining and whistling and has a

force to it that it is almost impossible to stand against. I wish you and the boys were here.

I received some slight attention from a nice little Southern bachelor, with a frank voice and manner and a pronounced drawl at breakfast this morning.

We were exchanging confidences in the usual ship's way when I told him I was leaving my wife in Europe for a year.

"Do you think that's a good thing?" said he quite frankly. "Well, we decided to do it," I answered.

He thought a while then continued. "It's a question whether a man can continue continent that long. Of course it all depends on the man."

To this I replied by saying I thought that nowadays there was as much question about a woman as a man in such cases.

"Oh no," says my bachelor, "a woman doesn't have any difficulty keeping out of trouble unless she goes looking for it, but a man is always billy-goating around one way or another." "Well," I said, "I'll tell you more about it next time we meet—next year."

He laughed and said yes, he'd be looking for me.

Love,
BILL

The sun is coming out. It's going to be a fine cold day.

More love,
BILL

The book Sylvia gave me, *Dead Souls,* by Gogol, is a wonder. Read it.

BILL

62: To Florence Herman Williams

On Board S.S. Pennland
7:45 A.M., Saturday, October 1, 1927

Dearest Floss: It is a perfectly glorious summer's day, scarcely the trace of a cloud anywhere in the sky, a gentle headwind and the sea just a great field of even small waves. This is the first really fine day of our trip, which in general has been most unpleasant as far as weather (and many other things) are concerned.

Today I feel cured of my desperate despondency. I do not sleep well. This morning as always I wakened early and discovered something interesting. All the rest of the time you are away from me after I arrive in New York you will be getting nearer every day, but during these two weeks you have been getting always further away. I'll feel better as soon as I get on shore and hear from you.

Another thing I discovered this morning: the sea as I looked at it is exactly the same sea, given the right day and weather, that Columbus, Eric the Red, and the Puritans looked at. Thus it annihilates time and brings us right up beside these men in the imagination. This is a delight to me.

Perhaps the change in wind yesterday, with the subsequent clearing of the weather, was due to the passing of one of the Carolina boys on board, who died of pneumonia. The ship was quiet all day because of this. We now have three dead men in the hold. Legionnaires who died in Europe. The song they sing, the Carolinians, is very appropriate in this case: "I'm tarheel born/ and I'm tarheel bred/and when I die/I'll be tarheel dead/So ra-ra Carolina, lina." Oh well, that's over, and there's no use thinking of that any more.

They closed the bar two days ago because of drunkenness, also yesterday they closed it at 6 P.M. It was getting too rough on board.

There are all kinds of people on this ship. Another man than myself might be getting wonderful character impressions, but I simply couldn't use the material so instinctively. I just keep by myself and ponder and think. A few people of course I try to know, and it is their essence that I am after. Such a one is a little aviator, the one I wrote of yesterday, from Tennessee. He is a wonder. I knew it as soon as I heard him laugh, looked at his eyes and head and saw him walking around. He is a reserve officer in the Combat and Pursuit Aero Squadron, but he can't quit flying actively. He has a plane of his own and uses it all the time in his business to cover territory. He loves flying and flying alone. He has flown for ten years and says it is the safest means of locomotion he knows: "I don't want to die any more than anyone else," he says, "If I didn't know it was safe I wouldn't do it." He is a solitary man, a perfect hawk, I am sure, small, powerful, but not heavy, and keen in his instincts. He flies every Sunday for rest, relaxation and sport. I admire such a man and enjoy putting him in my mental library to think about when I am disturbed by my own eccentric thoughts and not too satisfied with my general make-up.

But it's a great day today, sweetheart, and I'm at peace in my insides. The old ship is as steady as a ferry boat today and soon this bloody trip will be over and I'll be getting nearer to you every minute.

Love,
BILL

P.S. This is to remind you again to tell me what money you need. I rely on you for that. I'll tell you about my book as soon as I know what has been going on.

This month has been a world, a life in itself. Do you remember it all? The cabin on the *Arabic,* the roses, the obstreperous brats, bless 'em.

It is amazing how many thoughts and emotions we both have gone through. Such things are tremendously important if well used. It is like a farm that has been cultivated over a gold mine. But you can't live on gold. I'll be the happiest man in the world when I see you again "back on the old farm," and yet the "gold" of such an experience is proving—as we know. I keep rambling on. But soon I'll be getting letters and that too will bring you closer. It looks from what I say that to bring you closer is the only worthwhile thing on earth—and, one way or another, that's pretty near true.

BILL

Later in the day

Dearest Floss: Perhaps I've said too much of love and devotion and all that in my letters, but I have been mentally and emotionally disturbed by leaving you, so that I have wanted to speak to you as if I were holding you in my arms, that way I have let myself go freely to you and all I have said is true. But today I am wondering how it will look to you on the page. But even that is not quite what I mean, because I have no fear that you will not understand me perfectly.

I want here only to speak of the seriousness of my understanding what this separation is all about and what I will do with it. Persistence and hard work are the only means by which I shall be able to get the value out of our serious plans. I only want to tell you that I see clearly what I have to do and that I am going ahead with the keenest desire and interest. You'll see.

Your hubby,
BILL

Good beer on this ship.

63: To FLORENCE HERMAN WILLIAMS

On board S.S. Pennland
11:30 A.M., *Sunday, October 2, 1927*

Dearest Floss: The excellent cognac I swigged into myself an hour ago is still deliciously warming me. Since then I have been in the smoking room with scraps and loud talk and games going on around me, reading quietly. Then I had a strong desire to write to you. I fought it off for a while in order to go on with my book—but here I am writing, still in the smoking room.

This is the last day at sea—we must be approaching Nantucket Light. Early this morn the day was as perfect as one could imagine: no clouds, just a soft veiled blue dome over the quiet bright sea and just warm wind enough to make it pleasant to stand in it. Off to starboard a school of large fish, bluefish I think, were jumping. Since then a light luminous fog has settled down and the foghorn has been indifferently blowing, as much as to say, oh well, I might as well give a toot now and then for form's sake.

But I'd rather talk of the Luxembourg Gardens, which seemed

to belong to you. That was our great pleasure, wasn't it, just to walk there? I can see those dahlias, the lavender ones, topping the other flowers. I can see also some of the lesser flower borders under the trees, the very simple ones, white and green. That is the best of Paris, in one way.

This will be my last letter before leaving the ship. Of course I shan't write as often when I am at home, but it has been a great joy to me to be able to invoke your presence every day in this way. I love you. After I am home I'll be busy of course at first tearing around, getting things started; then I'll let you know. And, dear girl, you must promise me to cable if ever there is reason for it. Just shoot me a word, or you could even go to England and telephone, as it is easier to talk from there than from Paris.

Now we begin the next phase of our adventure, I mean with my landing. From then on the moves will be yours. I say little about you, since it is from you that I expect to hear all that. But I hope you are happy as may be.

Love from your husband,

BILL

P.S. Sunday, 9:30 P.M.

Dearest Bunny: Everybody more or less is drunk. This has been some wild trip. They have just had "Nevada" up on a table in the smoking room singing cowboy songs. It has been a rough trip in every way. It won't happen again in years. I'm mighty glad to have been here. Sore, sore, sore, that's the general feeling. There's been screwing (as always, I suppose) in the cabins and to cap the climax, last night some guy, presumably a member of the crew, went through some of the cabins and cleaned up several hundred dollars, five or six watches, travelers' checks, etc. There happen to be two detectives on board. If they catch the thief, there's going to be murder.

We passed Nantucket Light at 4:30 P.M. We're now off Long Island.

God, how glad I'll be to get off this ship!

BILL

"Down on the farm / they all ask for you / The chickens and the horses / They all ask for you" (drunken song).

1928

64: To Marianne Moore

9 Ridge Road, Rutherford, N. J.
March 16, 1928

Dear Marianne: Yes, there is a novel. I have just succeeded in finding a publisher. Macaulay & Co. are to bring it out "before the spring of 1929," whatever that means. It is called *A Voyage to Pagany. transition* brought out a chapter or two last fall. Something seems mixed in these sentences. I am dog-tired with running around.

But anyhow, it was a pleasure, as always, to hear from you. And it would be a pleasure for me to have *The Dial* display parts of the book. The trouble is, will my publishers consent to such a scheme? And will you still care to feature the work if a publisher already has it in hand? I dunno (1), I dunno (2).

Tell me by return mail whether or not you are still interested, under the circumstances. If you are I'll consult Macaulay by phone, asking their consent, and if they are willing for you to use a chapter or two for *The Dial* I will see to it that you have a copy of the MS for your amusement, delight, instruction or what not.

Somehow I get little time to finish work any more. The novel had to be pushed through, heaven knows with what success! But since then I have been doing more thinking than anything else. It would all be possible if anyone had sense enough (*vide* Ezra Pound's *Cantos*) to give me a salary for sitting on my tail and enriching blank paper by careful work. But intestinal toxemia and mastoiditis are more important to a prosperous community than impalpable directions and invisible (but damned important) pitfalls, etc. In other words, all I am doing is making notes, confused accuracies (I hope), which would not find a place in neat arrangements. I have now only interest in some place where I can do freely and unencumbered what I please. I don't

know why I am writing this to you. I wish I had a little more
time to work, really, that is all.

Best luck.

Yours,
WILLIAM

[*In 1928 Pound wrote Williams about Louis Zukofsky, a promising young poet. They met in New York and began a long friendship which flowered in the Objectivist Movement in poetry.
Mrs. Celia Zukofsky has set WCW's "Pink Church" to music.*]

65: TO LOUIS ZUKOFSKY

March 23, 1928

My dear Zukofsky: By "human values" I suppose Ezrie means
that in his opinion I can't write. Dammit, who can write, isolated
as we all find ourselves and robbed of the natural friendly stimuli
on which we rest, at least, in our lesser moments? But undoubtedly the old ant-eater didn't mean anything at all other than that
he'd like me to make your acquaintance, and you mine.

So you are responsible for *Exile*[1] now. Is that so? Come over
to this suburb some Tuesday, Friday or Saturday evening for a
country meal and a talk and explain to me what all has taken
place in "the center" while I have been rusticating. I'd like
greatly to see you, since you come with an introduction from my
old friend. But do call up since I am a laborer and my time must
be arranged to fit the advent of a guest. I have a good cook.
What do you like especially to eat?

Yours,
W. C. WILLIAMS

---
[1] *The Exile* (1927-28) was edited by Ezra Pound.

66: To Louis Zukofsky

April 2, 1928

Dear Zukofsky: Yes, yes. You have the rare gift. As with everything else there are plans—the tripping rhythm—but not always the tripping rhythm—just sometimes. It spoils the adagio effect. It is notable that the lines have such an excellent internal necessity that they must be read slowly. It is thoughtful poetry, but actual word stuff, not thoughts for thoughts. It escapes me in its analysis (thank God) and strikes against me a thing (thank God). There are not so many things in the world as we commonly imagine. Plenty of debris, plenty of smudges.

This has been a pleasure, the reading of your poem. You make me want to carry out deferred designs. Don't take my theories too seriously. They are not for you—or for you, of course, or anybody.

I'd give my shirt to hear the Matthaus "Passion" this week, but I doubt if it can be done. If I do get there in spite of everything, I'll cast an eye around for you.

But your work's the thing. It encourages me in my designs. Makes me anxious to get at my notes and the things (thank God) which I did not tell the gentleman. Thanks for the supper. As soon as work lightens a bit for me here in the suburbs, I want you to come out. I congratulate Pound on his luck in finding you. You are another nail in the—coffin. Damn fools.

Yours,
WILLIAMS

67: To Marianne Moore

April 9, 1928

Dear Marianne: It is very interesting to me to read what you have chosen for reproduction in *The Dial*.[1] The effect produced

---

[1] From *Voyage to Pagany*.

does not give an impression of the book, tho' it does give a taste of the writing. It is, in effect, something like what H. D. did to a poem of mine many years ago.[2] She (and Richard Aldington) edited the poem before publishing it in *The Egoist*. I liked what they did but I have since wondered if they really knew what I was talking about. I really wish I could have the benefit of your careful reading of the manuscript before it goes to the printer. Perhaps you will let me submit sections of it here and there to you, sections that puzzle me, for your criticism before I let them have it. I have in mind reading over the whole thing with a pencil in hand and with your present notes before me. Then someday I'll appear before you with the manuscript carefully marked for you to read a paragraph or two here and there. Or perhaps I'll not bother you at all.

Will you please return the sheets enclosed under separate cover after you have extracted what you desire.

Many thanks for your kindness.

WILLIAM

68: To LOUIS ZUKOFSKY

Easter, 1928

Dear Zukofsky: Was the Matthaus' "Passion" well sung? I wish I could have been there.

What meeting you meant to me was at first just that Pound had admired your work. I was amazed to see you, nothing like what I had imagined. Then just reticence.

I did not wish to be twenty years younger and surely I did not wish to be twenty years older. I was happy to find a link between myself and another wave of it. Sometimes one thinks the thing has died down. I believe that somehow you have benefited by my work. Not that you have even seen it fully but it proves to me (God Damn this machine) that the thing moves by a direct relationship between men from generation to generation. And

---

[2] The poem was "March"; see H. D.'s letter to WCW, *Kora in Hell*, p. 15.

that no matter how we may be ignored, maligned, left unnoticed, yet by doing straightforward work we do somehow reach
the right people.

There must be an American magazine. As I have gotten older,
I am less volatile over projects such as this (a magazine)[1] less
willing to say much but more determined to make a go of it
finally—after I am 70 perhaps—. Perhaps it will crystallize soon.

WILLIAMS

69: TO EZRA POUND

April 16, 1928

Dear Ezra: Your present letter rescued me from an oozy hell.
Your offer is generous. I hereby give up any thought of a new
magazine. Within two weeks I'll let you know what kind of
material—what kind of impetus it is that has been stirring me.
If you feel impelled to give me a whole number of *Exile* when
you have the material in hand, well and good. But I'll be content
with as much space as comes my way.

But it is a delight to me to feel a possible bond of workman-
ship being exercised between us today. Damn it, why don't—why
didn't I seek you sooner? *Exile* is a good venture; let me from
now on really throw my energy into it—not for my name or for
myself in any way, but just to do it. I'll do it. For a year at least
I'll shower you with anything I can rustle up or squeeze out.
I want to. I need to. I have felt sometimes of late that I am
sinking forever.

This is just to accept your offer. More later. I heartily support
your judgment of Zukofsky's excellence (in the one poem at
least) and he seems worth while personally.

BILL

[*Williams met Charles Demuth "over a dish of prunes at Mrs.
Chaim's boarding house" in Philadelphia, while Williams was*

---

[1] *Exile.*

studying at the University of Pennsylvania and Demuth at Drexel. Demuth was fascinated by his friend's poetry and interpreted several in paint, chief of which is "The Great Figure," now hanging in the Metropolitan Museum of Art. The poem was suggested by a hooting and clanging fire engine with the number 5.]

70: To CHARLES DEMUTH

May 12 or I guess 7 is right [1928]

Dear Deem: The unfinished poster[1] is the most distinguished American painting that I have seen in years. I enjoy it for five or six distinct reasons, color, composition, clarity, thought, emotional force, ingenuity—and its completeness. Well, it's very satisfying to me and I congratulate you.

I like the 5 better than I did at first, but the blankness of the red in the center bothers me. It should be blackened or something. I feel in this picture that the completion that was once felt and made the composition a whole has been lost and that you have tried twenty times to recapture and that every try has left a trace somewhere so that the whole is tortured. It needs some new sweep of imagination through the whole to make it one. It is no longer one but—not even 5. It is all shaken up.

Maybe to go back to 5 as a theme would solve it. 5 somethings, I don't know what.

Oh hell, I suppose you're tired of the picture. Maybe Stieglitz' suggestions are all that are necessary: to frame the picture better and to make the gold five a *smooth* metallic figure instead of pocky as it is now.

But my own feeling, as I told you over the phone, is to take the hint from the picture itself. That is, to use the overlapping of planes, one contour passing partly into the next. If that were used more through the solid red center (as it is used among the figures which surround it) the whole would gain by a unity of treatment which would cast a unity of feeling over it all. You

---

[1] "The Great Figure," in the Metropolitan Museum of Art.

have, in fact, done something of that with the very center of the picture but not enough.

The color of the biggest 5 is muddy, too.

Oh well, the thing's got to be imagined over again. See if you can't recall your first thought. *À la Recherche du Temps Perdu!*

I was delighted with the vigor of the whole show. Floss was wanting to buy the water color until we heard that it was taken —and at how much! Fine.

I wish we could see more of you, but Jesus knows it ain't possible. This summer I mean to drive out to Lancaster if it's my last act. Best luck and best wishes.

Yours,
WILLIAM CARLOS WILLIAMS

71: TO FLORENCE HERMAN WILLIAMS

Tuesday, June 19, 1928

Dearest Floss: I've just finished correcting the last of the galley proofs of the novel[1] this minute—8:30 A.M. I've been up since 6. It has been a drive, with all the other things I've had to do for the last ten days. But I got a great thrill from the last episode in the book to compensate me for my pains. It is wonderfully improved now and makes easily the best reading there is in the damned long-winded what-ever-it-is that I have written. Yes, I have to confess that I am not altogether disgusted with my newest child. And I'm glad it will not be out till you are home. That would be entirely out of place. You must be here to share whatever there is—blame and perhaps some praise. I really need you.

But I am an insane person—the longer I live the more I realize it—and the more I realize I am not much different from anyone else. We are all crazy—but I seem to be more so than some. Perhaps it is my only value. I simply crash all together. Here's Smoky come in to curse me for leaving her out last night, in the rain. She is on Billy's bed now licking herself. But she makes me tired. She hides in the evening, then comes out to play at 4 A.M. The

---

[1] *Voyage to Pagany.*

other night she twice jumped right on my bed, waking me up and scaring me. Finally, I had to yank her out by the back of the neck and kick her into the yard—at about 4:30.

How are you getting on? I hope you are not having to fuss much about baggage. In some ways it must be a real help to have the boys with you, since they are strong and can speak French now. Really, it must be a lot of fun. I can see you all as plain as daylight, damn it! Well, kiss 'em all for me. And the boat trip should really be fun. Just in itself it is something. And you'll be coming *toward* your boss, not going away from him, as I was when I was bound "homeward."

Less than four weeks now before you view the wreck! Yes, I'll see that the driver brings us back through the Hudson Tunnel. But it will not be my car. I refuse to have my long-legged family jam itself into that bus of mine. I'll get a big touring car. The four of us can then sit on the back seat. Good night! Good night! It sure seems strange. Sometimes I feel just as you do that it isn't really so. I get panicky, especially at night. Then I plunge into some work.

The Luceys were here for dinner on Sunday. Lovely people. We sat out on the back lawn on chairs we brought from the house and talked for two or three hours. I am just getting the cards you sent from Stuttgart.

Practice is quite active in spite of the summer season. Now I must get to work on the poem—but the proofs and the usual medical work have held me lashed to the mast for weeks. I'm crazy to get to the poem—please do not speak of it to anyone. Nobody but you knows of its existence. This is a pleasure I have reserved for you exclusively, if it turns out to be a pleasure.

Love, dear, from your hubby,
BILL

My gray suit just came back, neatly pressed. And that's life again.

The publisher wants me to dedicate the book to someone—and so: "To the first of us all, my old friend, EZRA POUND, this book is affectionately dedicated." (He doesn't know it. Perhaps he won't be pleased. But what the h. do I care?)

Your ramblers, by the way, are magnifique, all except the Star of Persia, which is no good. . . .

Remember me to all my old enemies in Paree. After all, Paris is right. How in hell are you going to get along together except by raising hell with each other? Therefore it can be said that France and Germany are perfect neighbors, almost married. In fact, man and wife—yes? It's a question of affection. Oh well, it's easier to talk than to write, and yet the firmness of the written word is a great thing. It is becoming more and more the center about which this small piece of protoplasm revolves—that and his distracting lady—and all that she means, and will mean in the days, and I hope years to come. I have begun to look into the next few years now that this one is ending.

72: TO EZRA POUND

June 25 [1928]

deer Editur: Your suggestions regarding—etc., etc., very welcome. At this time of the day, the week, the month, the year, I find myself, however, about as word sensitive as a three-toed sloth. I couldn't retouch those poems for any money in the ooniverse.

But I am more than willing to make cuts to this effect that the poems you speak of will be *spurloss versengt. Raus mit Ihnen!* Thus the following pomes will disappear from the script—and chuck 'em in the waste basket: Underwear poem (p. 1), First poem (p. 4), pome (p. 6), pome (p. 15).

Yes, that helps a lot.

I'll send *In the Am. Grain* to your Austrian lady in a few days. And now, me old frien', lemme tell ya what I done las week. Havin' writ a novel what I always sez I would never in the world do (nothin does, does, does as it use to do, do, do!), why, I sez to myself this is somethin'. Well, then who shall I hang it onto? Why, who else but my old friend and college chum Ezrie, sez I. So this is to let you know that I writ it all out fine and high sountin and it'll be print in the front of that there novel, as nice as you please. What do you think? Why it's dedicated to you. God help me. I hopes you likes it. But if you don't why you can tear out the dedication page in the copy I'm a going to have them send you—as soon as it's printed and as soon as I get around to signing my ugly scrawl into it.

Anybody you think should get complimentary copies? Send me their names. Official publishing date is "after Labor Day." But you should have a copy the end of August. Give me a little blurb will you? That is, of course, if you don't feel disgraced.

Remember me to Dorothy. I'd like very much to know what her reaction to the novel will be. I'm most anxious to have direct words from all whom I know—since there is to be another one, another novel (already ordered by the publisher![1] My God.) Please do not think, however, that I am going to do it to order. It will be much different from the current one. Meanwhile I have—many other projects. God what a fool. I am sick with work as it is but I suppose the Jew in me likes punishment. Anyhow that's the way I get myself into the terrible mill which writing is sometimes— and must be so. Wish I could find a publisher for a new book of poems.

I'm really delighted that you like Zukofsky's batch of choosings. You'd be amused to see the stuff he didn't take. Yet he did a fine job, believe me—

Yours,
BILL

73: TO LOUIS ZUKOFSKY

July 5, 1928

Dear Louis: Poems are inventions richer in thought as image. Your early poems, even when the thought has enough force or freshness, have not been objectivized in new or fresh observations. But if it is the music, even that is not inventive enough to make up for images which give an overwhelming effect of triteness—as it has been said. The language is stilted "poetic" except in the piece I marked.

---

[1] This was to be *White Mule,* published by New Directions in 1938.

Eyes have always stood first in the poet's equipment. If you are mostly ear—a newer rhythm must come in more strongly than has been the case so far.

Yet I am willing to grant—to listen.

BILL

74: To Louis Zukofsky

July 18, 1928

Dear Louis: Certainly the "Lenin" outdistances anything in the earlier book of poems as the effect of a "thing" surpasses all thought about it. It is the second poem of yours that I like, the first being the long one. In some ways this poem is your best work (that I have seen). It has the surging rhythm that in itself embodies all that is necessary to say, but it carries the words nevertheless and the theme helplessly with it. The word "continual" at the end is fine.

It is this, the thing that this poem is, that makes you what you are today—I hope you're satisfied! No doubt it is the underlying theme to me of whatever feeling we have for each other. It seems to me surely the contrabass for everything else we may do. If there is not that under our feet (though I realize that you are speaking of a star), then we cannot go on elaborating our stuff.

Sometimes though I don't like your language. It probably is me and not you who should be blamed for this. You are wrestling with the antagonist under newer rules. But I can't see "all live processes," "orbit-trembling," "our consciousness," "the sources of being"—what the hell? I'm not finding fault. I'm just trying to nail what troubles me. It may be that I am too literal in my search for objective clarities of image. It may be that you are completely right in forcing abstract conceptions into the sound pattern. I dunno. Anyhow, there you are.

I will say that in this case the abstract, philosophic-jargonist language is not an obstruction. It may be that when the force of the conception is sufficiently strong it can carry this sort of thing. If the force were weaker the whole poem would fall apart. Good, perhaps. Perhaps by my picayune, imagistic mannerisms I hold together superficially what should by all means fall apart. . . .

Yours,

BILL

Later: . . . virtue exists like a small flower on a loose piece of earth above a precipice. And isn't it a fine day.

Yours,

BILL

75: TO EZRA POUND

Monroe, N. Y.
Aug. 11, 1928

Dear Ezra: Thayer seems to have all but nothing to do with the management of *The Dial* at the present time—from what I am able to infer from a talk I had with Mary Ann.[1] The rumor I heard, that *The Dial* was for sale and might be bought by G., is perhaps no more than a rumor. I have heard nothing more of it since. If *The Dial* is sold and bought, I am sure that it would mean the retirement of our Mary. She will not sell out, I know, but would probably go back to the library—on starvation wages. Marianne gets little credit for her fight in New York but stands aces high with me for what she is doing, not—though—for what she is able to accomplish, unfortunately. *The Dial* is a dead letter among the publisher crowd. It almost means that if you are "one of *The Dial* crowd" you are automatically excluded from perlite society as far as influence in N. Y. goes. And yet I myself feel so disgusted with *The Dial* for its halfhearted ways that I am almost ready to agree with anyone concerning its worthlessness.

Marianne, however, is never included by me in my condemnations; she is doing quietly all she can to warp things toward a better policy—but she will not succeed. . . .

If Watson sells I will positively, for once in my life, stir every-

---

[1] Marianne Moore.

thing about me in an effort to have him support *Exile*. It is the first sensible proposal of the sort that I have ever encountered.

As to the Hart Crane-Josephson group—to hell with them all. There is good there but it's not for me. As it stands, Crane is supposed to be the man that puts me on the shelf. But not only do I find him just as thickheaded as I am myself and quite as helplessly verbose at times but that he comes up into clarity far less often. If what he puts on the page is related to design, or thought, or emotion—or anything but disguised sentimentality and sloppy feeling —then I am licked and no one more happy to acknowledge it than myself. But really I do not feel so violently about the group. I am quite willing that they shall be what they are for there is nothing there that I expect to be caught copying for the next twenty years. To hell with them. But if I can help them, I will. Ha, ha!

I'm on my vacation. Just finished *The Education of Henry Adams*. Also John Dos Passos' *Orient Express*. The first interested me enormously for its information and for the mental balance of Adams. Its style is probably all the style there was in the U. S. in his day. It was refreshing to me to find how much of what he said is—after all—pure style: never to be understood. Now I want to go at his *Mont-St. Michel and Chartres*. A fine old fellow, credit to his country and any country—or all countries, I should say, as any sensible person must be—being international.

I have Soupault's *Dernières Nuits de Paris* with me and the first volume of Gide's *Si le grain ne meurt*. Also *Conditioned Reflexes* by Pavlov. God! if only I had time! If only I could devote even ten percent of my days to what writing means to me. Oh well, oh well! if I had all the time in the world to devote to it I'd probably do no more than I do and it wouldn't have, probably, half the taste to it it has now.

I have heaps of undigested notes to thumb through both physically and mentally. Then there is a book of—theories! to design, and a new so-called novel to thrash out. Of course it isn't a novel at all. I can't write fiction. All I do is try to understand something in its natural colors and shapes. Since it must have some kind of shape to be seen by me at all it grows to be—if it please—a novel.

The first few pages of Soupault, by the way, are delightful reading. Easy, deceptive, accurate to the rules of conversation (which

I am afraid Hem doesn't at all understand, since it is rarely as expressive as he makes it and almost twice as succinct), just batting the air effectively and swimming in it—like an airplane. I like the Soupault better than anything of his that I have encountered. Perhaps it will grow foolishly fantastic later in the book—as much of the little modern French stuff that I have seen does.

What *transition*—per Josephson—wants to say is that you are a conservative. You are, what of it? It's just a class of radicals which wants to sell what it has high, whereas the rest don't know the value of anything, half the time. Anyhow with you it's constitutional, and being so it hasn't kept you from recognizing the best for twenty years or more before anyone else did so. Naturally you ain't God, and you are thickheaded when there's no need of it—on occasion—but I'll bet my everlasting shirt that if someone with extraordinary brains gave you and anybody else that I can think of half a million to do literature with, the Josephsons and Burkeses and Cranes and all of them would look old fashioned. That's not flattery but my frank opinion. And this would be so because you know what you are talking about, and they dont.— Or so it seems to me.

Under separate cover you will receive a copy of last Sunday's *Tribune Book Section*. I was invited up to see this here Isabel Paterson. She lit into you and wanted to larf you and Antheil off the stage. I was saying was there anything that could be done to get decent literature through the customs for private libraries without having it stole by the government. Then she started to laugh at your name, says she: "All he wants to do is to find fault with something. That's all he ever does." Then says I, "&S6 &$"! For once I got mad. She and Burton Rascoe and a couple of others listened very politely, I thought. Later I quoted them the gist of my article about Antheil. Again they listened. Isabel retorted, however, that she had heard the same sort of thing concerning some other N. Y. composer (Leo Arnstein) ten years ago and where was he now. Says I, "You didn't hear anything about him from me, did ya?" To which she had to admit that she didn't. Which is about as daring as I have ever been in public in my days. Who knows what the future may be?

The corn is almost ready for our lunch. After storm yesterday, lightning—which is very hopeful, in a way—and oppressive heat which usually makes me think of *South Wind*—etc.

I've nothing finished to send you just now. The novel should be out in a few weeks.

Remember me to Dorothy. . . .

Best luck,
BILL

76: To Marianne Moore

Monroe, N. Y.
August 23, 1928

Dear Marianne: It frightens me to have you accept my poem.[1] I know that you are not one to judge of a work save as it stands word by word on the page. But I am not used to acceptances at many hands so that I have become suspicious of my friends. Yet I am delighted.

The "are" in the last line was meant just to have it that the fly, the hummingbird, etc., as well as the lilies, were blossoming along with the lilies. Nevertheless, I too was uncertain of the syntax, or is it the grammar? As I reconsider the point I am inclined to have the printer insert "is" for the "are." Yes, unless you advise otherwise, please make the change indicated.

It will be a pleasure for me to do the review you ask for, but as I am far from my base of supplies and the book is unknown to me I'll have to ask you to send me a copy of it and as quickly as possible, as I'd like to do the work while I still have some time at my disposal.

The boys are here with us now and very charming too. Bill is almost fifteen; his voice is deepening; he is thoughtful, able and considerate; he has learned to speak rather good French. His mental development is indicated by his statement: "It's funny, sometimes when I see grownups I feel years and years older than they are." He is said to have been a month old when he was born.

---

[1] "The Lily." Reprinted in *C.E.P.*

Paul's state is different. When asked by Floss if he would lie to her his reply was: "I've already done it."

Demuth is very well, as well as a man can be who has to have two hypodermic injections every day of his life and whose food must be weighed at every meal. His mother is his patron saint. He will live on indefinitely, as long as we will. He told me he has just finished a large canvas with my poem "The Great Figure" (being the figure 5) as his subject.

Oh, and will you kindly look up for me a poem of mine in some back issue of *The Dial*, a poem whose name I have even forgotten, a longish poem in which there is a ballad in modified form with refrain.

Sincerely yours,
WILLIAM

77: To MARIANNE MOORE

August 30, 1928

Dear Marianne: It is strange, nothing whips my blood like verse. Sometimes I am dull to the point of feeling a defeat that appears to me synonymous with death. Verse lifts me up superbly. This is pagan and no real cure in a Christian's code. Mostly it is something I have written myself that rouses me. Often though, I get the same feeling from the work of others. The best of French painting does it. Matisse does it. Recently I felt it from all I could read of Donne's Poetical Works. Is this a crime? I mean how much may one deny life in order to satisfy this craving? Or should one devote himself blindly to this? The answer would be academic only, since I find my life fairly fixed. But still there come times when I feel that I would gladly give everything to which I am attached in order to let loose finally and completely in that stream and let it finish me if it wanted to and could.

The long and the short of all of which is that I have written another poem—inspired by your acceptance of the first—which I cannot change.

May I confess to your private ear that it is no longer a pleasure to me to be printed except by those—those two or three—oh well, oh well, oh well. It would be meeter if I said this after I had discovered more readers.

I hope you like the "Gay Wall Paper."

And—most important—please send me the single copy of *The Dial* containing "When Fresh It Was Sweet." Do not send the other copies. But if, at your leisure, you could have other work of mine that has appeared in *The Dial* copied—it would be of great help to me in getting up the contemplated collection.

Yours,
WILLIAM

"The Source" enclosed at last moment.

78: To EZRA POUND

Nov. 6, 1928

Dear Ezrie: Nothing will ever be said of better understanding regarding my work than your article in *The Dial*.[1] I must thank you for your great interest and discriminating defense of my position. Without question you have hit most of the trends that I am following with the effect that you have clarified my designs on the future which in turn will act as encouragement and strength for me.

Naturally I consider myself a fool for not getting out of Medicine. I do not consider myself a fool for having been a physician for the past twenty years. That was accurately figured out in its relation to my disposition and mental capabilities. It has all turned out precisely as I foresaw, save only that at my present age I planned to withdraw from active competition with the world and close up the gaps in my expositions, continuing at this till I was shoveled under or went daffy or satisfactorily convinced myself that I had failed.

I am now engaged in cutting out much of my medical work under the guise of becoming a "Specialist." Within a few months

---

[1] "The Position of Dr. Williams," November 1928.

I will have done with evening office hours, that hellish drag. But it is not going fast enough. I can't quit cold, for I would only torment myself into the grave if I did so. I ain't built that way, I mean to withstand financial worries or to discover ways of living aside from the work of my hands. I simply can't.

But things are moving, nevertheless, according to the plans. Perhaps I expect too much.

But I am touched by the sobriety of your review, that is what I set out to say, meaning to add that I am going on as best I can and that you have helped me there also. You also have grown older—without loss. In fact, I like your writing in what you have said of me as well as anything I have seen of yours in prose.

I have the new *Cantos* but there has been no time in which to read—as yet.

Yours,
BILL

[*"For a New Magazine" is a good inscription for WCW's activities in support of the little magazine, that phenomenon of advanced writing, which is forever dying and rising again like the Phoenix. Its name may be* Others *or* Contact *or* Blues *or* Pagany *or* Little Review, *but it is the same magazine. Standard procedure in launching a little magazine is to ask for a contribution (free, of course) from WCW, Marianne Moore, Ezra Pound, and a few lesser known poets, and to fill the rest of the pages with local and usually unpublished talent.* Blues *was edited by Charles Henri Ford and Parker Tyler, who became close literary friends of WCW.*]

79: To Charles Henri Ford

Nov. 12, 1929

Dear Ford: That's better—a swell cover. Yes, and under the economic pressure we all suffer, a quarterly is inescapable, forced on us, therefore a better face to the facts, and so better all around.

Blues is after all you. You must bear it yourself and make it go, no help to that, though help you must have.

There are four or five new quarterlies and what not. Some good, some (probably) bad. Each will be at its best a person, as I see it. Yours is the most unhindered of all—so far, most alert for the new—but not sure yet. If ever it will be.

But I like this issue. I like the English letter. I like the French scene. And the thing about the ferryman is clever as hell.

Rexroth is one of my favorites, though I like his present effort less than some others. His letter in the back of the number is well written. He has something, that boy.

And he is quite right in jumping me for my lack of lucidity and my statements which do not help. But all that means nothing to me at all but this—How can I do better? Time is lacking. The only reason I propound what I do, these bits of statements, is in recognition of the fact that they should be done better and more fully. Let someone else be lucid. I'd welcome it. Most are just dumb, say nothing, make no attempt to surmount the difficulties of a skeleton statement, they just leave their rags about.

I'd like some day to complete what I have to say, to articulate up the bones of my plea.

But *Blues* is coming on. Good, keep it up.

Yours,
WILLIAMS

[*Lincoln Kirstein and Bernard Bandler, while undergraduates at Harvard, projected* Hound and Horn, *which became distinguished not only for the quality of its contributions but also for paying its contributors, a rare feat among little magazines.*]

80: To LINCOLN KIRSTEIN

Dec. 8, 1929

My dear Kirstein: In reply to your letter of Dec. 5: I am delighted that you are pleased with the poem "Love in a Truck," it will give me great pleasure to appear in *H. & H.* a second time.

As to the last four lines: I believe you have spotted a weakness in my middle English! What I wanted to say was simply that spring had arrived or had come in. I was speaking in a mildly ironic vein, as much as to say: "Boy, it ain't half the dainty, sweet little affair of butterfles and daisies you think it."—What I should have said was simply "ycomen", mocking the old songs by using an old English form of speech.

Weeeel, let's make a change in the last line, let's say—

> the bounty
> of . . and spring
> they say—
> spring is here

Please make the change, indicated in the script. Many thanks.

Sincerely yours,
W. C. WILLIAMS

1930

March 13, 1930

Dear Ezra: Your last letter, *re Bifur,* etc., received. I'll tend to the various subjects therein mentioned during the next day or two.

As you may possibly have imagined, this is my mad season. Work is that which makes me maddest—not the weather. I'm rushing around trying to keep the medical lid on; only in the free moments between calls rushing to the typewriter to keep within sight of my literary—or what you will.

I've been up since 5.30 certifying the death of a man's wife (he cried) and now finishing the correction of the *Novelette.*

The latter will go forward to you by the next mail.[1] It is the prime provocation for this letter.

Naturally Nancy[2] will not want to print two books by me this year. And the poem should come first if she prints either. But the *Novelette* is very close to my heart—and no one will handle it here. You see what I mean.

The *Novelette* contains something I have been trying for half my life, yet—well, that's about enough of that. I hope you like the thing and that you will be able to find something in it suitable for *Variétés.*

What can I do? The answer is: Write.

Oh, Jolas will be using the first four chapters of the *Novelette* in *transition.* I'd suggest that you take the chapter called "Conversation as Design"—if I remember it correctly—it's in a drawer behind my back and I can't bother to turn around.

Hope Dorothy has some fun out of the thing. Floss and the ubiquitous Zuke are the only ones in this section of understanding

---

[1] It was published in Dijon.
[2] Cunard.

who have fallen for it. And no two people could approach the thing from a more divergent angle.

Yours,
BILL

[*Robert Carlton Brown was the Maecenas of the "Others Group" in Grantwood. He was also a poet in his own right, as this salute to Williams' Al Que Quiere! attests: "Petal-fingered for/humanity stroking/trim grim gray/gay American toreador/driving tall-scented shadows/down dusty/Yankee road for/freer greener less earthly pastures. Fresh-hearted daisy boy sitting/self-sunlit/on the wistful weather-beaten/front porch of America/holding out a bouquet of/damp inward-eyed violets/offering a trembling fistful of/nervous Fourth-of-July sparklers/shooting up to dazzle/bigger and better trans-Neptunians/suicidally giving themselves with him/-m—a spark-spraying bouquet/al que quiere."*]

82: TO ROBERT CARLTON BROWN

March 21, 1930

Dear Bob Brown: Who is this Gertrude Stein? It seems to me I remember an ambulance driver by that name whom I came across during the war. Anyhow I'm glad she likes me. It's funny about these women.

Gosh, man, I don't know what the hell to tell you about yourself. All I can think of is that you ought to have a Wasserman test done on you. Don't be offended—and maybe you've had it done already—but it's one of the things any man (or women) who is feeling fuzzy in the head ought to have done when he's approaching the mid-century mark.

Then have your blood pressure taken. It may be too high or too low. If your urine is wrong you'll have to take that into consideration too.

But those things aside, there's nothing like steady and remunerative employment to clear the head. When I am sick of life and myself in particular and ready to quit (so to speak), nothing clears my head like hard work which I cannot avoid. I begin to speed up and the sense of power that comes with that is the best tonic I know.

There's no use saying more. Anyhow I'm a children's specialist; I got sick of grownups and their ills years ago. To hell with them!

If this is anything to you, take it for the giving.

I'll look for the description of the reading machine in *transition* and tell you what I think of it when I see it. For myself nothing could possibly be more welcome. I am a slow, a painfully slow reader, anything that would help me speed the process up would be the purest bliss to me that I can imagine.

Best luck to you. Write again. If I can be of service I'm your man.

Yours,
W. C. WILLIAMS

1931

April 27, 1931

Dear Ken: Glad to hear from you. Glad you are on your way toward summer. I suppose "glad" is a Saxon word, sounds like it. I have been reading bits of translation centering around *Beowulf* recently. I like the place where Ethelwyn (is it?) comes down to the shore to tell the Danes to go to hell and they have to wait till the tide goes down before they can begin fighting.

Glad the new magazine is on or about to be on. What's its policy? Pro anything or just anti? Anyhow I have work for you whenever you want it. I write and there it lies, I don't even try to get published any more. But I haven't much poetry, just one short thing that's any good. But I have a ten page story that I like muchly—yes, I like it plenty and it ain't even censorable.[1]

Did you see Zukofsky's criticism of Ezra's *Cantos* in the recent *Criterion*. I think that it is fine stuff after he gets going. I'm sick of this God-damned hair-splitting that so many of the critics, the erudite critics, go in for. All that means nothing to me. But when Zuke speaks of Pound's excellences and lays the thing open for the eye and the ear, it is clear and it has power, and I can feel the weight of it and enjoy. If you haven't read the thing, do so. Skip the first page or two.

Then, as a diversion, read what I myself said on the same subject in the last *Symposium*.[2]

I've been looking for your name recently but found it not. What t'ell? whatche doin' these days? And yes, we'll be up to see you soon. It may be age, but I've been physically fat but exhausted this spring. Not that it has made much difference in what I have done

---

[1] "The Paid Nurse."
[2] *Selected Essays,* pp. 105-112.

—only spring ain't what it has been other years. Probably a good sign. Let 'em bloom, is the way I feel this year.

My best to your lady and the brats.

Yours,
BILL

84: TO MARIANNE MOORE

Sept. 26, 1931

Dear Marianne: You have elated me—and made me miserable—in that there is no world in which we may refresh each other—we, I mean all of us. There is none since you have shown that it exists here and there—but nowhere. We so rarely communicate, any of us even when we talk or write. What a delight it is to read you again. Bless you! It goes down through me as the doxology used to and then didn't any more.

Rhapsodic? Not at all. I mean every word of it in the strictest sense of which I am capable.

The book is being gotten ready but whether the bridegroom will come or not I cannot say. In any case I'll have it fully resigned to the publication when wanted. Sam Putnam, I have heard, is far from well. I think however that he'll go through with the business.

What a life we might live were writing permitted to us as a life. Now we write from prison, which is too barren an existence for the exuberance which writers, of all people, need for their—for the fullest exuberance which you show as by flashes in your work—

Many thanks for this refreshment—I'll let you know the course of events later.

Yours,
W.

85: To Ezra Pound

Dec. 8, 1931

Dear Ezra: Aw can't see that Zuke[1] needs Urup just now, not at any pussonal sacrifice on his friends' part leastwise. And he has a couple uv friens, here and there, who might help him. Now his place just now is here facing the harbor and the whited Statue of Miss Liberty—which his cubicle in Brooklyn faces very pleasantly —if it does face north and a French window his only bulwark against the wind. But he has a private bath and toilet to boot. Leave him lay for the moment at least. In the spring it may be different. In fact he might need a change by that time if he survives.

He has just completed (during the past month) an anthology which Putnam has. Now I don't know Putnam well, but I've written to him and had no answer after having been led to believe that he might answer very substantially, etc., etc. New ef you wants Zuke to see Yurup, have Put. bring out that anthology first, and if you can't do the second why think of the first.

Fer meself, I've a book of poems doing a Nurmi around these here book publishers, I think they used to call 'em in Nieu York. It's a nice book too, big and fat and willing to go to bed with almost anyone for a price. But I don't want no cheap guys. I wants a reglar publisher what knows how to do it, you get me, with a limousine, flowers, a swell feed and, you know. . . . I ain't no Lesbian, I don't care for violets.

If I get any bids I'll let you know. No real ones yet, but one good nibble at least.

Then I'm editor of a new quarterly, *Contact!* up again and soon to be at 'em. And we got a couple of guys Bob[2] picked up when he was last in New York who are backing it. I say they are backing it, but it's their mag. I'm just the, you know, editor—until we meet again or something. All I does is to pick out what goes into the

---
[1] Louis Zukofsky.
[2] McAlmon: Moss and Kamin.

magazine—if it ain't too dirty or lood, whatever that means. The first issue is to appear in January. I'll see that you get one.

There are other projects in the offing but none sufficiently certain to talk about. I go on writing *White Mule,* a few pages every three months and Johns goes on publishing it in *Pagany.* For my interest in *Pagany* continues, tho' I have little or nix to do with it.

My boy Bill goes to college next year if he makes it and I don't get caught by the depression. So far, although I am badly in the hole on stocks I bought, I can still hold my head up, tho' not very high. The kid was captain of his soccer team. The other brat played end of the second football team. The wife is well and getting buxom. My mother, who lives with me, busted her hip two years ago and walks little. We just found out that my grand-mother who died in 1920 left sixty dollars in the bank at the time! her total estate. I hope I can get it out.

Anyhow, here we are, and there we are and what t'ell. I write all the time and get less done or more or different and I hope my pomes gets published because that would be a help—as they say.

I read what you said about me in the May, June, July *The New Review*—and it embarrassed me—but I know you're right and it's to the point. It's just a temperamental job to feel anything but the force of what is being said, and still I felt embarrassed and still you're right. Maybe in this new *Contact*—

BILL

1932

[*Wayne Andrews was coeditor of* Demain, *undergraduate leaflet in French mimeographed at Lawrenceville.*]

86: To Wayne Andrews

March 10, 1932

Mon Cher Andrews: *Vous avez bien raison, mon temps est precieux et, de plus, mon français est mauvais. Mais ça m'a fait grand plaisir de voir un interest si grand en vous et votre confrere dans la littérature en général et en particulier la littérature française-moderne.* Hell, I can't go on like that. It's good to get the feel of you fellows daring to take an interest in international letters and having the hardihood to speak of it in the French language, as you have done. Naturally you will be sat on. What do you expect? All intelligence is taboo save to those possessing red, white and blue tickets.

The French poets have had no influence on me whatever—unless it be something so occult and subtle that I myself have been unaware of it. I have never read one modern French poem that I can remember having seen, though I must say I have stumbled on bits of poems here and there from time to time. It may sound odd, but it is the truth.

I have, however, been influenced by French painting and the French spirit, which, through my mother, is partly my own. It would have been pleasant to answer you in the language you used to address me. It wasn't possible. Good luck to you.

Sincerely yours,
William Carlos Williams

[*In the summer of 1935 T. C. Wilson and Ezra Pound collected an anthology of Modern English and American Poetry, to which WCW contributed, for* The Westminster Magazine *of Ogle-*

thorpe University, Georgia. Williams had become interested in
Wilson's writing, which he tried to get published.]

87: To T. C. WILSON

March 10, 1932

My dear Wilson: Let's have another short story—of the quality
of that last paragraph, down in the cellar with the butter smells.—
But, honestly, we've got to keep away from the adolescent emotions. It's stupid to say that, a man will write what he will—but
we've got—somehow—for the time being at least—to show ourselves more tormented. Our life is putrescent about us. We've got
to live in it. We're not kids any longer. What have we to say to
the god-damned offenses which we as writers and supposedly intelligent men and women and these here United States—etc., etc.?

I don't care how young you are, you've got to live in it as well
as I. Your intelligence doesn't have to be mellow—sophisticated
—what you will: but it must at least realize what we are up
against. Let's at least probe our immediate hells to the bottom.

I'll keep the poem on the cross—I can't promise to use it at
once but I may.[1] And let's have a story that turns back a—that
opens up your phase of the imbecility which keeps us all in-
effective.

Yours,
WILLIAMS

Guess I'll keep them all for a while—at least.

[*Marsden Hartley, the painter, used to circulate easily and affably*
through the Greenwich Village parties of the Others, Little Review *and* Dial *days, acting as "granddaddy to all, male and*
female," as Williams notes. To one party he brought Robert
McAlmon, one of his models. Williams was very interested in

---

[1] For *Contact* II.

*and highly critical of Hartley's paintings, which he viewed
chiefly at The American Place of Alfred Stieglitz.*]

88: TO MARSDEN HARTLEY

[Fall, 1932]

Dear Marsden: I envy you the pleasure of reading my book, especially the chapter "The Destruction of Tenochtitlan," in the public gardens of Mexico City. By this book you will see how heartily
I am in agreement with you when you damn the Spanish Con-
quistadores and how little you need to fear treading on my toes in
anything you say. Your letter is a magnificent document, I had
no idea you were still so thoroughly up and coming. The "health"
of your views about art is still sticking by me, it helped me greatly
to—or it, the "health" I mean, helped me greatly in the writing
of still another chapter of a book I have in hand, the story of an
infant who is getting herself up to the age of ten months in the
thirteenth chapter now.[1] I'll be sending you the book some day
if we both live long enough. Do you want a copy of *In The American Grain* for yourself in the meantime?

Floss was not feeling so well the day your letter arrived so I sat
on the edge of the bed to read it to her. She much appreciates
your speaking up for her that she has been such a help to me in
my progress toward retrogression into some sort of sanity of existence—back to the alphabet—though Lord knows I don't mean
Gertrude Stein for the present. Floss is fine, these days, and so are
the boys, though the younger one has arrived at the stage where
he steals my cigarettes, and Bill, the older, is away at college so I
don't know so much about him as I used to think I used to.

The typewriter was a great improvement. My regards to your
sister!

Really that was a real west wind of a letter, the best I have received from anyone for a long time.

I can't tell you anything of the happenings among the painters
in New York, for I seldom go into the city these days to see the

---

[1]*White Mule.*

shows. All I seem to find time for is work at my practice and work at my writing. Meanwhile the old head goes on refining itself, I believe, and the zest grows stronger—every sort of zest I've ever taken a delight in. I think the writing is firmer, less frothy in spots and has a better direction. Only I can't get published very easily, which may be my saving for all I know. I look forward to twenty years of continued development, however, with time for summations and reminiscences after that. Concretely I have just ended an editorship of another small magazine (*Contact,* revived) with the resolution never to do that sort of thing again. People who have money to put up for such ventures are too slippery for me and my time is too limited.

A book of poems should be coming out this spring, the work of the last ten years. The rest of this year I want to spend on my novel, of which I spoke earlier, *White Mule.* Here's hoping.

If you go to Germany, as you plan, please do not forget us but write as you say. Floss sends love and says that if you enjoy coming to this house, this house will always enjoy having you, so don't ever feel that you can be in N. Y. and give us the slip again.

Yours,

BILL

89: To MARIANNE MOORE

June 2, 1932

Dear Marianne: The first poem especially—but I have read all three only the once as yet. That one, however, is reward enough for any waiting.

Why should I not speak in superlatives? It couldn't be to a more discerning listener: there is no work in verse being done in any language which I can read which I find more to my liking and which I believe to be so thoroughly excellent. You have everything that satisfies me. I omit the catalogue. No, I won't. Your words have an immediate quality which only comes when the intelligence matches the acuteness of the sensual perception to which you add an aimed heat of the emotions, without which there can never be anything but blur. This would sound horrible on the jacket of a book, but it can be said to you in private. The poem itself proves that you cannot be marked by it.

And to me especially you give a sense of triumph in that it is my own scene without mistaking the local for the parochial. Almost no one (or very few) has felt the full and conclusive impact of that necessity in the writing. The meaning of the objective, the realization of its releasing quality, instead of its walling effect when badly comprehended, has been nowhere so well forced to the light. It is the underlying reality as well as the supreme difficulty of an art.

Allow me to congratulate you without reserve. I wish only that what you have said in the make-up of your compositions—especially the first one—were more. It is my only reservation in the praise I want to shower on you, that you are not everywhere, abundantly, instead of just one, now and then, with long intervals and miles between.

I suppose there is nothing to do about it but to write, also, as well as I can. Still I must be permitted to say that I regret that I cannot actually see you oftener in the rare light of such work.

McAlmon wrote me recently from Majorca urging me to try by every means at my disposal to get you to send me some writing for the magazine *Contact*. He spoke of the appreciation which everyone, so to speak, has for you. That even when you publish nothing many people here and in Europe wait expectantly to hear from you. This is quite true. Send me what you may wish to at any time, I will be proud to print it.

Affectionately yours,
WILLIAM

P.S. Perhaps you'll be interested to know that I took my elder son, Bill, to Williamstown last Sunday to see the college there. That's where he wants to go. And in September! He is eighteen now. He says that it looks bad, he acknowledges that, for William Williams to want to go to Williams College in Williamstown—but somehow or other he plans to live down the imputation. He's a reasonably attractive young gentleman whose sole difficulty relative to his getting into that college seems to be an ingrained detestation of

Latin. But he has had to swallow four years of it for all that and will take the examination on June 23d. Just the one subject. He has passed in everything else. A blond gray-eyed son—

The brown-eyed one is a sophomore in high school here in Rutherford. He is trying for the baseball nine, substitute catcher —but he can't hit the ball very well as yet. And that crushes him to the earth. Yesterday I thought he would faint after striking out and hitting an easy one to third. Poor kid. But I tell him he'll grow older—even in a year! He hardly believes me.

Floss is, I think, in better shape generally than she has been in years—. And I'm wearing glasses. Also my hair is vanishing. That's an odd thing—to find oneself growing toward fifty. Not that I mind it in the least. But I don't like not being able to see dust flecks quite so distinctly as formerly—and the grains of pollen in the flowers. There are many compensations however. And I am convinced that they far overbalance the losses, especially when one has wanted only one or two things from life after all.

Last summer we went to Labrador, but this year we have built a balcony over my office on the third floor. The rail is of teak in imitation of that of a steamer. When the family, the boys, my mother and the maid are gone, Floss and I shall use that balcony extensively.

Ezra writes from time to time. They tell me he is getting fat in spite of tennis. I hear from Zukofsky, who is in California. Bob Brown is in New York. Rosenfeld had me in to supper a month ago. A certain Angel Flores who is in Ithaca has published a book of short stories of mine.[1] He's a good friend. I met the two children who edit *Contempto* from Chapel Hill, N. C.[2]

The garden is full of iris—and all the rest of it. Next week the roses. George Antheil wants me to do the libretto of an opera on an American theme for him.

Here's Floss who says she is going out on the promenade deck. She sends you her love. And so do I.

Yours,

W.

---

[1] *The Knife of the Times.*
[2] Milton Abernethy, A. J. Buttitta.

[*Sometime early in the thirties Williams met Nathanael (Pep) West and was exceedingly taken by his wit and ability. They teamed up to edit* Contact II, *which faded from lack of good material and preoccupation of the editors with children or women.* Miss Lonelyhearts *and* The Day of the Locust, *with their acid wit, will perpetuate West's fame and "talent, as fine as any of his day," Williams notes.*]

90: To Nathanael West

Quatorze Juillet, 1932

Dear Pep: After further thought I decided to write Kamin asking him to postpone his Communist number until the winter. I don't feel justified in putting off those who have so generously sent us their scripts any longer.

By this we should be able to get up a better Communist number, besides which we really cannot afford to go off into the special feature business until we have placed ourselves far more thoroughly than we have now as a forum of good writing. All we'll get by a Communist issue is a reputation for radicalism and not for good writing—which is our real aim. But later we can appear with an air of: there's good writing among the Communists too; they're not just propagandist crazy. Or that's the way I feel. Hope you'll back me.

See you next Tuesday.

Yours,
Bill

91: To Ezra Pound

June, 1932

Dear Ezra: I've been playing with a theory that the inexplicitness of modern verse as compared with, let us say, the *Iliad,* and our increasingly difficult music in the verse as compared with the more or less downrightness of their line forms—have been the result of a clearly understandable revolution in poetic attitude. Whereas formerly the music which accompanied the words amplified, certified and released them, today the words we write, failing a patent music, have become the music itself, and the understanding of the individual (presumed) is now that which used to be the words.

This blasts out of existence forever all the puerilities of the dum te dum versifiers and puts it up to the reader to be a man— if possible. There are not many things to believe, but the trouble is no one believes them. Modern verse forces belief. It is music to that, in every sense, when if ever and in whoever it does or may exist. Without the word (the man himself) the music (verse as we know it today) is only a melody of sounds. But it is magnificent when it plays about some kind of certitude.

Floss has just brought me up an applejack mint julep which I enjoy.—We do produce good applejack in Jersey—and Floss can mix 'em.

Confusion of thought is the worst devilment I have to suffer— as it must be the hell itself of all intelligence. Unbelief is impossible—merely because it is impossible, negation, futility, nothingness.—But the crap that is offered for sale by the big believing corporations—(What the hell! I don't even think of them, it isn't that). It's the lack of focus that drives me to the edge of insanity.

I've tried all sorts of personal adjustments—other than a complete let go—

Returning to the writing of verse, which is the only thing that concerns us after all: certainly there is nothing for it but to go on with a complex quantitative music and to further accuracy of image (notes in a scale) and—the rest (undefined save in individual poems)—a music which can only have authority as we—

I'm a little drunk—

Contact can't pay for verse or anything else. I mentioned to Pep West that you had more or less objectionably asked me if I was doing this (editing, publishing) *Contact* in order to offer you a mouthpiece—I told him I had told you to go to hell. He said he'd be mighty glad to have a *Canto,* that he thought them great.

But we can't pay a nickel—

(After another two hours)

The Junior Prom at the High School: Bill is taking his first girl (after an interval of five years). The fishing period and girl-hating has passed again. This one has taught him to dance—he is getting ready to take a bath—now when it is almost time to leave the house.

Yes, I have wanted to kick myself (as you suggest) for not realizing more about Ford Madox's verse. If he were only not so unapproachable, so gone nowadays. I want to but it is not to be done. Also he is too much like my father was—too English for me ever to be able to talk with him animal to animal.

It's the middle of a June evening

No news—much I'd like to do.

Yours,

BILL

92: To Lincoln Kirstein

July 23, 1932

Dear Mr. Kirstein: Certainly I shall be glad to wait for the check until you find it convenient to send it. Though few of us are able to do it, those of us who are publishing new work I mean, it should always be recognized that everything we print should be paid for. Which is to say that though *Hound & Horn* could get much of the material it prints today from its writers and not pay for it, your continuing to pay is particularly to your credit.

Your last issue gave me good reading. I heartily dislike the Leighton criticism, which is ill-tempered and short-sighted from the viewpoint of a modern technique which we Americans are in the act of creating for ourselves. There is a fundamental misapprehension in most opinions emanating from men who occupy teaching positions in the universities and who attempt to criticize new work, work created by conditions with which they do not have an opportunity to come inexorably into contact. They must fall back on something, something "universal," an ideal criticism which is somehow more related to what might be wished than to anything that is. I can't see that Radiguet's work has any bearing on our difficulties.—But the issue as a whole attracted me, particularly the translation from the French. My poem was beautifully printed.

WILLIAMS

93: To NATHANAEL WEST

Aug. 2 (late at night) [1932]

Dear Pep: May I take lunch with you this Friday at about 1 P.M. or a little earlier? That's a funny way to put it, but convenience is the objective. I want to get away again before three. This new *Contact* (if there is to be one) must be gotten under way. And it must not be dull, at all costs, if we can make it otherwise.

This is what I've been thinking: everything must be put aside for the sake of interest to the reader. Ruthlessly we've got to turn down anything that doesn't fit that purpose even though we make virtual blackguards of ourselves. And the first objective must be not to make this issue just another series of short stories. There's no trick in that. In a way, though it was bad otherwise, our first issue was much better in point of diversified interest than the second. This issue must be different from both those.

The reproduction is worthwhile. Follow it by the—not Brown but perhaps Jonathan Edwards. Then Brown. Then maybe Villa. Then Oppen's fragmentary poems. Topping. The Long poem—(maybe).—The essay by Parkes. And maybe after all I will do a Commentary. Maybe the Ben Franklin—*Miss Lonelyhearts*

Let me know if Friday will be convenient for you. I have a long thing by Sherry Mangan which we may run in two issues. It's censorable tho, I'm afraid. A terrific story of death and perversion.

Yours,
BILL

[*Kay Boyle, an inveterate contributor to the little magazine, came to know Williams first through her poems published in* Contact I. *The editorship of* Contact II *revived the relationship, and Williams attempted a complete assessment of literature and writers in a letter to her designed for* Contact.]

94: TO KAY BOYLE

[*1932*]

Dear Kay Boyle: You say: "Some kind of poetic form has to be found or I'll go crazy. I can't go on taking what you (and others) make possible and beautiful. I think I've got lots to say in poetry and no, no, no form. Lousy—loose—*no punch*—no shape—no agony of line like the back-side or a lovely thigh or whatnot."

Precisely—and a timely reaction of the first importance; it means the present moment for what it is, a formless interim—but those are periods calling more for invention which mask or should mask a feverish activity still out of sight to the generality of observers. There is no workable poetic form extant among us today.

Joyce and Stein have been paramount in knocking the props from under a new technique in the past ten years and enforcing it. They have specifically gone out of their way to draw down the attention on words, so that the line has become pulverous instead of metallic—or at least ductile. Your comment marks clearly for me the definite departure from that sort of thing toward a metrical coherence of some sort—not a *return* to anything, for God's sake let us be clear on that at the beginning. Let us once and for all understand that Eliot is finally and definitely dead—and his troop along with him.

But what remains? For myself, I have written little poetry recently. Form, the form has been lacking. Instead I have been watching speech in my own environment from which I continually expect to discover whatever of new is being reflected about the world. I have no interest, as far as observation goes, in the cosmic. I have been actively at work (if such sketchy trials as I employ can be called such) in the flesh, watching how words match the act, especially how they come together. The result has been a few patches of metrical coherence which I don't as yet see how to use—but they seem to run to groups of lines. Occasionally they give me the feel of authenticity.

You know, I think, enough of me to understand that I have no belief in the continuity of history. To me the classic lives now just as it did then—or not at all. The "Greek" is just as much in Preakness as it was in Athens. Everything we know is a local virtue—if we know it at all—the only difference between the force of a great work and a lesser one being lack of brain and fire in the second. In other words, art can be made of anything—provided it be seen, smelt, touched, apprehended and understood to be what it is—the flesh of a constantly repeated permanence. This must be a lot of bosh to anyone who isn't intimate with the materials. But to one who is working with the stuff it may mean something. If not—

But it doesn't mean enough to create form. It means this however—that whatever form we create during the next ten years will be, in excellence, like all the classic inventions, a new thing, a thing intrinsic in the times. It will probably foretell the decade that is to follow it. It will take its shape from the character of its age, not the "social" character, if so positively, not satirically. It will not be the symptom of a chronic bellyache or—something else. It will be like no classic which has preceded it. Why do we not read more of Juan Gris? He knew these things in painting and wrote well of them.

I have been working with prose, since I didn't know what to do with poetry. Perhaps I have been in error. Maybe I should be slaving at verse. But I don't think so. Prose can be a laboratory for metrics. It is lower in the literary scale. But it throws up jewels which may be cleaned and grouped.

I don't think any poetry ever originated in any other way. It must have been inherent in the language, Greek, Latin, Italian, English, French or Chinese.

And this should blast that occasionally pushing notion that the form of poetry (as that of any art) is social in character. Such an opinion is purest superficiality. The form of poetry is that of language. It is related to all art first, then to certain essential characteristics of language, to words then and finally to every-thing among all the categories of knowledge among which the social attributes of a time occur. The work of Einstein also merges into it, hardly a social phenomenon. It is not formed "like" the society of any time; it might be formed in a manner opposite to the character of the times, a formal rigidity of line in a period of social looseness. That is, the outstanding genius of such a time might, in his attic, be writing that sort of poetry.

This is difficult ground. One might sink in it. All that I wish to point [out] is that poetry is related to poetry, not to social statutes. It will, nevertheless, make its form of what it finds. And so does *seem* to be a social eye. It is nothing of the sort. It remains itself. It remains related only to poetry. Much more could be said about this. I myself can be accused of contradictions. Pos-sibly I have contradicted myself.

Bosh! All I want to do is to state that poetry, in its sources, body, spirit, in its form, in short, is related to poetry and not to socialism, communism or anything else that tries to swallow it; to reconcile this with the equally important fact that it deals with reality, the actuality of every day, by virtue of its use of language. Doing so, naturally it reflects its time, by coincidence. It does, that's all—or may, or may not.

As I have said, for *me*, its virtue lies in relating to the im-mediacy of my life. I live where I live and acknowledge no lack of opportunity because of that to be alert to facts, to the music of events, of words, of the speech of people about me. As well as to the speech of the muse, the intangible perfection of all ex-cellent verse.

And so some of the young men seem to me to be too much influenced by the disintegrationists, the users of words for their individual forms and meanings. They are after meanings (Joyce) and their objectivity as things (Stein). Well, as far as poetry is concerned, what of it?

Ezra Pound is too "like" the classics. He is a classicist, almost a pedant, according to some. His actuality is what has been forced on him by his disposition and the mode of life he affects. He

writes in American as far as he writes in any language, but his
meter is the purifications of older orders used with modern words.
He has brought back the modern language to the water of excellent poetic usage, then what the hell? He is teaching it classic
dancing. A dash of grotesquerie thrown in with a great sense of
time.

Pound is one of the few moderns worth reading. One can
differ with him so easily and excel him only with the greatest of
difficulty. He is still a worthwhile beginning for any poet writing
in our language. I don't think that he has solved anything for us.
His line is classic adaptation, no more.

Who else? Jeffers has not been able to overcome poetic diction.
Possibly he has something. I doubt it.

Robinson? Well, if you can find anything there. To me it seems
stiff English. I can't see a flicker. He has passion, tho, and a flare
for the story. His versification seems to me pure stucco. It loosens
nothing for thought, for feeling, for inclusion of a variety of
understanding. It seems closed, tight closed to me.

Wallace Stevens has something more than his play with sequences of sound. His line, under that, was sometimes fluid.
Worth reading again.

Yvor Winters seems to me bogged in ideas. His line has a
self-inflicted tendency to become short and to stay so. It excludes
too much. It has no largesse for the mind or the emotion.

As far as I can see, when we let go we get a loose nothing, a
rhythmical blur, a formlessness which is abhorrent now no matter what it may have been formerly. And when we close down
on the line we get classic imitation or tightness. The bucolic
simplicity of Robert Frost seems to me a halt.

English writers I exclude axiomatically. It may be that someone will later prove me blind. That must be my misfortune.
There will be time to judge of that later. Perhaps we should
turn to France, Italy, Russia. No.

Either I build here or there will be no building as far as I am
concerned. I'd rather feel Russia, France, or what have you as
it comes up here (including newspapers, radio despatches, etc.),
than get it direct. Oh, but that doesn't mean that I do not enjoy
excellence wherever it is. But that is a personal matter which I

will manage as I please. I am talking first, though, of poetic invention. In that I am a rival of France. I acknowledge them as overwhelmingly successful but I do not (henceforth) lean on them. That's past.

A poet should take his inspiration from the other arts too. Picasso? Which line is significant? Damned if I know. Maybe there is something running through it all. But he seems so intent on proving that he just doesn't have to work after any particular mode that I have lost interest in him. The dance? Angna Enters has a line which passes through her satire, but it doesn't seem, on second thought, much of an invention.

All I can see finally to rely on is the seriousness of poetry itself, that it stands equal to any endeavor. The fact that it takes us, turns over the mind, because the required form is not easy to come at, discloses its pertinence to the time and the intelligence. That must be the beginning, as it is about all there is to take hold of. There is, you see, in our minds the possibility of a technique which may be used. It must be large enough, free enough, elastic enough, new enough yet firm enough to hold the new well, without spilling. It must have a form.

Why? There's no use making a mystery of what we know and don't know about poetry. Though there is no clear perception of poetic form operative today, and we must understand precisely that there is never a poetic form of force and timeliness except that which is in the act of being created, there is no poetic form in theory, in the rules, there is no grammar of poetry—there is only poetry—it is the very essence of the thing that this is so.

No one can say what poetry will accord to, what it will be like, for the fact of its existence is in its nature a supersession, an assertion, one of whose minor attributes is the efflorescence, not surpassing rules—but disintegrating them.

Though there is no clear perception of poetic form today and though there can be none until the poem itself appears as the rule in fact, yet it is silly to make a mystery of the pre-masterly period. It is a period without mastery, that is all. It is a period in which the form has not yet been found. It is a formative time whose duty it is to bare the essentials, to shuck away the hulls, to lay open at least the problems with open eyes.

It is a time to use the intelligence on the problem and not in groans and ritual, no matter how "beautiful" or "old" that may be. It should be possible to state a minimum of what we can find that is—until we know better—true of modern verse. What it, leastwise, cannot be any longer as compared with the past. We ought to be able to make up our minds to a few things.

At least there is no use forgetting what we have learned in the past twenty years, there is no use in doing worse work than has been done, there's no use in going backward. That's a good place to begin. When I say backward I by no means intend to signify that we should not look back at past mastery. Look and be sure what you're looking for and at. But by backward I mean don't try to make the mistakes that can be made by lack of intelligence and information as to what has been going on. Personally, I'd like to start by saying, don't write sonnets. The line is dead, unsuited to the language. Everything that can ever be said from now until doomsday in the sonnet form has been better said in twelfth-century Italian. But I am speaking only figuratively now.

Poetry is creation of new form—

A minimum of present new knowledge seems to be this: there can no longer be serious work in poetry written in "poetic" diction. It is a contortion of speech to conform to a rigidity of line. It is in the newness of a live speech that the new line exists undiscovered. To go back is to deny the first opportunity for invention which exists. Speech is the fountain of the line into which the pollutions of a poetic manner and inverted phrasing should never again be permitted to drain.

That T. S. Eliot knows this (mainly) is at present the sole reason for reading him. He is concerned with the line as it is modulated by a limited kind of half-alive speech.

Then, the inclusiveness of the diction must be preserved. Local though the spring of genius may be, we do not live in medieval times, in the cities of northern Italy nor a walled Paris, Madrid or London, there can be no new enclosure of manner. The line must be pliable with speech, for speech, for thought, for the intricacies of new thought—the universality of science compels it. There is no use pretending that we live in a closed "poetic" world in which we do not need to know what is going on about us and then think we can invent poetry. Asinine presumption. Just as it is to look to the past for assurance—or perhaps we should look to the past for assurance and nothing else.

The modern line must at least exclude no possibility of intelligent resource. Thus it will include the age as the Homeric line included Greece, the Renaissance line its age and the Shakespearian line England. It need not be supposed that it included everything, every offshoot of English genius, it would be the end of a race if it did. But it cannot be great and exclude any major element of the civilization in which it exists.

It is this difficulty which makes present invention so excessively difficult—if at all possible. In the form, the form of the line (of which diction is a part) it must have room for the best of Joyce— the best of all living, terminal, bud-end reflection of thought and—Einstein—the Soviets. This is compelled (though the diagnosis of genius may exclude much that we think now is important). This is the seriousness of poetry itself.

So far I believe that Pound's line in his *Cantos*—there is something *like* what we shall achieve. Pound in his mould, a medieval inspiration, patterned on a substitution of medieval simulacra for a possible, not yet extant modern and living material, has made a pre-composition for us. Something which when later (perhaps) packed and realized in living, breathing stuff will (in its changed form) be the thing. That, at least, is my best estimate of Pound.

That, as your letter intimates, implies foreshadows—and this is the power that has set me going—next, the modern line must have an internal tension which is now nowhere.

Free verse—if it ever existed—is out. Whitman was a magnificent failure. He himself in his later stages showed all the terrifying defects of his own method. Whitman to me is one broom stroke and that is all. He could not go on. Nature, the Rousseauists who foreshadowed Whitman, the imitation of the sounds of the sea *per se,* are a mistake. Poetry has nothing to do with that. It is not nature. It is poetry. Whitman grew into senseless padding, bombast, bathos. His invention ended where it began. He is almost a satirist of his era, when his line itself is taken as the criterion. He evaporates under scrutiny—crumbling not into sand, surely, but into a moraine, sizable and impressive because of that.

The line must, as a minimum, have a well-conceived form within which modification may exist. Without this internal play upon the stops, it cannot achieve power. Thank you for bringing the point into prominence.

But there we are almost at the end of our resources. To be more specific would be to get into the guessers.

One more positive thing though—or minimal requisite. It seems to be that the "foot" being at the bottom of all prosody, the time has come when that must be recognized to have changed in nature. And it must be seen to have changed in its rhythmical powers of inclusion. It cannot be used any longer in its old-time rigidities. Speech for poetry is nothing but time—I mean time in the musical sense. That is where the real battle has been going on.

The new verse is a new time—"rag-time" is only a penny sample; "jazz" is excessively limited when looked at thoroughly. Its rigidities are exactly like that of all that we have outgrown. Take away its aphrodisiac qualities and it is stale. But time is the root of the matter.

Quantitative, qualitative, these things have lost all clear meaning for us. Then just there is the place for invention. The metronome beat of doggerel makes us restless, lowers us to nonsense. The forced timing of verse after antique patterns wearies us even more and seduces thought even more disastrously—as in Eliot's work. But a new time that catches thought as it lags and swings it up into the attention will be read, will be read (by those interested) with that breathlessness which is an indication that they are not dragging a gunny sack flavored with anise around for us to follow but that there is meat at the end of the hunt for us—and we are hungry.

Yours,
WILLIAM CARLOS WILLIAMS

1933

Jan. 26, 1933

Dear Ken: Yes, of course. The examples are missing, tho present in my head as circus performers, net makers—anything but machines—possessors of knowledge in the flesh as opposed to a body of knowledge called science or philosophy. From knowledge possessed by a man springs poetry. From science springs the machine. But from a man partially informed, that is, not yet an artist, springs now science, a detached mass of pseudo-knowledge, now philosophy, frightened acts of half realization. Poetry, however, is the flower of action and presents a different kind of knowledge from that of S. and P. If I am wrong then it is just too bad—but I should never want to write reading matter that would be dull: hence my reluctance to show anyone my notes save as "my mode of procedure."

I thought what you were after was something to print which would amuse, puzzle, entice people suffering from the depression or their equivalents in some other category. I didn't expect you to be convinced, I sought only to present to you an object.

Your letter would make an excellent prefatory note with my own abject apology following it. My object in much that I do has also an ulterior motive. I have to go on and want to go on living for a few years more perhaps. As I grow older I hope to get rid of medicine—the sooner the better, if only I can fulfill certain obligations and still have enough money for bread, wine, honey, beefsteak—travel, and a nice garden, maybe a swimming pool—and guest rooms. So, I have gradually made enough notes, here and there, to keep me busy clearing them up and developing them for a long time after I retire—if ever. I should dread an old age divorced from the thoughts and actions of my more vigorous years. Age should be a commentator, and what better than to comment upon one's own existence? Thus I have many

137

projects in mind. And if I never catch up with them—wouldn't that also be a misfortune. But I intend to try to do so. These notes on what the hell would then be straightened out, illustrated. I do want to make the thing clear and I fully intend to drive myself into all the corners possible. What the hell, I'm no bigot. If I could convince myself or have anyone else convince me that I were merely following in the steps of Dewey, I'd vomit and quit—at any time. But for the moment I don't believe it— the poetry is offered not too confidently as proof.

If you want the object to print it's yours, if not I have absolutely no feeling about it. Send it back, I'll love you just the same.

Regards to the family, I doubt that I shall be able to come in on Sunday, these are working days.

Yours,

BILL

96: TO EZRA POUND

March 15, 1933

Dear Ezra: I've selected twenty-one typewritten pages of verse for you. They go forward to Zukofsky today. They may not be exactly what you expect, but I refuse to go back over the old books to rake up "favorites." I have made this selection from my present, unpublished, volume. If you don't like the group and there is time I'll make another for you or add to this one. Twenty pages do not, after all, give much leeway. But I for myself find the group excellently representative and would wish that it remain as it is.

What shall you say about me? That I have a volume of verse which I have been in the process of making for the past ten years, that it is the best collection of verse in America today and that I can't find a publisher—while, at the same time, every Sunday literary supplement has pages of book titles representing the poetry of my contemporaries. And when I say I have sought a publisher I mean just that, for I had the best agent in New

York fairly comb the city for me last year. I'll try again this spring.

This must mean something. No doubt it means that my conception of poetry is not that of my contemporaries, either in the academies or out. This should be a distinction. It means that I believe poetry to be the mould of language as of feeling in any world and that its importance as a mechanism for correct thinking makes it too difficult for ordinary use, not that my own work is anywhere near what it shd. be, & that it is my constant effort to make it.

I don't care what you say. Any one of the poems, or some one of them, should be capable of saying all that is necessary.

But I've had a letter recently from a young fellow named Brittain[1] who first sent me a short story and then a long poem, both of which are on the verge of being very good indeed. I believe him to be very young as I know him to be somewhat influenced by Eliot. I immediately threw up a red flag, warning him to come to life if he wanted me to help him and to get off Eliot as soon as he could. When I know more of him I'll say more. He looks to be worth watching. He gives me something to say at least in reply to your query about—Any new ones coming along? I'll report later on.

Yrs.
BILL

Thanks for the working drawings, etc., re. the catamaran.

97: TO EZRA POUND

March 23, 1933

Dear Ezra, Fer the luv of God snap out of it! I'm no more sentimental about "murika" than Li Po was about China or Shakespeare about Yingland or any damned Frog about Paris. I know as well as you do that there's nothing sacred about any land.

---

[1] Robert Brittain, then at Princeton.

But I also know (as you do also) that there's no taboo effective against any land, and where I live is no more a "province" than I make it. To hell with youse. I ain't tryin' to be an international figure. All I care about is to write.

When I write badly, sock me, I like it. But you gotta agree that the sort of thing you pointed out to me in your last, the "dark kisses" sort of thing, is not the first thing that hits you in my work. I acknowledge, however, that it does occur—but less and less frequently.—It won't occur again. It's less than half of one percent anyway.

I'll be sending some typescripts soon to augment the ones which I presume Zukofsky forwarded yesterday. Go ahead with your selections from *Spring and All*.

(Wait a minute, I can't chew gum and smoke a cigarette at the same time.) Fer myself I—well, I admire your choice—adding only the ones I added in the script Z. sent you. I must confess I do like the ball-game—Is that sentimentality? So-s-o-o-o-o-o! Let's say: (*ing· my preferences) I

By the way, Floss almost dropped dead at the expression of your love! . . .

Soberly, I'm bound to agree that your criticism about the "soft spots" is valid. No doubt an immediate reaction from proximal pals would be the greatest thing in the wurrld for me. But, writing the way I do, soft spots must occur. I cannot stop for them. I *must* count on the well-inclined reader. In the end I've got to get over the bad slips but I can only get over them by writing, chucking up the diamonds with the marl. If I didn't do it this way I'd be hamstrung, nutted, sunk in two minutes. But I do realize the difficulty.

Thanks fer wishing twenty more years life to me. In that time I may school myself to a purer product—also less of it.

Yrs.
BILL

98: To T. C. Wilson

July 12, 1933

Dear Wilson: The *Contact* version, as you correctly observed, is the final one.

Poetry (a magazine of verse!) has had a group of poems of mine for several months past among their treasure trove. Why they do not print them is beyond me; perhaps Harriet feels a certain antagonism in me against her—and so reacts by leaving me lay. You might ask Zabel what it's all about, tho his reply would very properly fall back upon, "more important work has the precedence." I seldom succeed in finding a publisher. Not a bad sign, really.

You're right about the stupidity of a "southern tradition" as something which might be helpful to letters in the United States. Yet no region on earth has a tradition more vital to modern letters than America. Why it's the New World itself in the very blood and ghost of Dante's *Vita Nuova*. Blast them all if they can't see it. And they can't. Eliot is at the head of them too. First he runs away from it, then he looks back with what? A wish to correlate and understand, as a scholar should? Not at all but with a desire to shut it away for "tradition." Good God! it is nothing less than stupid, that also. For me, without one word of civil greeting (a sign of his really bad breeding, which all so-called scholars show—protectively), he reserves the slogan "of local interest perhaps."

Mind you, I feel no resentment against the treatment I get from those who should be working with "me," even tho the heat of the preceding paragraph might seem to imply it. I feel only impatience that we are so slow at our tasks. The real resentment I have is for the sluggardly Harriets with their soft wish to be helpful—while they stick the few self-conscious workers in the back by their niggardliness and delays. But one line of excellent poetry is worth them all—so write.

No group will form. Why should it? Especially asinine is it

to try to coordinate the efforts of men who do not wish to be bound together. Occasionally a book gets into print, that's all that matters, no matter how seldom or how poorly it may be done. The thing to do is to be sure of what gets into that book— by sweat, by exercise of brain, bone, nerves, drive. All the rest of the books printed are self eliminating. It is as sure that good work lives (if any be written) as that scientific discoveries into the depths of physics and chemistry will not be lost. But one must be at the advancing edge of the art: that's the American tradition. It is especially *not* a matter of families but exists—in Indian relics—anywhere. In fact you can't escape it and live.

Yours,

WILLIAMS

["*But then writing is not, of course, your* métier," *said Miss Gertrude Stein to Doctor Williams, when he suggested she throw away most of her typescripts. Actually, however, he thought highly of her best work, and defended her in articles written in 1931 and 1934 (see* Essays of W. C. Williams). *She perhaps forgave his unfortunate advice, admitting him at least as an* amateur *of poetry. (Compare Williams' letter to Milton Abernethy, Oct. 16, 1933.)*]

99: TO GERTRUDE STEIN

[*Sep 16, 1933, I'll be 50 tomorrow*]

Dear Gertrude Stein: You have been exceptionally thoughtful in having them send me your recent *Autobiography* and in sending me, with the words of greeting, the *Américains d'Amérique.* It's pretty hard for me to say just the pleasure I have experienced. A rare pleasure. Too damned rare for a life of the sort I had imagined.

Nothing much ever gets said, so why should I waste breath? Perhaps I should spend every bit of breath I have in the attempt.

Many thanks. It would be worth while exchanging gifts with you if there were anything I could send.

Keep it up.

Yours,

W. C. WILLIAMS

Thanks for being so exceptionally accurate as to put down the facts about Contact Press—the bastards make a virtue of forgetting.

W.

[*Milton A. Abernethy was editor of* Contempo, *"A semi-monthly review without plan or policy, provocative and complacent," started in Chapel Hill in 1931. He was an admirer of WCW's verse, for one hundred copies of "The Cod Head," by WCW, were printed by the Harvest Press by the Friends of Milton Abernethy.*]

100: TO M. A. ABERNETHY

Oct. 16, 1933

Dear Abernethy: Confusion worse confounded: your recent contributor S. S. may be a Czechoslovakian. I think it likely, but if so not one of whom his people can be very proud. There must be Czechoslovakians who have brains and know how to use them.

The everlasting stupidity of attempting to criticize a piece of work, a machine, a page of written characters or a painting, say by some such person as Paul Klee, by attacking the body of the author is something that beggars all patience. It is the last resort of a defeated man. Defile that which you cannot understand. It is the child vilifying his teacher's name since he cannot do his arithmetic. It is the familiar escape mechanism. But the only escape permissible to sanity is not that but a resolution of the elements of the work itself as it lies into its component parts, showing their order or disorder from which a significance is drawn.

Notice this: S. finds in Gertrude Stein's work what he seeks to show as the "word salad" of a schizophrenic. The observation is trite but legitimate. Then he goes on to an impassioned apostrophe to our times. "There is agony in Manchuria, etc., etc. Man moans piteously in the night of his despair. In his delirium he imagines God committing suicide in a speak-easy, etc. What's there left to believe in? etc."

Is he trying to kid us?

But, were he in the vaguest way qualified as a critic of literature, might it not occur to him to lay the work of Miss Stein side by side with his grandiloquent ranting and see them to be the same thing. But she has done hers deliberately, while he seems to be merely jerking out the sensibilities unconsciously.

How can anyone who has not been decapitated by his own incapacities fail to know that Gertrude Stein is an extremely capable and intelligent individual, well able to manage her affairs, the intimate of many leaders in the thought of the day and one who has besides produced at least two books of the most lucid and thought provoking prose? I refer to her last success and to the superb *Three Lives*. What possible excuse can anyone have for comparing such an individual with some unfortunate degenerate who may be the helpless inmate of an asylum? The only possible excuse is the one I have intimated to be here operative.

Gertrude Stein has kept many minds at tension, persistently and profitably for many years, but this is the first instance I know of one breaking down under the strain, if it exists.

WILLIAM CARLOS WILLIAMS

1934

[*In the second number of* A Year Magazine *appeared a survey of opinion about the position of the advance-guard magazine. Thomas Uzzell stimulated Williams to this trenchant statement.*]

101: TO THE EDITOR OF *A Year Magazine*

April, 1934

Mr. Uzzell ably and sympathetically states the terms on which the never-to-be-ended battle against "The existing, old, reliable, literary magazines" must go on.

My comment on his categories would be:

1. The magazines which pay and still pretend to keep a literary standard, even though we cannot accept their shrewdly whittled codes, can print no more than about 200 short stories a year in the aggregate. The larger section of the field is occupied by nonpaying periodicals. Furthermore, it is this "radical" enterprise which has always dragged the paying magazines out of their own filth finally. Mr. Uzzell is too genial and forgiving toward the sluggardly offenses committed against good writing by the "old, reliable, literary magazines" which he cannot quite keep from somewhat defending. They have only one virtue, they pay.

2. Americans in general are infantile in their reactions to sex. It still remains a burning topic with us; fully three quarters of the scripts that come into the small magazine offices have sex for theme; and they are terrible in their unenlightenment. I doubt if we shall ever achieve the French viewpoint or deftness here. We are not much better at the pathology of it than at the physiology. What to do with all this steam is something that has puzzled me a good deal. I am glad that Mr. Uzzell recommends further investigation. It's something we simply cannot drop, we haven't done anything distinctive with it as yet. But the dirty mindedness of the pay magazine editors with their lists of censored words is the

direct cause of forcing the thing underground into the frankly
sex toilet-paper rags.

3. It's a hard thing for a young writer to find time for reading;
he can't get to the books and he is probably so harassed by
parental, economic, and sacredly national impedimenta that he
hasn't even a hardwood chair to sit down on before table for
writing. Compared with Europe, America is completely bare of
books and they cost too much for every damn-fool reason. So,
we don't read. It hasn't happened yet to us to have a literary
saturation of the atmosphere. Therefore we don't know what
Europe has done before us. We think, then, that because we put
down what we see (and what else, primarily, can we do?) we have
thus achieved realism and so interest. I am emphasizing this
from Mr. Uzzell's statements because it is important. I say all
this just to thank Mr. Uzzell for having mentioned Zola. Zola
makes more of our realism look pretty sick.

"The high art of the realist is much more subtle and profound
than most youthful experimenters believe." Then comes the most
interesting portion of Mr. Uzzell's article. He gives three sub-
categories: (a) simply physical or external realism, (b) psycho-
logical realism, and (c) biological realism. He should have extended his comments on this last. I take it that he means what
we see in Shakespeare. Hadn't it better have been called, imagination? "Use your imagination" is the common American term.
It amounts to realistic observation related into an equally real
schematic whole. But I'd like to say a word for the first of these
three sub-heads also:

"Simply physical or external realism" has an important place
in America still. We know far less, racially, than we should about
our localities and ourselves. But it is quite true that the photo-
graphic camera will not help us. We can though, if we are able to
see general relationships in local setting, set them down verbatim
with a view to penetration. And there is a cleanliness about this
method which if it can be well handled makes a fascinating
project in which every bit of subtlety and experience one is
possessed of may be utilized.

Plot is like God: the less we formulate it the closer we are to the
truth.

For some time I have maintained that the "radical magazine" is not a series of failures, always dying, but one continuous success, impossible to kill. It is an unconscious cooperative division of effort. Some of the cruder faults in its make-up have been dissected out and profitably laid bare by Mr. Uzzell. I'd like to know more about *Anvil*.

WILLIAM CARLOS WILLIAMS

102: TO MARIANNE MOORE

May 2, 1934

Dear Marianne: The thing that I like best about your review of my book[1] is that you have looked at what I have done through my own eyes. I assure you that this is so. Had it not been so you would not have noticed the "inner security" nor the significance of some of the detail—which nobody seems to value as I have valued it.

The inner security though is an overwhelmingly important observation. I'm glad to have had you bring it up. Not that anyone will notice it. It is something which occurred once when I was about twenty, a sudden resignation to existence, a despair— if you wish to call it that, but a despair which made everything a unit and at the same time a part of myself. I suppose it might be called a sort of nameless religious experience. I resigned, I gave up. I decided there was nothing else in life for me but to work. It is the explanation for the calumny that is heaped on my head by women and men alike once they know me long enough. I won't follow causes. I can't. The reason is that it seems so much more important to me that I *am*. Where shall one go? What shall one do? Things have no names for me and places have no significance. As a reward for this anonymity I feel as much a part of things as trees and stones. Heaven seems frankly impossible. I am damned as I succeed. I have no particular hope save to repair, to rescue, to complete.

---

[1] *Collected Poems: 1921-1931.*

Brooklyn is the place where Washington stood after his defeat at the Battle of Long Island! One might go there to visit a dear friend—Heaven knows, one wants to—

I am working on a libretto for an opera. It will have to do with the life of George Washington. The composer is an unknown. I admire him. We have made a few more or less futile passes at each other so far but by next fall the work should be in full blast. It should prove an interesting engagement if we don't fall apart from each other in disgust before we accomplish anything.

—and the inhabitants. Florence bit her teeth into that one.

Affectionately yours,

WILLIAM

103: To EDWARD B. ROWAN

Aug. 28, 1934

Edward B. Rowan
Assistant Technical Director, etc.
Washington, D. C.

Dear Sir: Taking you seriously, if it is the object of your plan to give a certain number of writers, presumably creative, a certain amount of money for mere subsistence, I can think of nothing better for it than to draw up a recommended list of names, pay them, and tell them to go ahead with whatever they have in mind—and if anything of value is produced that it will be published. In any case they get paid. [*Written in longhand in margin:* The writers to be paid for sustenance while writing.]

But if excellence in itself, literary excellence, should by chance be the prime objective, as it should be, the difficulty is insuperable, or almost so. Some will be too radical in thought for the government, others will be thought obscene, etc. There's nothing you can do about that.

I'd like to see a National Dep't. of Letters or, lest it become a literary mausoleum, a department of creative letters, or living letters. I wonder, in the spirit of Geo. Washington, whether the country is sufficiently broad-minded for that. A monthly periodical, paying its contributors, could be maintained, well printed, free from the necessity of putting boodle in someone's pockets; it should print whatever is well written, regardless of its political complexion, the emphasis being only on the writing. But this, I am afraid, is too French. After a year or two the best that had been published in the magazine should be put into book form. It would be a safety valve for us all, but it would have to be edited by a superb spirit, altogether unfamiliar in these temperatures. The gesture would be superlative, though only a small number of writers would be helped.

What might prove better would be an issue of paper books, the books to be selected by individual publishing houses, a limited number by each according to its equipment and importance, the Dep't of Letters (as we may call it) standing back of the publications in the character of a subsidizer. And again, quality of writing should be the objective. Prizes might be offered in the form of republication on a national scale. *And* to the publishing houses.

Wonders might come from such a move as you propose, for letters are the wave's edge in all cultural advance which, God knows, we in America ain't got much of.

Sincerely yours,
WILLIAM CARLOS WILLIAMS

[*Ronald Lane Latimer* (alias James G. Leippert) *progressed from the editorship of a Columbia College literary journal to a Buddhist monastery in Asia. Between careers he edited* Alcestis, a Poetry Quarterly, *in the early thirties and also the* Alcestis Press, *which published a limited edition of WCW's* Adam and Eve *and* An Early Martyr.]

104: TO RONALD LANE LATIMER

Nov. 26, 1934

Dear Latimer: It's all right with me—if I can find the time for it. The best thing to do, no doubt, would be for me to begin. Later on we could decide on the issue, whether to choke it or to let it live. There can be no thought of writing for publication, I couldn't say a word that way, I'll just have to let you have it, come what may. And boy! when ah comes—sometimes it ain't pretty. We'll see, I dunno that I can do it.[1]

It mightn't be a bad idea at the same time to try and get hold of some old letters that have been written in the past to friends here and there—recent letters. They could go in with the rest if we can find any. Most people throw letters away, I should imagine, as soon as they have read them. I've tried saving them at various times, letters from friends, and have them by the hundreds in careless files. But recently I've let even brilliant letters go. If you want letters, though, from all sorts of people, some of them twenty years old or more . . . No, let that pass. I haven't time to sort them and I shouldn't like to lose the best ones just yet.

It's not easy to release the mind to flow; that, I suppose, is why there is so little really good writing. It's there and we may know, "know," how to write but we go on writing and exhibiting all we "know" and what we know damned well ought to be said remains right there where it was before we started and failed to release it. Yes, I doubt very much that I can really say anything to you about myself. Yet I'm full of endless things I want to say. It's precisely an informal opportunity like this that I have desired for years. It's just another man of fifty before a willing virgin, who just can't come up. Yet he knows he can perfectly well— and yet he can't. It's a sort of pity, a sort of lack of interest—a good deal a matter of resentment that it hadn't been so easy formerly when it would have meant infinitely more. What the hell. He looks and finds the situation rather anatomical.

You see, I'm trying to start myself into something and wondering all the time with my head full of material just what I'd better not say. If only I could make a bolus of it of some sort, one grand pill, the whole mess of it squeezed into a lump and let you have it simply and quickly. But to have to tiresomely string it out—Nuts! I can't see what it could mean to you or anyone. I'm no journalist and autobiography doesn't mean a thing to me.

---

[1] A projected autobiography.

All I'm interested in—or almost all—is impersonally, as impersonally as possible, to get the meaning over and see it flourish—and be left alone. That's bitter enough, I know that, but the early dreams of a communal life, of being important to my friends and neighbors, have almost evaporated forever. I don't think they can be made to come back by "revolution." Too many have been injured.

Yours,
WILLIAMS

But I'll try.

1935

Feb. 25, 1935

Dear Latimer: Certainly, I'd like to have a book of verse by the Alcestis Press. I haven't a damned thing to send you for #3—not even a line of a poem. Everything has been snatched out of my hands the moment it's written. I am even starting to write them to order now. If I can find anything in the air for you during the next week or so—but that's no promise. How big a book do you want? Tell me again. And when do you want it?

This is what I'd say to our academic critics, if I were asked: . . . You are thinking of something very dead and likely to be smelly very soon—one of the first things that is done at an autopsy is to meaure and weigh the corpse. But the danger to the difficult present art of verse-making in our language which you gentlemen are likely to fabricate is great, unless you grow more careful with your teaching. You will be the losers too, not the inventive mind of some possible poet.

All right, what then do I want you to do? I want you to DISCOVER not necessarily in my verse, but mine may do, what the new measures are to be. I want you to reject the slag of what I write and pull out the NEW, that which relates to the American language and modern times—and give it the benefit of your unquestioned erudition and training. Do as critics what the artist cannot do, hasn't time for in the performance of his task of perception of truth piecemeal—you to join it into a grammar if you will.

It makes me weary for some instructor at Columbia to come up to me after a reading and ask me why I put a certain verse in the form in which I put it. How in hell am I going to answer him and why should I if I could? Let him rather look into my verse to discover where the formal occasion lies—and find perhaps a lead for his deductions. I know he is important, I know what my difficulties are—but I'll be damned if I'll have the onus of proof put on me.

Very well, you may reject me and all I do, place me far down your table of values. That's perfectly all right, you do it at your own peril and that is your business—but if you are interested in fertilizing me as a producing poet you won't classify me lightly—

Sincerely,
W. C. WILLIAMS

[*William Eric Williams, his elder son, was then in his senior year at Williams College.*]

106: TO WILLIAM ERIC WILLIAMS

March 13, 1935

Dearest Bill: This I can say for certain, you seem not far different from what I was myself at your age. I don't mind saying I went through hell, what with worrying about my immortal soul and my hellish itch to screw almost any female I could get my hands on—which I never did. I can tell you it is almost as vivid today as it was then when I hear you speak of it. Everything seems upside down and one's self the very muck under one's foot.

It comes from many things, my dear boy, but mostly from the inevitable maladjustment consequent upon growing up in a more or less civilized environment. Any bum on the street, any crook who is his own master at the expense of the law is happier than the man who is trying to mould himself to a society which revolts his entire manhood. We do not want to fit into anything, we want to be free, potent, self-reliant—and that society cannot and will not permit. Nor would we be really satisfied if we found ourselves antisocial in our success. That is the situation of the great fortunes, the Morgans, the Vanderbilts, as well as the Al Capones of the world. They are "free" but at a terrific cost.

But more immediately, your difficulties arise from a lack of balance in your daily life, a lack of balance which has to be understood and withstood—for it cannot be avoided for the present. I refer to the fact that your intellectual life, for the moment, has eclipsed the physical life, the animal life, the normal he-man life, which every man needs and craves. If you were an athlete, a powerful body, one who could be a hero on the field or the diamond, a *Big* Hero, many of your mental torments would be lulled to sleep. But you cannot be that—so what? You'll have to wait and take it by a different course.

And after all, the athletes haven't it as easy as it seems. They may be soothed during the difficult years, but they've got to face the music some day, and that some day may be too late. They can't always be physical figures, and when the real test comes later, they often fold up and disappear completely.

You, dear Bill, have a magnificent opportunity to enjoy life ahead of you. You have sensibility (even if it drives you nuts at times), which will be the source of keen pleasures later and the source of useful accomplishments too. You've got a brain, as you have been told *ad nauseam*. But these are the very things which are tormenting you, the very things which are your most valued possessions and which will be your joy tomorrow. Sure you are sentimental, sure you admire a man like Wordsworth and his "Tintern Abbey." It is natural, it is the correct reaction of your age in life. It is also a criticism of Wordsworth as you will see later. All I can say about that is, wait! Not wait cynically, idly, but wait while looking, believing, getting fooled, changing from day to day. Wait with the only kind of faith I have ever recognized, the faith that says I wanna know! I wanna see! I think I will understand when I do know and see. Meanwhile I'm not making any final judgments. Wait it out. Don't worry too much. You've got time. You're all right. You're reacting to life in the only way an intelligent, sensitive young man in a college can. In another year you'll enter another sphere of existence, the practical one. The knowledge, abstract now, which seems unrelated to sense to you (at times) will get a different color.

Sooner or later we all of us knock our heads against the ceiling of the world. It's like breaking a record: the last fifth of a second, which marks the difference between a good runner and a world beater is the hardest part of the whole proceeding. I mean that you, Bill, will be one of the minds of the world tomorrow. You will be the one, you and your generation, who will have to push knowledge of all sorts that inch ahead, which will make life tolerable in your day. Knowledge is limited, very limited, and it is only because you are in the preliminary stages of knowing that you think men, certain men, know so much more than you do. They may know a little more, but not the great amount that you imagine. For this reason, wait! Believe in yourself and your generation. Take it with a smile. That's what they mean when they speak of humor. It doesn't mean a guffaw or a grin. It means steadiness of nerves that is willing to bide its time, certain that with time a human adjustment can and will be made. It is the most that any man has ever been able to do.

Jumping to practical things: Have the Ford put in condition up there if you think the local mechanics can be trusted. Send me the bill. . . .

Mother and I both send love. Don't let *anything* get your goat and don't think you have to duck anything in life. There is a way out for every man who has the intellectual fortitude to go on in the face of difficulties.

Yours,
DAD

107: TO MARIANNE MOORE

Oct. 18, 1935

Dear Marianne: I'm glad you have the book[1] and that you liked it well enough to speak freely about it. I thoroughly sympathize with your position. But to me a book is somewhat of a confessional. It is just because I do not say things that-I-would-say that I must write them. It would not be fair to a reader for me to hold back knowledge of the matrix from which comes the possible gem.

It goes further than that with me. There is a good deal of rebellion still in what I write, rebellion against stereotyped poetic process—the too meticulous choice among other things. In too much refinement there lurks a sterility that wishes to pass too

---

[1] *An Early Martyr.*

often for purity when it is anything but that. Coarseness for its own sake is inexcusable, but a Rabelaisian sanity requires that the rare and the fine be exhibited as coming like everything else from the dirt. There is no incompatibility between them.

My dear Mother is perhaps my example. Cruel to blame anything on her and through her to blame a certain Latin influence. She exasperates me too but there are times when I see her eye light with a curious fire and I know what is coming. It comes from the manure heap sometimes. It clears the atmosphere.

You remember that Strindberg wrote "Snow White." I feel that there is an inescapable relationship between that and Strindberg's other work, much of it sordid. Heaven knows how much satisfaction Dante got from the hell which he wrote of better than he did of Paradise. In any case I am made up of hells and heavens which constitute a truer me than my face-to-face appearance could possibly suggest. This, I think, is that which should make a book. And over everything, good and bad, if possible, poetry.

Always, to me, poetry seems limitless in its application to life. If a man were able there is no subject or material which can rightly be denied him. But if he fails, he fails through the lack of power not through the material he employs.

Forgive me for defending myself from a loved adversary. You may be right and I may be wrong. Hilda Doolittle attacked me somewhat along the same line many years ago—at the very beginning. Maybe you are both right. I feel that you are wrong. If the stories of the mythical saints and virgins could be known, understood and tolerated, dogma might get an enlightening that would be fiery in its purging effects. I'm no reformer though. And God knows I'm no saint or virgin!

We're coming to see you.

Yours,
BILL

1936

April, 1936

The American cultural tradition appears to me to stem directly from that of Western Europe of four hundred years ago in its most liberal phases. From that point it became a separate thing, or attempted to become so. It failed in large part because of the inability of the men of that day to absorb the new ideology, faced as they were by a life-and-death struggle with their primitive environment and also, of course, the inevitable fallibility of all human flesh—the dishonesty, self-seeking which characterized every phase of crude plenty in the world.

The essential democracy upon which an attempt was made to found the U. S. has been the central shaft about which all the other movements and trends of thought have revolved—without changing it in any way. This deeply embedded feeling for a democracy has defeated the more radical thought of each era, such as that of Tom Paine, Gene Debs, Bill Haywood, making their movements and thought seem foreign to the environment. It is this same democracy of feeling which will defeat Marxism in America and all other attempts at regimentation of thought and action. It will also defeat fascism—though it may have to pass through that.

This is an idealistic foundation which America has been able to protect because of its isolated geographic position. Only the rather myopic European or Asian could fail to sense the essential good humor of the American democratic spirit which permits the brutality of the self-seeker to go its way in the perhaps misguided notion that essential democracy will triumph finally. Be that as it may, the democratic spirit is still the same as it has always been in the U. S.

My opinion is that the American tradition is completely opposed to Marxism. America is progressing through difficult mechanistic readjustments which it is confident it can take care of. But Marxism is a static philosophy of a hundred years ago which has not yet kept up—as the democratic spirit has—through the stresses of an actual trial. Marxism to the American spirit is only another phase of force opposed to liberalism. It takes a tough theory to survive America, and America thinks it has that theory. Therefore it will smile and suffer, quite secure in its convictions that through all the rottenness, all the political corruption, all the cheap self-interest of its avowedly ruling moneyed class—that it can and will take care of itself when the crisis arrives.

My opinion is that our revolutionary literature is merely tolerated by most Americans, that it is definitely in conflict with our deep-seated ideals. I think the very premises of the revolutionary writers prevent an organic integration with the democratic principles upon which the American spirit is founded.

W. C. WILLIAMS

109: TO J. JOHN MUNSON

May 14, 1936

Dear Mr. Munson: It would be an honor to have you dedicate your book to me and one which I should greatly appreciate. I wish you the best of success in your venture.

The above sounds rather cold and formal whereas, to tell you the truth, I was much affected by your kind note. My writing, such as it is, has followed a fairly unswerving and unpopular drift from the beginning. The result has been that it goes out, wherever it goes, and almost never do I hear anything direct concerning it from that time forward. Oh, you know what I mean, I put everything I have into it and then find that that is the end of the matter.

Therefore when a total stranger writes to me as you have done I am fairly knocked off my feet. Or perhaps we have met somewhere and I should know who you are. Well, such things happen also.

Sincerely yours,
W. C. WILLIAMS

May 24, 1936

Dear Marianne: Do we grow duller as we grow older? I suppose
so. Or is it rather that we know better what little we know and
are less bedazzled by appearances, so that the world seems smaller
and smaller to us? I am referring to your poems and, indirectly,
to mine. You still bewilder me, happily, with your writing, but
it seems less a mystery and more an accomplishment now. You
are a most amazing person. Far at the end of the narrowing horn
I see a spot of sunlight toward which you are conducting us—.
But I detest such symbols. Everything is getting smaller but seems
moving, as always, to some—the same—climax as always. But
what in the world it is I cannot say. Perhaps no one can ever say.
It does, however, seem a way OUT. It indicates a day. So I fall into
my symbol again. I should never speak that way if I could help it.

Best to let it go at that. We were very happy to see you both
again. In many ways it was a greater pleasure than formerly.
Maybe the instinct for defense: the more the world hems us in
the closer we are pressed toward our friends. Anyhow, it was a
pleasure.

I scarcely realized that you had given us your book[1] until I was
in the car and on my way home. Naturally, you don't want
any thanks for that but I should have liked to have said a few
words of appreciation. I've read the book twice since then, it is
extremely good. I see many scripts, through the years, but today
(I *am* getting old) they seem to lack the invention I used to look
for. It makes me doubt my own sense and intelligence when I
look at most work now-a-days. I wonder whether my wit is not
decaying. Or has theirs long since decayed—in a lump? You
have a savor, a ripeness that doesn't always need to be the best
apple in the sack. The craftsmanship is distinctive, the form has
been liberalized but retains its solidity, the words rest firmly in
place—

---

[1] *The Pangolin.*

"Bird-witted" has more of the older quality but it stays on the subject better and more easily. The others have a lift at the conclusion that, sometimes, was all over the other pieces (ten years ago). Now you gather your forces more carefully.

Nothing I can say. These are just rambling fumblings after what you are which escapes—

Please send us the leaflet of the leper colony. Do not for a moment believe we shall do anything we don't want to about it.

Heaven knows what one should feel about a work of art. I always feel disturbed by what I like. It torments me at first because I cannot understand it completely—unlike a nut and bolt that one knows at once belong together. You do disturb me—I don't know what you want to make me think or do—except I know that it is extremely simple and difficult, the most difficult thing in the world—you are yourself restless in a Poe-like sense, intricate to disguise a great lucidity—I give it up. And enjoy—as I may. You are in the full tradition of the artist throughout time—you are impatient of everything else—and that's a most dangerous thing.

Yours,
WILLIAM

[*James Laughlin IV, editor of* New Directions *for over twenty years, as an undergraduate at Harvard was an admirer of Ezra Pound, through whom he was introduced to WCW. He was destined to become the first commercial publisher of WCW. He also is a poet who has had the benefit of WCW's trenchant criticism.*]

111: To JAMES LAUGHLIN

Sept. 22, 1936

Dear Laughlin: Thanks for the pamphlet. Your introduction to the O'Reilly is seductive, but I haven't had the moment to read into the text itself as yet. The weather is hot, my mind is at sea or the equivalent when one is so solidly on shore as I am today. But it's good to know you're alive and doing what you're doing. *New Directions* had better remain in the plural—I almost said pleural cavity, so flighty is my imagination today.

This would be a good day for me to go nuts—

You're right to make the distinction between the American Grain type of inquiry and this newer (and older) type of process. They're not far apart, really. I can remember the feeling that in an abler, later, more studied form, the French and O'Reilly are attacking now. Once grounded one can afford to spring into the air. It is the solidity of the take-off that insures the flight. One plays into the other.

There seems no possibility of our meeting and talking. It won't happen, either. We're too far apart in years and neither of us would be able to beat down the bushes enough even to look through them—or over them.

Anyhow, thanks and please don't ever forget to send me anything you think I should see. I'm always greatly interested—and think that you have something of peculiar merit to say or do. Haven't, by the way, heard from dear Ezrie for years.

Sincerely yours,
Williams

112: To James Laughlin

Oct. 27, 1936

Dear God: You mention, casually, that you are willing to publish my *White Mule,* that you will pay for it and that we shall then share, if any, the profits! My God! It must be that you are so tall that separate clouds circle around that head, giving thoughts of other metal than those the under sides of which we are in the habit of seeing.

Anyhow, nothing could give me greater pleasure than for you to undertake that task. I accept the offer quickly but without any thought of a time limit of any kind. Think the thing over, going at your own pace, and when you are quite ready for the script let me know.

There is one point I have to make. The present script, or the script as it stands, amounts to about 22 chapters, about 300 typed pages. It is the first part only of a much longer book which may or may not someday be written. This book is a unit. It has a beginning and a fairly satisfactory end. It will be called Book I. It needs touching up toward the end, something I have clearly in mind to do at once. In a month (or less) it will be ready subject to your call.

I'll be looking for the *Advocate* and the anthology. As soon as I can get to it I'll let you have a list of names and addresses— as many as I can think up. I'll try to do it this afternoon. I'm extremely curious about the anthology. Most books of the sort are tooted about so much before they appear that they are stale before the seeing. Best luck to you in the matter of distribution in which I'll help you all I can.

The New Caravan, 1936, is out this week. I'll send you one as soon as I get my copies.

Mrs. Williams joins me in sending greetings. Where are you week-ends? I suppose here and there. What I have in mind is that if you're in Connecticut as a general thing and can be reached by phone you might like to drop in on Charles Sheeler some Sunday afternoon when we are there. I think you'd enjoy the experience and I'm sure he'd like to meet you.

Sincerely yours,
W. C. WILLIAMS

113: To Ezra Pound

Nov. 6, 1936

Dea Rezra: Always delighted to hear from you. I began to think you had gone up into some more rarefied stratum than that to which I have grown accustomed. Truly, truly, my friend, you have greatly alleviated the passage of my years—. Don't stop now. My only regret has been that you have not been closer to these here diggins. Damn it to hell, it's been a serious loss to us all that you haven't set your flowers to clambering on our walls.

I planted three small clematis vines in my back yard this morning. Very mild weather here so far.

I approve of your proposed manifesto and think that this is of all times the most propitious in which to release it. The American political upheaval having for the moment practically eliminated the Communist party from our midst, it would seem to be THE moment for redirecting sane minds toward the need for an actual radicalism—which would concern precisely the things your nine or ten categories included. . . .

And James Laughlin (bless his heart) has just offered to do my *White Mule. That* finished me. It sure was a bolt out of the blue of almost despair. His impetus has set me polishing (that is, rewriting) the last chapters to make this a definite Book. It is to be Book I and ends with proper regard for an ending. I'm going to like this book. It's put ten years on my life; out next spring.

Besides which I've about made up my mind to write my mother's story this winter. I have an idea for it that I can't detail now. I've been collecting her sayings and letters for years. You'll see.

And I've done seven new short poems—two of them as good as anything I've ever done, maybe the best.

And then there's that magnum opus I've always wanted to do: the poem PATERSON. Jeez how I'd like to get at that. I've been sounding myself out in these years working toward a form of some sort. . . .

Oh yeah, there's a good guy named Bernard de Voto; he has taken the place of Henry Seidel Canby as editor of the *Saturday Review of Literature* and MAY come to something. He's got a face like a spoiled potato but they say his heart is in the right place. I'm going to meet him first, through a woman, a real fine woman, and we'll see what happens.

I'm never hopeless, as you seem to suggest—but I have always been hopeless of doing anything with other people. I know I am wrong, but then, that's the way I am.

You see, I live a very obscure but very complete life in my own petty world, I know its smells and its bouquets. They are not to be ignored. I tell you when I went in to Rockefeller City today and saw that beeg building and then entered it and rode on the escalator and walked about the book show—I tells you my little suburb just bust right out laughing. SUCH a lot of cheap crap I NEVER encountered. There in the middle of everything was our old, very old friend Edwin Markham parading his innocent white beard about, wanting to be spoken to and admired. I tell you I was not envious, nor did I wish I had been paraded about the walls to sell for them.

Me Mother is helping me translate an old book I think it was you left here once: *El Perro y la Calentura,* by Quevedo.

Well, write me again. Floss is fine. Best to Dorothy. I'd enjoy playing you a game of tennis.

Yrs.,
BILL

114: TO MARIANNE MOORE

Dec. 10, 1936

Dear Marianne: These are the three best that I have recently written. Use "The Sun" if you have a place for it. The others are for your pleasure. I think it might be wise not to let them get into other hands just now—a pair of scissors will do the trick.

We may be governed by our stripes, but we all run on the ground, swim or climb trees—some of us can fly by beating our wings: to me the sonnet form while lovely must remain 12th-century Italian—not to be imitated save as a purely secondary exercise, a sort of poetic St. John the Divine, by which I am not stirred any more than I am by the blatancies of a Rev. Manning. They may be good but there are better possibilities. As there were in 1492—perhaps not to be realized.

Milton with his latinities mutilated the English language for centuries following him. Wordsworth went far to correct that. His sonnets seem to me to be the place at which his genius stopped.

Yours,
WILLIAM

115: To Marianne Moore

Dec. 23, 1936

Dear Marianne: I laughed and Florence laughed over your fright at the sudden appearance of your embassy to the *Daily Eagle*. What a pity they printed the poem so badly, leaving out a whole, if short, line to leave the end of it completely vague. But your own statements about the book touched me deeply. You are very kind, very wise and your critical observations hit the nail on the head. The whole statement you make about the book seems to me particularly alert and colorful. I wish I had a few more copies of the paper to send here and there to friends.

The poem was not promised to anyone. But what about the longer poem, "The Sun?" Wasn't that the one you were most interested in? There is no hurry about it, just that I am interested.

If only—I keep saying year in year out—it were possible for "us" to have a place, a location, to which we could resort, singly or otherwise, and to which others could follow us as dogs follow each other—without formality but surely—where we could be known as poets and our work be seen—and we could see the work of others and buy it and have it! Why can't such a thing come about? It seems so brainless and spineless a thing for us to be "exiles" in too literal and accepted a sense. Being exiles might we not at least, as exiles, consort more easily together? We seem needlessly isolated and we suffer dully, supinely. I am not one for leading a crusade, but I'd lead a little group through the underbrush to a place in the woods, or under a barn if I thought anyone would (or perhaps, could) follow me. Or I'd follow. The basis for an agreement is the thing that is perhaps lacking. And perhaps your catholic breadth of character, more than your mind, even, might be that thing—and the thing we admire. But nobody moves—or moves only singly. Is this hope?

Whatever we think of you here, anyhow, is Christmas. And to your Mother.

Yours,
WILLIAM

1937

[In the American Grain *was a* succès d'estime *and attracted a small but discriminating audience in its original format. Among its readers was Alfred Stieglitz, who wrote enthusiastically to WCW about it, and took the title for his new gallery on Madison Avenue, "An American Place," from the book. WCW made a practice of dropping into* An American Place *to see the pictures of his friends Marsden Hartley, Charles Demuth, John Marin or some other new American painter. Although he makes little of it in the* Autobiography, *Williams has maintained a keen interest in painting ever since his own Sunday painting at the University of Pennsylvania. And over the years he has published essays on Matisse, Stieglitz, Charles Sheeler, Tchelitchew, and American primitives.*]

116: To Alfred Stieglitz

June 27, 1937

Dear Stieglitz: May I ask a favor of you? Two weeks ago Mrs. Norman asked me if I would meet her at An American Place for a talk relative to a project which she had in mind in which she suggested that I might be interested. I was prepared to go but found myself held up at the last minute. I wired her and presume that she received my message. In my telegram I said that I would write later. This is the letter, addressed to you rather than to her asking that you communicate to her its contents.

I have been extremely busy during the last two weeks. Among other things I had four maternity cases due, three of which have come off, one being on the way this afternoon. I could not leave town with a clear conscience. Perhaps now I shall be a little freer.

Mrs. Norman mentioned in her phone conversation that the project in question was a magazine devoted to art in general, perhaps paintings in particular. I was to be an associate among

166

those responsible. I think that was the way of it. It is to be launched this fall, or at least there is thought of launching it this fall.

I think you know my state of mind and my obligations here as a physician pretty well. I don't see how I can take a very active part in the publication of a new magazine under the circumstances. I'd enjoy it, it isn't that, but I simply can't load myself up with editorial work just now. I can't afford it for many reasons, one of the chief of which is that if I am to go on writing, as I get older, my time has to be conserved more and more. And maybe, by that, I shall be able to give all my time to writing and the allied activities of an artist before I quit or rot.

I don't wish to grow too heavy about this. I'm afraid of my natural tendency to overload my schedule, that's all.

Also, this new book of mine, *White Mule,* which seems to be on the way to some sort of a success, places an obligation on me to do another book or two next year. What the hell? I can't do much more than I'm doing at present. Do you understand?

Please tell Mrs. Norman that she may count on me for every bit of assistance I can give her in a collateral capacity, but that I can't just now assume any principal burden. Nevertheless, if she wishes still to talk with me I'll be delighted to run in, sometime before July 10th, at her convenience, to give her what assistance I can—to talk it over with her, that is. Maybe that's all that is asked of me.

One day last April, I think, I went into the city on several errands, if they can be called that, one of which was to take a look at Marsden's new pictures. When I entered The Place no one else was there. I looked into your office and found that too empty. But there were voices coming from the back room. I walked about looking at the pictures for about a quarter of an hour, being glad to be alone and then left, not having seen anyone the whole time I was there. I didn't feel much like talking about the pictures.

This was the strangest show of Hartley's I have ever seen. It taxed the good will of the spectator pretty hard because of the monotonous tone of the pictures and the similarity if not identity of the sizes, one next to the other along the wall. It was a tough session. I don't know. All I seemed to see was black. Some seemed not to have come off at all, they looked flat and lifeless. Others were so full of mannerisms that the good of them seemed buried, completely buried. The best I could discover was in the drawings and in one or two of the simpler compositions which I cannot remember now. The effect was desperately sad and no doubt that was the major effect. I wish I could see one at a time, perhaps in a gay setting. I could not understand the heavy black outlines to the forms—as paintings, that is. It seemed to me too much for the effect desired. After all, death is not sad. It's life that's sad. Is that what is meant? Life takes the shapes of crabs, of shells—I don't know. Nor can I quarrel with Marsden. I see it but it repels me—graphically. Marsden has himself *too much* to heart. Call me what you please. He has tried to paint *too much* of that into his forms. The forms have been distorted by that not in an effective way but rather to obscure their true effectiveness FOR HIS PURPOSE. At least that is what I think. He might better let his wit go into discovery, into showing what there *is,* with the candor of his drawings, some of them, rather than in overloading them with emotion which, in a sense, makes them sentimental. A painter needs to be more of a scientist. We exaggerate our own importance and all exaggeration—unless more accurately aimed than Marsden has aimed it in these pictures— is questionable practice.

My regards to Georgia O'Keefe.

Sincerely,
WILLIAMS

1938

March 30, 1938

Dear Ford: Looks good to me. More power to you. But not my autobiography just yet. That will have to be a monastic, brooding, gay sort of lonely thing that cannot be hurried—cannot even be put on the spot but will have to come about in the manner of the seasons. I don't feel up to it at present. There's too much to do before that.

To me the title *View* is much better than the other, tho' less dynamic, more passive, but it *should* be a "view," the work contained therein being left to supply the drive.

I'll have some prose of one sort or another for you by fall or sooner; whenever you want it. Let's hope you get started before a war engulfs us all again. The times are too like those of 1913 to suit me. At that time it looked as if we were really building up to a period of major expression. They did not let it occur. As then there are too many now who do not want the artist to speak as only he can. They'll slaughter the world before they'll let a Lorca live. Be sure to have something on Lorca in your first issue. He is very important to me.

And Éluard. When you are in Paris if you can pick up a book or two of Éluard's work lying around, not too expensive—I don't know which to choose—send it to me collect.

Congratulations on the new venture. I saw Virgil Thomson at your suggestion and had a profitable talk with him.

Yours,
WILLIAMS

[*Dorothy Norman, a close friend of Stieglitz, launched a new magazine,* Twice A Year, *and called on WCW for help.*]

118: To Mrs. Dorothy Norman

May 8, 1938

Dear Mrs. Norman: You'll be getting some pages during the latter part of the week which, if you still want anything of mine, you'll have to use in lieu of an article. I've plundered my brain trying to find the sort of thing you wanted, but the cupboard was bare. If I kept at it much longer I'd have to say that you had finished me. You'll finish me and maybe yourself too if that sort of thing is to be kept up. I got so I wasn't good for anything. With my daily job, sometimes completely absorbing all the energy I possess. I found myself writing nothing at all but going on week after week wondering what I ought to say. To hell with that sort of thing. Either I had to give my life away and make a book of it or quit. I was in a daze. And besides I became convinced that it wasn't worth it. All you have to do is look around and you'll find a hundred good books coming out, being squeezed out from between the bricks. Let them say it.

What I've done is to do some writing under the title which, after all, gives the whole thing. The writing is not bad, in places. That's really what I intend. There was much more of it getting steadily worse as I proceeded. So I cut it off. That's what it needed, to be stopped! I stopped it and left a row of dots.

I hope you haven't set up the two versions of the poem "Morning," because I have since sending them to you combined them into the final version. Please return the two to me so that I may send you the one which I wish to show.

The note for the biography[1]—which I hope to God I'll be able to work at now that I've had a bath—are still in your hands. Do what you please about that.

You realize of course, as I do, that you have given me no promise to print the thing I have written as spoken of above. I'd

---

[1] Of his mother.

be glad to have it appear—as it is but I must tell you that I am
completely through with it. I will not touch it again unless to
make minor changes at your request. This is the end. Use it or
not, I am through with it. Though I will say for myself, now that
I realize what has been going on, that I could not wish it to be
in other form.

Sincerely yours,
W. C. WILLIAMS

119: To ALVA TURNER

June 27, 1938

Dear Alva: No, I'm not dead, just existing along. Today especially with the cold rain falling this way, approaching the
Fourth of July, I'm just barely existing. There has been no use
in my trying to keep pace with your letters. My mind has been
too occupied most of the time with disturbing cases and all the
other detail of a life such as I lead. There are a thousand things
that keep crowding me in my efforts to get through the day with
anything like the number of things done that stare me in the
face each morning. At times I must shut off certain interests in
order to be able to preserve something of my health and approximate sanity.

I have all your letters and the various documents and clippings
which they contain. I wish I could find it possible to collate them
and put them in order for the book I should like to do on you.
I wish I could find time to finish the book on my mother. I am
told that it is my duty to write the biography of Martha Graham,
the American dancer. Meanwhile I receive in royalties for my last
two books the munificent sum of one hundred and thirty dollars—covering the work of a ten or fifteen year period, about
twelve dollars a year. One must be a hard worker to be able to
stand up under a luxury of those proportions. Nothing but the
best for me! But the price is a bit high. I can't afford to buy
much more of it at the moment.

Your letters are interesting too. I admire your guts and political acumen.

Just remember that I do not forget you. Whether or not we can get out to see you this summer still depends on too many ifs and ands for me to say for certain that we shall come—but if possible. . . . I don't know. Maybe in October.

Best luck and keep your health.

Sincerely yours,

W. C. WILLIAMS

[*Norman Holmes Pearson, one of the first college professors to teach* Paterson, *met WCW when editing the* Oxford Anthology of American Literature *(1938). He showed a sympathetic understanding of WCW's poetry, rare at that time among professors.*]

120: To NORMAN H. PEARSON

Oct. 3, 1938

Dear Norman: If I have pleased and satisfied you by anything that I have written it is because the best in it has been able, in spite of gross defects, to find its way through the words. Anything I have ever done might have been better in more expert hands. But I will join you in your unexpressed feelings that with the magnificent opportunities there are for good work today there are very few who address themselves to excellence for its own sake. I hope I can at least keep the objective in mind without rancor and the jealousy I sometimes admit to feeling when I see what succeeds about me.

Just this morning I was talking to a woman who was laughing at a painter for saying, "Who couldn't paint potboilers if it were possible to drag himself so low?" And anyone must always lay himself open to such a taunt.

. . . At the moment I can't write a thing. I haven't written anything to speak of for almost a year. The poison is lacking. A man has to have a fever to write and I've not had a fever.

Maybe I am drying up. Maybe the incentives have been punc-
tured too often to be incentives any longer. One has to write for
someone. When we are pretty destitute we write. Anyhow, at my
age I've got to have something else to write for. Not easy to find.
I'm a severer critic than I was and I've done the easy part of the
work. The rest will be hard as hell. Maybe you'll notice the
difference if I ever get to it. . . .

Sincerely,
Bill

121: To Norman Holmes Pearson

November 7, 1938

Dear Pearson: Living forever is an awful job, one wishes sometimes that one didn't have an immortal soul, writing would be so
much more a pleasure. Now that I find it impossible to write,
my mind is fast winding itself into knots of despair. This
morning Floss and I in our agony started to clean a large boxlike
semiornamental catchall that lies like a coffin across one end of
our front hall. Books, magazines, pamphlets—a steadily mounting
stream and none of them so much as looked at—pile up and are
pushed under a lid against such a day as this one. What are we
to do? Where shall we turn for relief? I don't know. My own
books dismay me. I wonder why I too have been so mad as to
add to the horrible pile.

One thing I can do. I can send you one of my new books of the
collected poems. That will reduce the accumulation by at least
one item.

It must be change of life. It must be the weather. I go about
forgetting to cork the cleaning fluid bottle. I strike my dwindling
thighs against miraculously obstructing chairs. I pick up a book
and dance with it vaguely, then lay it down again without having
found a place for it. But that is only the surface. Inside I possess
the heart of a fly, not even so much heart, for a fly will at least
struggle against the spider. I hit the wrong keys. I am not even
ashamed to speak of these things.

Meanwhile four or five books must be written, at once. And I must help others who appeal to me for advice and assistance.

One must eat too. And one must work, hard at times, to no purpose other than the bare mechanics of the work itself. A failure more of fate than ability, the infection being a few points more virulent in one case than another, brings permanent hatred. Success is passed over as *selbstverständlich*. One rescues a poor specimen of humanity unfooled that it will turn out to be a genius, knowing, on the contrary, that it will surely develop into a charge of the municipality or the state. One's own family distrusts one—at a distance of three feet—barring one.

(An hour or two later)

Just had a nice, big, fat young woman in here, age 41—the place still smells of her, not too objectionably so long as you know where it comes from—she has a pain in her coccyx and her poor head feels (as mine does) as if it were packed with cotton. . . . Her difficulty comes from a fibroid tumor of the uterus which makes her periods irregular and dotty. She doesn't want to go to the H. hospital because her sister died there two years ago. The sister had a bad heart and her doctor wanted her to get rid of it in the second month, but the husband was religious (O God! give me relief from my afflictions!) and didn't think it was right. So she said to herself, Lots of times doctors tell women they should not have any children and after that they have five or six and it never bothers them. So she went ahead with it and in the seventh month she began to swell up something awful. You wouldn't know she was a young woman. She swelled up to twice her size and all she could do was sit up in a chair and gasp. The doctor wouldn't take her case but he felt sorry for her, so he got a specialist from the city to help him. When she couldn't go any longer they had to do a Caesarean section, but she died on the sixth day.

Now I feel better. I am always better when I can spill my stupid soul into the emptiness—with someone foolish enough to stand below my window and perhaps get it on his coat.

So now I'll go into the house and tell Floss I'm going to see my little mother who is in the hospital in N.Y. where she is expecting to be operated on for a second cataract after having had the first removed (miraculously well by a young Spaniard) two weeks ago. It's a new technique. They take the opaque lens out by way of an incision into the anterior chamber of the eye, drawing it up through the pupil itself.

My mind is beginning to click again. It is raining. I have tried to read Louis Zukofsky in Laughlin's new *New Directions*. I admire Louis but his work is either the end, the collapse or the final justification of the objective method. He is building up a literary argument for Marxism. He is placing sentences, paragraphs, slices of speech in a line—for their flavor and special character—by that to build (the opposite or the same as Gert Stone the People) a monument, a literary creation. It is very difficult to grasp and impossible to follow with a mind of my type. Yet it is very good (in theory) and solid in practice. But is it literature? I dunno. I don't know. I do not know. It seems an impossible method, without sequence, without "swing," without consecutiveness except one have the mind of a mathematician plus the inventiveness of such a poet as never existed in this world. So maybe it is good, if it is good.

I want to be drunk and I'm beginning to feel drunk. With the only drink I know that intoxicates me: words at flow. My own words pouring out of me, the steam from them rising and the sound of them splashing in the bowl—even the rank smell of them rising as if from the green shell of a walnut. Nuts!

So go on and get well. The whole damn works ain't worth it, but go ahead and get well. Why not? What for? It's a world unfit for literature but maybe, as Malraux says, through blood and daring it may be made fit for us—cheap cowards that we call ourselves at times.

Yours,
WILLIAMS

1939

April 26, 1939

Dear Jim: One of the most difficult and important things, I should say, for a young man to learn would be the limitations of his teachers, at Harvard as elsewhere. It's forbidden ground in most cases, deliberately hidden and desperately defended against attack. The facts of the case aren't desired, besides which the natural modesty of youth makes us susceptible to just the sort of deceit that those in positions of authority practice against us— when we are young—to hide from us just that which we should know.

It takes us most of our lives to find out how limited the world is. Very little is understood other than that which has been underscored by authority. Nobody will take the trouble to really get down to work on new proposals. Perhaps the university as such must inevitably place itself as a barrier to the new just by being a defender of the old and the established. I once heard the elderly and intelligent and tolerant Dean Gauss of Princeton (much to my surprise) discourse on that subject. He was overruled later by several of his hirelings.

Aristocrats with their blanket lack of esteem for any one who is not an aristocrat are often, I suppose, in an advantageous position toward the beginnings of their lives because of that. It is hard otherwise to grasp that we know, that we are able, that others are barriers to our progress right from the beginning. I for one have hung back just from a lack of conviction of the dullness of others. I have said, Why should I presume? when I should have said, For God's sake, get the hell out of my way and at once! So much time is lost.

Damn the bastards for saying that you can't mix auditory and visual standards in poetry. Who the hell ever invented these two categories but themselves? Those are the questions that set up all academic controversies. The trouble with them is that they aren't real questions at all; they are merely evidence of lack of definition in the terms. Define your terms and the question disappears. Philosophy is full of them until someone who knows what he is about shows them up.

What they, the formulators of that particular question, do not know, is that an auditory quality, a NEW auditory quality, underlies and determines the visual quality which they object to. Let it pass, Jim, it's one of the limitations of the present grade of teachers. Do your stuff, listen hard and make discoveries. If we're right, we'll turn out to be termites in their wooden legs. If we're wrong, the birds will eat us.

Yours,
BILL

123: TO ROBERT MCALMON

May 25, 1939

Dear Bob: Ford and Biala[1] are leaving here for France next Tuesday, I went in to see them for a few minutes this afternoon, to say good-bye to them and found that they were expecting the Ezra. He however failed to arrive. He's been very mysterious about his comings and goings while in this country, keeping his whereabouts more or less secret and all that sort of thing. Perhaps he's somewhat uncertain as to the sort of reception he might get if he came out too outspokenly with his fascistic opinions.

He is now protesting that he is not a fascist—at least that is what Ford told me today. What the hell difference does it make anyway? They have been arguing with him in favor of lechery— or anything at all to keep him amused or distracted between poems. I understand he did get a chance to lecture at Harvard once, tho' whether or not he was paid for it I can't say. He says he is returning to Rapallo in about a month.

I happened to see him in Washington. I don't think I have told

---

[1] Mr. and Mrs. Ford Madox Ford.

you about it, have I? Floss and I badly needed a little rest, so she and I drove down to Norfolk, Virginia, one day and then worked slowly back north, seeing the reconstructions at Williamsburg on the way, Yorktown, Jamestown, etc., a five-day trip. Pretty fine country in April. We enjoyed every minute of it, though it rained the whole time. Well, just before we left home Skip Cannell, who has turned up recently, wrote me that he hoped we'd be able to drop in on him and his family while we were down that way. I replied that I knew Ezra Pound to be in Washington and that if he could pick Ezra up we might all have dinner together.

When Floss and I arrived at Skip's home in Washington we found that he had done even better than I asked. An old friend of Skip's, Dorsey Hyde, had been able to have Pound paged through the administrative buildings, where they found him wandering around more or less blindly, and invited him to Sunday dinner with us. It turned out all right. Hyde has a responsible government position and did the thing up brown.

Pound looks like Henry VIII of England. He was wrapped in sweaters and shirts and coats until I thought him a man mountain, but after a while he returned to normal measurements again —I think he was afraid of our damp spring weather! Can't blame him much. He ate wonderfully well of Mrs. Hyde's fare. We had a very brief talk together after an affectionate greeting—with nothing said on either side and that's all I've seen or heard of our hero except from the Fords.

To end this story of the Fords. They are taking a villa on the French coast near Le Havre for the summer and have invited us to stay with them in August. Damned thoughtful of them. I wish we could do it, but it would cost all of $500 for a two or three weeks' vacation. I don't think we'll be able to afford it, what with the time it would take to make the crossings. Still, it sounds attractive—provided there would be no war. Not much chance of our doing it unless Paul gets a job.

We're having the "Friends of W.C.W."[2] out here for a final party the evening of the first Tuesday in June, about 40 of them. Ford will be in France by that time or near it. The group, that is to say Ford, will be awarding a prize for a script, finished or

---

[2] Founded by F. M. Ford.

unfinished, submitted before next January. I think the prize is going to be one thousand dollars! What do you know about that? Somebody has donated that sum for us to award, some woman friend of Ford's I think. Oh well, why not? I confess it all means very little to me except as it relates to Ford. I've gotten to like the man. If I can be of use to him toward the finish of his life, and let me tell you it is toward the finish of his life unless I'm much mistaken, I'm willing to let him go ahead. He understands perfectly well how I feel about it.

They had a party at the Gotham Book Mart in honor of Joyce on the occasion of the appearance of *Finnegans Wake* a week or two ago. All kinds of people showed up, mostly no friends of mine—including Nancy Carrol of the screen and Hollywood and that sort of crap. We all had our pictures took. Good beer anyhow.

Then there was another party of the same sort only smaller for Katherine Anne Porter and her *Pale Rider*—a new book of short stories. More beer and such. She was charming as usual. I met Wm. Rose Benét for the first time. Strange how one doesn't meet people—luckily. . . .

Driving myself to it, I've plugged on through the first six chapters of *White Mule* and the seventh is half written. But it's a hell of a job. I wonder whether I'll ever get twenty-four such new chapters written this year. Not that I don't like what I've done or the prospects of more, but what in hell am I going to do for time? I'm sunk before I start. As soon as the typist has finished with what I've just given her I'll bundle it off to you. Better return it, as there will only be two copies besides the original script.

Paul is entered at the Harvard School of Business Administration for the next two years, but now that I've signed a bond for $500 to cover his room rent he is beginning to think—to hell with it, he'd rather get a job—for which I do not precisely blame him. I suppose I could get released from the bond by getting somebody else to take it up if it comes to that. With Bill only one year from his M.D. all this means plenty to the old man. If the boys were on their own we'd be in a position to dictate a few terms to fate, which might make it a bit easier for us.

Paul says, God damn it, he wants to write! Now ain't that sompin? He says he's going to get a job writing if it has to be in Oshkosh (which they say is quite a place, by the way) and start from there. More power to him. We'll see what the summer brings.

It might possibly amuse you to hear of American collegiate doing—as related by my kids: anyway, Paul and his pals and their girls danced at the usual Ivy Ball last week-end until 5 A.M. then breakfasted on beer and dumped the girls at their hotel. Now feeling exhilarated, just before dawn or so, they decided to go fishing in the miniature lake in the Botanical Gardens—Paul had found an old rusty deep-sea hook in the cubby hole in the dashboard of his car. They fished, in their tuxedos, sitting in a row on the bank, until finally—to Paul's amazement he got a terrific bite on his hook and, to make a long story short, yanked a two-pound catfish out of the pond and onto the grass behind him. That, by the way, is Paul! so perhaps I'd better let him alone. He once went fishing with Bill (an expert) and, catching a trout (bigger than any Bill had caught), dropped his line with a piece of worm still on the hook back into the stream by accident and, while examining the first fish, caught another. Nothing to count on, perhaps, but an attractive trait for all that. The cook at the fraternity house ate the catfish.

I'm sitting out here in the office more or less at loose ends tonight. Two patients have been trying frantically (and uselessly) to drag me out for nothing but their own god-damned nerves. Floss is in New York with a friend hearing Marion Anderson, the colored soprano, sing at Carnegie Hall. God how that woman can sing!

Took Mother in to New York yesterday afternoon to get the final verdict on her eyes and was told that she would never be able to read again. Christ, that gets me down. It's a problem that will never be solved except in the one way. She's lame and deaf and now more or less blind. I have no place to put her and couldn't do it if there were a place. Not that I give much of a damn about myself. It's tough on Floss though.

Oh well, Charlie Sheeler has married a swell Russian girl to whom we introduced him last year and is as happy as a man can well be. She seems happy too. Anyhow she's all right. It is working out nicely. He has money now and lots of work to do at top prices and she is a decoration. . . .

There was a grand opening at the new Museum of Modern Art in New York a few weeks ago. It really was a stampede—what a mob! Art has at last achieved its objective, it has served in America as an occasion for the rich to come out and root for it—just once, just once. The bastards. But the show is a great one and well worth repeated visits I'm sure. It will be on until October.

No new ideas! There are dozens of new magazines coming up almost every day. Can't bother with them any more. I don't write much. Did I tell you I'm being sued for $160,000? A big lummox of an Irishman, while drunk, fell downstairs after beating up his wife—so much so that she walked out on him after the accident and started divorce proceedings against him. He finally died as a result of another fall, on top of the first one and after being twice in the hospital, drunk as hell in between and generally out of control—he weighed 250 pounds if he weighed an ounce. So she is suing me because I neglected him! And me after sitting between the two of them through it all. Just because he didn't get double indemnity because when he fell he was drunk and I said he was drunk. So if the case comes up and I have to start over again on a nickel—won't it be a joke, it will. I'm insured for $25,000, but what's that? They say I have nothing to fear— it all happened over three years ago now—but at times it disturbs me. Life is sour enough without that.

But Floss is worth having lived to discover—and she to have lived through it for me. The damned kid is in better health of late than formerly and, when she isn't cursing me to hell for my bad habits, does everything in her power to make life worth living in every way for me. I'd like to give her a break before we both die of this that or the other—you never can tell when it may get you, any day now—something or other. . . .

I want to read more. But I also want to write. I can't do both. Remember me to Bill Bird if you see him. I was sorry to have to

refer Jim Higgins to him as you had already told me there was
little chance of a job in Paris, but what could I do?

Yours,
BILL

124: To *Furioso*

June 7, 1939

Dear *Furioso*:[1] Please let me have three more copies of Vol. 1,
No. 1. We had a gang of lights and less lights here last night,
and many of them saw my copy of your baby and liked it. Miss
Steloff of the Gotham Book Mart was one. Someone said it was
the best little mag. he'd seen in twenty years. It is. Go to it.

Pound was here day before yesterday, he saw it too—I don't
know whether or not for the first time. He seemed pleased though
distant. He has taken the attitude of being little interested in the
intermediary steps, his attack and thoughts being occupied with
nothing but the peaks of interest. I hope he wears the right glasses
or he may in the near future trip over the hem of his skirt. He's
an old friend and an able poet, perhaps the best of us all, but
his youthful faults are creeping up on him fast and—you can't
avoid issues forever by ignoring them or attempting to change
the topic of conversation. Even the lion finally gets a horn through
his guts.

The best of luck to you and courage be yours. You have made a
good start in a difficult game; don't for one moment allow yourself to forget that you will be watched with eagle eyes from now
on—whether evidences of the watching appear to you or otherwise. You've definitely put yourselves on the spot. You will find
plenty of friends willing to root for you if you keep up the clean
front, but if you slip, they'll crap all over you with glee. Print
the kids, print 'em bald, fragmentarily, scattered, in part, a line,
a bit and paragraph FOR THE GOOD IN IT. I'd like to see a fragmentary issue of the kids, kid stuff, at its best—eliminating everything
but the good piece which MAY later appear as a considered work.

---

[1] A Yale poetry review.

But do print more of the unknowns. It's all right to salt in a few like myself, but it's not the major function of *Furioso,* unless I mistake your aim. The issue seems to me a little tight, too ordered —coming from two kids. I want to see what might be presumed to be more of you, as you, in it. Well.

Sincerely yours,
W. C. WILLIAMS

125: To James Laughlin

June 7, 1939

Dear Jim: By all means have Lorca in the 1939 *N.D.* There's so much of the Spanish stuff that is unknown, old and new. Geez, how I'd like you to use some of the *novella* by Quevedo I've been translating, 1627 stuff, right on the ball. I could give you anywhere from twenty to forty pages or more if you had room for it. Maybe ten pages would be enough—the only difficulty being that unless the whole business is offered, it might be too puzzling for the ordinary reader to get the drift of it. I'm using the whole *novella* as a framework to hang my mother's biography on. Probably best not to fool with it now.

The one to look up in connection with Lorca is Rolph Humphries, who is in Mexico on a Gug. now I think. Maybe you have his address, if not, he could be reached through *Kenyon Review.* I'm not familiar with Alberti, don't know him at all.

We had a gay party last night. Too bad you didn't show up, everybody wanted to see the wonder child. There were about twenty here, including Higgins and his girl, more of a child than I had suspected—but maybe I'm wrong, I usually am in such matters. Marsden Hartley and my new Scotty pup (6 weeks old or so) were the heroes. Hartley was well primed by my Bill and a pal with good Gordon gin so that he positively glowed. Haven't seen him so young and happy in years. But we didn't do any reading, just talked and drank and ate. A marvellous night was accorded to us by God in the matter of the weather,

superb. We started it in the back yard among roses and lilies and
ended after midnight indoors.

Pound spent the night here Monday. He spread himself on the
divan all evening and discoursed to the family in his usual indis-
tinct syllables—at that it wasn't bad, if you believed him. I
found, unfortunately, that he has acquired a habit of avoiding
the question at issue when he is pressed for a direct answer. Not
so good. But he does go, he does see the important faces and he
does have some worthwhile thoughts and projects in hand. I like
him immensely as always, he is inspiring and has much information to impart but he gets nowhere with it, "a static explosion in
a granite quarry" is the way Munson spoke of him. The man is
sunk, in my opinion, unless he can shake the fog of fascism out
of his brain during the next few years, which I seriously doubt
that he can do. The logicality of fascist rationalization is soon
going to kill him. You can't argue away wanton slaughter of
innocent women and children by the neoscholasticism of a con-
trolled economy program. To hell with a Hitler who lauds the
work of his airmen in Spain and so to hell with Pound too if he
can't stand up and face his questioners on the point.

Enclosed is a story that has been batted around everywhere
without acceptance. If you care to use it in *N.D. 1939* I'd like
to see you do so. I like the thing, but because of its length and a
slightly diluted quality no one wants it. If you also do not
want it, say so. It's about all I have now aside from the Quevedo
translation which is probably unsuitable.

Tooraloo, must get at the new *White Mule*. By the way, I've
decided on the title for volume two: "A Taste of Fortune." It
has a somewhat musty flavor at that but it goes, I think, with the
story. I did think of using, "In the Money." Like that better? The
second is snappier and more up to date. And, my dear publisher,
what about the publication of the book? This time it's got to be
pushed hard.

I didn't set out to write a letter as long as this. What the hell's
the matter with me?

Sincerely yours,

BILL

[*In 1938 Horace Gregory was directing a poetry seminar at Sarah Lawrence College and invited WCW as a guest speaker. The two poets soon discovered a deep bond not only in poetry but in personality.*]

126: To Horace Gregory

July 22, 1939

Dear Gregory: It really thrills me that you're doing the preface to this new edition of *In the American Grain*. I've said that before but now after reading your letter I say it again. I'll dig up the facts you want and send them with this letter.

Let me begin by telling you something of how I came to write the book. Of mixed ancestry, I felt from earliest childhood that America was the only home I could ever possibly call my own. I felt that it was expressly founded for me, personally, and that it must be my first business in life to possess it; that only by making it my own from the beginning to my own day, in detail, should I ever have a basis for knowing where I stood. I must have a basis for orienting myself formally in the beliefs which activated me from day to day.

Nothing in the school histories interested me, so I decided as far as possible to go to whatever source material I could get at and start my own valuations there: to establish myself from my own reading, in my own way, in the locality which by birthright had become my own.

As I recall it now, I started with the Columbus essay. I wrote and rewrote that ten times before I got hold of the idea which I finally adopted. The problem was to include all the four voyages and yet make the essay end on the high point of the successful termination of the first voyage with the tremendous emotional power centered there. Mrs. Williams and I were on our way to Europe when that chapter was finished, on the boat.

Meanwhile I had been reading the letters of Cortez to his king —not in the original Spanish, unfortunately, but in translation.

I also read the translations of the Norse saga, the famous Long Island saga, I think it is called. I am sorry I didn't keep a record of all the things I read. But whatever reading I did was done at the N.Y. Public Library in the American history room.

I remember a comical incident that happened there. I didn't have much time at my disposal so I would crowd as much as I could into the Friday afternoons of my one day a week off. One day when I was plugging away on the Ponce de Leon material, I think, I got out my source book but before I opened it (I had been working at the same task the week before) I suddenly got an idea and started to write, furiously. Right at the height of my flight I felt a tap on my shoulder and the son of a bitch of an attendant there, with a British accent (in the American history room!) told me that this was a reading room and that if I wanted to write I would have to go somewhere else. Christ! I could have murdered him. But I couldn't be stopped that easy in those days, so I merely opened a book, propped it in front of me and went on writing as before. What a bastard that bird was. I imagine he's still there. I'd like to see him cremated.

Oh well, I thought you might be amused. Now let's see what I can find in the attic.

Oh yes, about Hart Crane. I don't think I ever met Crane. I may have met him, he may even have been out here to Rutherford but I can't for the life of me remember it. We had a lively correspondence for a year or so toward the beginning of his New York period, but nothing much came of it. I remember I bought a water color through him painted by some friend of his back home.[1] That too must be up in the attic. I liked the man but I stuck on his verse. We were too far apart there. I have some letters of his in the file, I'll see what is in them. I was stumped by his verse. I suppose the thing was that he was searching for something inside, while I was all for a sharp use of the materials. We just were on different tracks. This has no bearing on what you're doing but since I'm writing a letter I'm just putting down whatever occurs to me.

Mrs. Williams helped me a lot with my reading. She would sometimes dig up the material, read it and tell me about it. I

[1] William Sommer.

always like to get things that way. In college I got quite as much from lectures as from books and always remembered more vividly what I heard than what I read. Anyhow, she did all the reading for the Aaron Burr chapter and it was, besides, her enthusiasm which fired it and which I took over complete, my part being merely to decide on the form of the make-up and go ahead.

And this brings up something else. The book is as much a study in styles of writing as anything else. I tried to write each chapter in the style most germane to its sources or at least the style which seemed to me appropriate to the material. To this end, where possible, I copied and used the original writings, as in the Cotton Mather chapter, the Benjamin Franklin chapter and in the Paul Jones chapter, of which no word is my own. I did this with malice aforethought to prove the truth of the book, since the originals fitted into it without effort on my part, perfectly, leaving not a seam.

This month, by the way, a French magazine, *Mesures,* is using several things from *In the American Grain* in translation. It's a beautifully made periodical. If you're interested I'll let you see my copy—when it arrives. They're using the Paul Jones thing, "Advent of the Slaves," and, I think, something from the Franklin chapter. They're also using several poems.

Floss just showed me the review of my poems in the N.Y. *Times* which came out today! I'm just short of being one of the best, it seems. That's too bad.

"The Destruction of Tenochtitlan" appears to have been the first of the chapters published, in *Broom,* Vol. 4, No. 2, January 1923. What a magazine that was! Too expensive for its time but superb to hold in the hand and to read. There were reproductions of Mayan sculpture and architecture all through the issue.

Then came "Red Eric," in *Broom* also, Vol. 4, No. 3, February 1923, followed by "The Discovery of the Indies," the next month, March 1923, "De Soto and the New World," Vol. 5, No. 3, October 1923, and finally "Sir Walter Raleigh," Vol 6, No. 1, January 1924. That was all for *Broom.*

As I recall now, the heavy reading for these chapters was done in the fall of 1922. The Columbus chapter, while it was the first written, was revised so many times that it was really not finished till after some of the others. I worked myself into the scheme on that one and then ran off several others rather rapidly. In that way some of the others were ready for publication earlier.

Now we jump somewhere else, I'll have to go look again. Wait a few minutes, I'll be back.

SPECIAL NOTE: To show the frailty of human witnessing, Floss has just reminded me that we sailed for Europe January 8, 1924! That means that all the above work was published a year before that time. Yet I am sure still that I worked on the Columbus piece on the boat, a sheer impossibility. The magazine dates are correct; therefore please ignore everything relating to dates in the early part of the letter.

To go on:—Christ only knows where the rest of the stuff is. I began to look but it is nearly six o'clock Sunday afternoon and I ate too much dinner to keep up with guests and must go out in an hour to eat too much again to keep up with my hosts. Anyhow I'm all balled up.

I'm sure *transition* published several things from the book, and in a day or two I'll find them and tell you about it.

I hope I haven't confused you too much.

Best luck.

> Yours,
> WILLIAMS

1940

[Harvey Breit, now the well-known editor of "In and Out of Books" appearing in The New York Times Book Review, *adopted the* nom de plume *of "Foka" in his early writing days, appealing for critical help, as so many other fledgling authors have done, to WCW.]*

127: To Harvey Breit

January 25, 1940

Dear Foka: Whether or not the fiery demon that possesses the world is going to destroy us or give us a new birth I cannot say. All we know is that only a few years ago we were too smug in our beliefs touching the ultimate triumph of man's coming humanity to man. We know now, hit or miss, that love is far more remote a power than we suspected, that it is a difficult master and that if we expect to realize it in any part we must labor with all our zeal toward its realization. We were too glib, too sanguine, too languid in what we thought and said and too doctrinaire in our praise and service. Imagine a Savonarola!

Either we are to be enslaved forthwith and all our reasons for living are to be removed from us in punishment for our guilty laxness or we shall grow serious as we have never been serious in the past and love again desperately with an abandon which we have been ashamed of. It is all very well to speak of Patchen as a mystic who hopes that love by some strange magic is to save us —and to laugh at him. But you point out that he aims at the heart of the matter. He does not have to advocate a scheme of ideas. He is an artist, a poet. How weak the argument seems.

Your thesis is important. As a matter of fact Patchen is only accidentally its theme. It sweeps him up into the theme. But you dignify him by identifying him with it.

I have no entrance into magazines generally but I agree with

189

you this should be widely read. My only idea would be for you to send the article (or thesis) to Laughlin himself at Norfolk, Connecticut, % *New Directions,* with a letter asking Laughlin if he knows where it can be used. Perhaps *The Saturday Review of Literature,* I don't know. Maybe you can extend the theme and have Laughlin bring it out later in *New Directions 1940.*

Anyhow, my congratulations. I think you are one of those who will, with labor, build the world again. Again, how weak.

Sincerely yours,

W. C. WILLIAMS

Don't let me appear sentimental. I'm not kidding myself. A work of art is no more built of sentiments than ideas. You know that as well as I or better. We are alike in that we recognize the structural basis for a criticism in what Patchen says and is. It is difficult and dangerous skating to keep objective, but it has to be done.

[*Written by hand on back of the letter:* Thanks for mentioning Silone with understanding. There's a man who is the type. It begins to be an addition, one here one there—yourself.

A worse letter I have never written. How in hell you can get anything from it but a false impression is more than I can say—but I can't write it over.]

128: TO JAMES LAUGHLIN

Sept. 25, 1940

Dear Jim: It's easy to forget, in our dislike for some of the parts Ezra Pound plays and for which there is no excuse, that he is a master of language. That goes far. It might be his only virtue and still be a mark of greatness. It is hard to appraise as it is hard to achieve, hard to isolate for criticism as for the honors earned. It is even possible that Pound himself is self-deceived and performs his miracles unconsciously & makes mistakes too sometimes while he frowns over some asininity he proposes and leans upon so heavily. His language represents his last naiveté, the childishness of complete sincerity discovered in the child and true poet alike.

All that is necessary to *feel* Pound's excellence in this use of language is to read the work of others—from among whom I particularly and prominently exclude E. E. Cummings. In the use of language Pound and Cummings are beyond doubt the two most distinguished American poets of today. It is the bringing over of the language of the day to the serious purposes of the poet that is the difficult thing. Both these men have evolved that ability to a high degree.

Two faulty alternatives are escaped in the achievement of this distinction. There are plenty who use the language well, fully as well as Pound, but for trivial purposes, either journalism, fiction or even verse, I mean the usual stroking of the material without penetration where anything of momentous significance is instinctively avoided. There are on the other hand poets of considerable seriousness who simply do not know what language is and unconsciously load their compositions with minute anachronisms as many as dead hairs on a mangy dog. These latter are the more pernicious, their methods well accredited by virtue of all academic teaching, simply make their work no good. They would need to go through the crises both Pound and Cummings experienced in ridding themselves of all collegiate taint.

It is impossible to praise Pound's line. The terms for such praise are lacking. There ain't none. You've got to read the line and feel first, then grasp through experience in its full significance how the language makes the verse live. It lives; even such unpromising cataloguing as his *Cantos* of the Chinese kings, princes and other rulers do live and become affecting under his treatment. It is the language and the language only that makes this true.

Bill

129: To James Laughlin

Dec. 14, 1940

Dear Jim: Before it is too late, please send me four copies of *In the Money* to be charged as usual to my account. I want them before Christmas. Many thanks. . . .

The world's nuts; I can't keep up with the mere reading I ought to do touching it. There is so much, so much, so much I might do that I, more than ever in my life before, feel desperately in need of giving all my time to writing (considering reading, serious, persistent reading as merely another phase of that.) How am I to do it? Yet I must do it or confess myself a failure. I planned my life (apart from a ten-year lag due to wars, economic catastrophes, etc.) to march through a tunnel at the far end of which was sunlight. By that I mean time, TIME to do what I knew I must do to breathe again! If I do not end as a full-time writer then I have not succeeded in my plan. Everything depends on that.

Ezra is an important poet, we must forgive him his stupidities; I do, no matter how much he riles me. But I prefer not to have to do with him in any way. He wants to patronize me. Don't tell me this isn't so, for I know better. His letters are insults, the mewings of an 8th-grade teacher. That's where he thinks I exist in relation to his catastrophic knowledge of affairs, his blinding judgments of contemporary values. In one sense he is quite right to protect himself as he does. But my perceptions overtook him twenty years ago—not however my accomplishments. When I have finished, if I can go on to the finish, there'll be another measuring.

Meanwhile I salute his native sensitiveness, which try as he may he cannot quite live down. It makes me laugh to read of his being spoken of as a musician and of a high order. He has a complex ear for metrical sequences, marvellous! And he has a naively just concept of the value of knowledge—in other words he is a poet, a great one, but a musician—never!

What the hell, all I started out to do was to ask you to send me four books.

Yours,
BILL

1942

March 18, 1942

Dear Harvey: This paper was a well-intentioned gift. I'm still making excuses for it, even though the gift touched me. Your letter struck C major with me. I had one brother, we were like one person all during our early development, breaking up finally over a girl whom neither of us got. I know what masculine identity of thought and feeling can mean and welcome it whole-heartedly. Your expression of it does not embarrass me in the least. Its resolution is the production of works of enlarged understanding and greater resourcefulness and felicity of design. Nothing of that sort is likely to occur today—save in the mind. I understand and thank you for your words.

I'll look for what you say about Patchen in *Poetry* when it comes out—though *Poetry* has gone Geo. Dillon of late, much to my mistrusting. I'm still a subscriber. It's the old respectability gag, the academic shuffle—they don't even know they're doing it. . . . I'll look for what Stevens says but don't know where to look. Did you say *New Republic*? I'm always grateful for tips on such things as, due to my life, I miss so much that I'd enjoy seeing if I could get to it.

You might have taken the words out of my mouth in what you suggest of Patchen's new book. I threw it aside in complete disgust when I saw how Evangelical he had become. After all, does he mean it or doesn't he? Is he spoofing or does he want us to take that crap literally? I think he's serious and if he's serious it's bad. It's second rate. I'm surprised and a little shocked. BUT THEN, here and there, a first-rate, clean poem appears. I was equally astonished at that. The book should be gone over and the bad and good poems checked, a, b. Enough good poems could be saved to make a first-rate small book I think. But many are spoiled now by this strange streak.

I think Patchen is obsessed by a divinity streak. He thinks he is God and that everything he says is good. He isn't self-critical enough—unless he really thinks he is John the Baptist. That won't do. It's all right to give the subconscious play but not *carte blanche* to spill everything that comes out of it. We let it go to see what it will turn up, but everything it turns up isn't equally valuable and significant. That's why we have developed a conscious brain.

Of course the conscious writers, who know everything and must keep everything in perfect order—the ones I was railing against above—want us to believe that they KNOW, that the church and its INTENTIONS are indispensable and right. They despise me. But I say and I believe it is true that in despising me (microscopic as I am) they are in reality despising an essential part of the poetic process, the imaginative quota, the unbridled, mad— sound basis of all poems. They won't even consider me or what I intend. So be it. The academy must be served.

But isn't poetry, at its most significant, the very antithesis of the academy? You see how the field divides. An armed assembly (we are not talking of the completely uninterested, outside the pale of literature), armed, that is by detailed knowledge, the academy, the Eliots, the hard students of literary history, men who fight for hard knowledge—and I respect that kind of knowledge. *Poetry,* under Geo. Dillon, is leaning toward that side. Then there are the dirt men, the laborers who try to keep alive the *geist,* the undisciplined power of the unimaginable poem. . . .

Some sort of synthesis is necessary between these two groups. It usually takes place in some one man at some propitious moment in history—an essentially ignorant Shakespeare, etc., etc.

Patchen must discipline himself, not as the academics want to discipline him—they hate him!—but to keep within the bounds of the art. He's trying to run out of bounds. We can't do that. If you run out of the bounds of art you make imbecilities.

Can you follow this vague adumbration of what I am trying to say? I hope so. I hope you want to follow it and do not find it trivial.

I'm not writing any poetry now. I can't. I hope I shall be able

to surmount present difficulties. Write again. We'll get together.
I hope you find a way to earn something in order to eat and
have a reasonable security.

Yours,

BILL

[*Charles Abbott, when he became Librarian of the Lockwood
Memorial Library of the University of Buffalo, determined to
build up a superior collection of modern American poetry. His
appeals to WCW were met by a mass of letters, personalia, drafts
of poems and stories, which fill four large filing cabinets. This
sheerly literary relationship flowered into a close friendship, and
Dr. and Mrs. Williams have spent some of their happiest vaca-
tions at Gratwick Highlands, the Abbott home outside Buffalo.*]

131: TO CHARLES ABBOTT

May 15, 1942

Dear Abbott: . . . I'm sending you a batch of my early letters to
my brother and to my mother. They were written during my college years and the years of my internship in two New York hospitals . . . but the tone of them all is so very immature that I am
astonished. Certainly they are not for general investigation. You
may keep them all, though I should prefer it if you selected a few
and destroyed the rest. There is nothing much of good in any of
them and much that is close to infantile. I can assure you that
the letters do not by any means reflect what I was thinking in
those days. The probability is that I did not have the courage or
the ability to place my most intimate actions and reactions on
paper for anybody's eyes. I can distinctly remember many, many
details of those times that the letters do not even adumbrate.
    . . . If the mind permitted it I'd hire myself out at food and
lodging to be your gardener for the next ten years with the special
privilege only—to write. I'd probably claim other privileges, as
Flossie says: an occasional whisky binge, hot and cold running

water, refrigeration, electric lights—a trip to the great city occa-
ionally and to the library frequently. . . . I'm good at caring for
children though. . . . Most of all I want long periods of silence
and loneliness. . . .

Yours,
W. C. WILLIAMS

132: To LOUIS ZUKOFSKY

June 21, 1942

Dear Louis: All right, it isn't a philosophical novel then. Perhaps
you're right. In that case, God damn it, you've got to kill the old
couple in the end. Who cares about "truth"; you've got a presumptive work of art on your hands; it's ridiculous to sidestep
the situation in the way you have. Either you should kill everybody and follow through with the "truth" of the story as a story.
Or else just don't do anything. Don't even have the hallucination
of an accident but make them come our perfectly safely into a
beautiful sunny green California valley and have a picnic lunch
on the grass.

Your explanation makes the story more comprehensible to me,
but in that case a little tighter writing here and there, a little
more care with the sentences, removal of hanging clauses and
some play with the sentence structure to avoid monotony would
be of great help. I didn't indicate anything because I wasn't ast
to, but I saw several spots that needed touching. With more
briskness in going over, without transitional explanation, from
incident to incident (as you have very well done for the most
part), stronger *lines* to the composition would be indicated. It
needs sharpness of compositional lines in several places.

What to do with the girl at the end is something of a problem.
He might find himself wanting almost irresistibly to turn back to
her, but, after a struggle, going on. I certainly do not like the
phantasm, the fantasy—which seems very definitely manufactured
and anything but "true" at the finish.

I think the whole might easily be brought down to ten or at

least eight pages less than it is by judicious clipping here and there throughout. Nothing like careful snipping for the bringing out of the profile. Even a word cut out will very often brighten a whole paragraph miraculously.

Wish you luck,
BILL

133: TO WILLIAM ERIC WILLIAMS

September 7, 1942

Dear Bill: Your last two rather short letters, in which more seemed to be withheld than stated, came to us very quickly. It disappoints us that our own letters do not at least occasionally do so well. There must be two dozen on the way to you with several small packages, but you do not appear to be getting them as you should. . . .

There's all kinds of news to tell you—where shall I begin? First, I wrote to Mrs. Biggers a week ago but have had no reply . . . Monnie's ear is still discharging. Doc Ehrenfeld says it probably comes from Eustachian tube and a few granulations in the middle ear impeding drainage. He suggested snuffing out the snot instead of blowing it out, sleeping on the opposite side (for drainage) and the use of ear drops as follows: Boric Ac gr X, Resorcin gr. V, Sp Vini Rect. oz ½ and Sol Bichloride (1-10,000) q.s. adoz I. Wipe out the canal and instil 4 gtts 4 i d. Hope it works. Monnie's scared to death they'll call him up for the army and then turn him down flat. He doesn't want that.

(Several hours later.) We've just returned from Isabel Pope's wedding to one of the Roehrs boys, a home wedding that went off all right, a pretty girl. They got off to a clatter of tin cans at about 6:30 after which Mother asked me to take her for a short drive—to settle our stomachs after the junk we had eaten. I drove to Rutherford Ave., then out on the new road. It was just at evening, the road dry as hell, so I went very slowly. . . .

I enclose a ticket I'm distributing to my patients. One of the doctors in Passaic who is going into the army next week has asked

me to hold office hours in his office once a week. I'm going to do
it on Tuesday afternoons. I'm taking no other vacation than the
four days I spent seeing the new baby. I don't want a vacation
and couldn't enjoy it if I had one. I want to work and to keep
working, it soothes my mind. I feel then that I am doing my part
as I want to. For wherever we are every stitch of work we do all
helps in the general cause. I am trying to keep to more or less
military discipline. It isn't that I get up on time or anything like
that, it's in the mind. As the younger men go, we older men must
do their work—there's no question about that. To do it, we've
got to give ourselves up to it and be ready, in our minds, to go—
because it's going to be pretty damn hard this winter unless I
miss my guess. We're going to be doing a number of things we
haven't done in years and we're going to have to like it. I'm going
to like it.

These last two weeks have been buggers. The principal cause
of this has been a strep throat infection that starts without many
physical signs other than prostration and high fever. The local
symptoms don't start till the next day with redness of the pharynx
and fauces. But the fever goes sailing and stays there. I had one
bad case two weeks ago that taught me a lesson. I tried sulfanilamide and things seemed to be doing all right. Then I switched
to sulfadiazine as the patient was getting pretty blue. But the
temp took a jump. I went back to sulfanilamide, but the temp
didn't come down until I gave maximum doses. I start with six
tablets gr 5 Sulfa and gr V Soda bicarb followed by three tabs
q 4 h, day and night. It didn't stop a strep pneumonia, but after
two weeks the guy is getting well at last. It seems to hit little kids
as well as adults.

Ran into a lousy case of a ruptured appendix, badly neglected,
in a twenty-six-year-old woman, seven months pregnant. Carlisle
opened her up day before yesterday. General peritonitis, the
appendix rotted off. Put in ten grammes sulfanilamide, but
couldn't pull the peritoneum together because of the pregnancy.
He put in through and through silkworm sutures. She aborted
the next morning. Have her in an oxygen tent after intravenous,
plasma, more glucose and saline, and finally a transfusion. Her
temp is down, so is her pulse and we have a Wagenstein tube in

her. I hope she can get something through. Except for that, she is doing fine.

Delivered a nine pound 13½ oz kid the other day from a woman who weighed only 93 pounds a year ago. Low forceps. I broke the clavicle getting the shoulders out. Everything's all right though. I've been going nuts. So yesterday, Sunday afternoon, I decided to do a little work in the back yard—it's been terribly dry of late. But then I thought of some leaks in the roof, so changed my mind and got my tar bucket and a stick and went at that. There was one leak I remembered right in the middle of the top roof. So I got on my rubber-soled shoes and went up there, worked my way up one of the gutters. It gave me quite a thrill to straddle the peak of the house and look around. A lot of fun. Found the leaks too, and plugged them—I hope.

Speaking of the front terrace, it looks fine this year. We had such a rainy August that the grass wasn't burned in the least. And now it is coming back strong. . . . The last of the red mallows appeared today, but the roses are just beginning their fall show and the morning-glory at the corner of the back steps where the stones from the shore have been placed is up to the very top of the office roof. . . .

Yeah, it must be tough situated where you are, with so very little to do and with so little contact with the world at large. But can't you even tell us about the natives? I suppose not. Oh well, there's not much use in telling you the news, for by the time it reaches you it'll be so stale that—even you will know it. The best to date is that the British and Americans in Libya have stopped Rommel's recent putsch. . . .

Last night, after my ruptured appendix case and the roof-climbing incident, I was all in. Mother hadn't been feeling any too chipper, so we both went to bed early. We must have fallen asleep very quickly and deeply because this morning I heard that there had been an air alarm in the night. An unidentified plane had flown over. All the whistles were going, so they say, but we both slept through it solidly. It turned out to be a friendly plane, but that didn't help us any. We just slept. . . .

Many thanks for your good wishes on my birthday coming up. It's amazing how quickly your letters come through—so that you

were way ahead of time. Damned thoughtful of you and I appreciate it. 59 years, not a hell of a long time as the ages run—and
what it's all about is far from clear. I'd trade 'em all in a minute
to see a little more light among the peoples of this world—and
who wouldn't? I'll work it—or take it out in hard work this
winter, the best I can. Thanks again.

Love,
DAD

The President speaks tonight at 9:30. I'm going to listen.

134: TO WILLIAM ERIC WILLIAMS

Sept. 13, 1942

Dear Bill: I don't know what's come over me recently. I don't
write as easily as I used to—not, that is to say, as confidently.
I find it necessary to go over and over things and to work at
them at times until I am damned sick of them before I am
through. Not always of course, but most of the time. I suppose it's
a change of some sort that's come over me, perhaps a part of my
education. Let's hope the final effect is beneficial and not fatal.

The enclosed I have been doing this evening for a small magazine run by a bunch of fairies. What the hell. I never care where
my stuff is published—or even, most of the time, whether or not
it is published at all—though that isn't quite true. I do like to
see the stuff in print and consequently out of my mind.

Funny how a thing sometimes crosses one's mind out of nowhere; as I was writing the above paragraph it came across me
that I haven't seen the Tylers all summer. Queer.

So here's my little essay—thought you might find something
to occupy your mind with in an off moment. I'd appreciate any
comment you care to make, anything from total rejection to the
liking of a word or a phrase here and there. No hurry.

Here's the clover I forgot to put in the previous letter.

Love,
DAD

135: To William Eric Williams

Sept. 25, 1942

Dear Bill: Your letters recently have shown me the changes that are taking place in you, a maturity which I want to salute and acknowledge. Generally speaking, your present experience has been of decided benefit, something you could not achieve, at least not so quickly, in any other way. Part of it has been the enforced separation from any protecting influence I may still have had on you, a very good thing. What you're facing is your world, a world in which I haven't the slightest part. We are now two individuals, two men, closely bound by mutual beliefs and interests but completely independent as to the future. Strangely enough, this separation has brought me much closer to you. I'm glad that early phase is at an end.

That relationship between father and son is one of the toughest things in the world to break down. It seems so natural and it is natural—in fact it's inevitable—but it separates as much as it joins. A man wants to protect his son, wants to teach him the things he, the father, has learned or thinks he has learned. But it's exactly that which a child resents. He wants to know but he wants to know on his own—and the longer the paternal influence lasts the harder it is to break down and the more two individuals who should have much in common are pushed apart. Only a sudden enforced break can get through that one.

But I've sweated over wanting to do and say the right thing concerning you boys. Certain things stick in my mind—I just didn't do the right thing and I suffered for it. Once when you were a little kid some question of veracity came up between you and Elsie, that goofy girl we had here. I should have known that you were just a baby but I lost my temper, insisting one of you was lying when I should have known, if I had thought for a moment, that it wasn't you. Or if it was, then what the hell anyway? It might have been from fear—no doubt of me. Then one day at the close of Watty's camp in Maine you were in some sort of a canoe race and were about to win when someone quite unfairly cut you out and you cried. I like a God-damned fool laughed at you. Why? Just to hide my own embarrassment. You looked at me and said, "It was my only chance to win anything!" I tell you that hurt. I've never forgotten it. Such are a father's inner regrets. Stupid enough. And what in the hell is a parent to do when an older child is tormented by a younger child, finally smears his younger tormentor and then comes up for punishment? I've never solved that one. I've done many more seriously stupid things than those mentioned—but I wanted so hard to give you the best.

On the other hand, when you say you've got so much more in the bank than some of the men you have to deal with, I feel that what we did for you wasn't too bad. The same for what you say about the kitten and the spiders. That you can get the good out of such trivia is a tribute to your mind which I have always respected and which I'm glad to see maintaining itself with distinction in the situation in which you are placed. I don't know what kind of a father I was but in things like that at least something "took" of what I intended and that it wasn't all beside the point.

You say you'd like to see my book of poems. What the hell? Let 'em go. They are things I wrote because to maintain myself in a world much of which I didn't love I had to fight to keep myself as I wanted to be. The poems are me, in much of the faulty perspective in which I have existed in my own sight—and nothing to copy, not for anyone even so much as to admire. I have wanted to link myself up with a traditional art, to feel that I was developing individually it might be, but along with that, developing still in the true evolving tradition of the art. I wonder how much I have succeeded there. I haven't been recognized and I doubt that my technical influence is good or even adequate.

However, this is just one more instance of the benefits to be gained by breaking entirely with the father-son hook-up. It was logical for you not to have looked at my poems—or only casually to look at them. You had me in my own person too strongly before you to need that added emphasis. You did the right thing and I never cared a damn. Now, separated from me by distance and circumstance, it may after all be permissible for you to look at the poems. Not to do anything more than to enjoy them, man to man, if you can get any enjoyment out of them, I'll send them. I have a gold-edged copy reserved for you, one of the de luxe copies, but I'll not send that. Look, if you care to, at whatever I have done as if you had never known me. That's the only way for a father and son to behave toward each other after the son's majority has been reached. Then, if you still find something to cherish, it will be something worthwhile.

You in your recent letters have shown that you have a style of your own—another testimonial to your own character and a tribute to your parents for not trying, really, to press themselves upon you. You have an interesting prose style that everyone who reads your letters admires. It's really comical. Some say, "A chip off the old block;" others say, "He writes better than you do," and so it goes. You are entirely different from me in your approach, and yet we are alike in our interests. . . .

They finished insulating the attic today and are putting storm windows all along the front of the house. Better to be prepared for what may happen the coming winter.

Love,
DAD

136: TO WILLIAM ERIC WILLIAMS

November 8, 1942

Dear Bill: The papers are ablaze today with news of the U. S. invasion of French North Africa. Details are coming through every hour; tho I have not listened, others tell me what they have heard. It seems to have been well planned. The French seem to have been caught off guard, let's hope they don't put up too serious a battle for it. The latest is that we have taken over all of Algeria, if so it begins to look as if the program of attack is off to a good start in the west.

This new information has momentarily obscured the news from New Guinea and Guadalcanal as well as that from Egypt but only momentarily. The British are doing all right, being conservative in their claims as usual but going ahead with devastating speed and power for all that. I hope they can get behind Rommel before he escapes to Libya and destroy him quickly. But even if he does get away with a few divisions now he's going to catch something else from Algeria that will surprise him. It looks as if the whole of North Africa will soon be in the hands of the United Nations, if so the beginning of the end is close at hand—though no one is kidding himself this time, it will still be a hard fight.

MacArthur also is beginning to make himself felt. If he can take all of Papua with its conveniently located airfields then the rolling-up operations in the Pacific will also be on the way. I have always suspected that when this does take place your gang will be moved up behind the front line.

In a few minutes I'm taking Mother to the ball field, it being Sunday afternoon, to see a demonstration of defense measures against incendiary bombing by experts. I'll tell you about it when I get back. It's a half-cloudy day, very quiet and with most of the leaves down. It looked as if it might rain earlier this morning but no rain materialized. We haven't had any frost as yet, though it is the end of the first week in November. A few roses are still blooming and just now Mother counted six buds on the bushes in the new beds. We have taken out unsatisfactory bushes and replaced them. In another week or two I'll be piling on the compost. The new grass out front looks fine.

I told Nana W. about the guava tree in bloom in front of your quarters. "A guava bush," she said. Well, bush or tree I told her the blossoms must be lovely. She said they were. Interesting about the honey. Charlotte brought us a pot of coffee flower honey a week or so ago. We thought it too astringent but the last time she was here she brought a different sort, avocado honey. This was delicious, I strongly recommend it. Maybe that's what your men found. I've never been able to get anyone to salvage the honey from the big maple in the Sylvan Street block near the school. There must be plenty there over all these years, the shade tree commission isn't interested.

6:18 P.M. news just came over the radio that the French in Algiers have signed an armistice with U.S. troops. I hope it's true.

Well, the anti-incendiary demonstration at the ball field was somewhat of a washout. We sat next to the Tamblyns in the east stand, so as to be out of the smoke! As it happened we got the works, including falling ash, like snow, a whiff of phosgene gas, though this was hardly noticeable, and smoke all in our faces. To add to it all it began to rain halfway through the proceedings so that many went home before the climax.

The people sat on the usual stands about the football field on which temporary structures resembling the interiors of rooms with one side knocked out, a small skeleton frame house with balloons red, blue and green tied to it (full of oxygen, hydrogen and oxygen-hydrogen) and a skeleton framehouse of three stories, at the south end of the field, had been erected. They showed us how magnesium, phosphorus, sodium and several other types of bombs burned, showing us the effects of water as a spray, as a stream, etc., etc., worked. A voice boomed from a loud-speaker in a booth erected over the west stands. But the thing was slow getting started; too many small officials had to throw the bull first including our idiotic mayor—until a person wanted to retch. No seriousness, no sense, no ability, no nothing. Undignified and unexcusable. Then came the rain. Oh well.

We came home wet but not too disgusted; each had a bottle of Coca-Cola, after which I lit a wood fire in the grate.

Annie Spence ain't had her brat yet but several others of my November batch have already produced, including a Helen Martin who knew you in high school, a dark-haired girl and a beauty, has the guts too, refused an anesthetic. She brought the head down almost to the perineum, then just quit having pains, sat there smiling and kidding. So, since the cervix was about fully dilated, I put her on the table and gave her 2 minims of pit. She took one good breath and let us have it. Pow! No tear, no nothing. Quite a gal. I think Annie will be on deck soon, her hubby is coming home on furlough tomorrow.

The cases of virus pneumonitis I've been seeing are a real entity. I had two kids, two boys, aged about 5 and 15, two brothers who had it beginning about a month ago now. The beginning is almost negligible, the person has a slight sore throat, not much, maybe a headache, and then begins to cough. The God-damned cough is the thing that wrecks them. They cough and cough and then really cough, day and night. Nothing does any good. The sulfa drugs have no effect, there is little fever. When you come to listen it sounds like a resolving pneumonia but it sounds like that from the first, loose rales everywhere, though usually one lobe is more affected than the others. The prostration is severe and protracted. Finally the fever quits, after two or three weeks, then the cough quiets and the patient staggers to his feet. I tried massive doses of vitamin C together with aspirin but I can't say the effect was very favorable. They just stay sick. The sputum is white and glarey, no sign of pneumonia. The prognosis is invariably good even when the chest sounds like imminent collapse.

Speaking of collapse, Mrs. Mahon, the mother of the two boys I spoke of above, now five months pregnant, contracted the infection from them and has she been a sick puppy! The fear of an abortion has made the course of the disease particularly troublesome in her case, together with anxious relatives, nurses almost impossible to get and all that. She herself has been splendid. But the cough all but ruined her and me. She has coughed until she was hysterical, I have given her codeine until I was ashamed of myself, even by suppository. Finally I listened to her right chest about five days ago and thought I had a consolidation—but her temperature was normal. She had ruptured her right lung. I didn't tumble until about two o'clock the following morning when I woke out of a sound sleep with the realization clearly in my mind. I have kept her down with M.S. $\frac{1}{4}$ at bedtime since then and strapped her chest for two days. She's on the mend now. Very unusual cases, watch for them—they don't seem to be dangerous but no treatment so far has proven successful, as I say. The circulation seems to be the thing to watch in older people.

By the way, Mrs. Mahon told me today that the younger of the two boys who had been so ill so long is desquamating at his finger tips, the skin of all his fingers and both his thumbs coming off almost like a cast of the fingers now.

I think I told you I have or had 14 maternity cases for the next twenty-eight days. Two down now and only twenty-four days left. Took pictures of two cases I thought might be breeches but they turned out to be L.O.A. both of them with enough room—one though is thirty and a primipara. Due to war jitters I suppose I am terribly pestered with night calls. They start in around supper time and if I gave in to them I'd never stay home.

Paul sent pictures of the brat who now weighs 10:5. He is a good-looking little punk. The family, Paul and Jinny I mean, have moved to the Carnes house in Massillon. I hope they can stay there for the winter at least. Paul's new job, though he may have written you all this, brings him into contact with a German metallurgist, a graduate of the U. of Munich, I think, or some other German Un. Paul is crazy about him, says he has been longing for some intellectual contact which this definitely supplies. The guy has no respect for authority as authority which suits Paul down to the ground.

That God-damned telephone bell keeps ringing and ringing, sure sign it's getting near 7 P.M. Ma will deal with them as far as possible; I don't know where I'd be without her.

I did my first examination of recruits for the draft last Friday afternoon, twenty kids including one of the Siri—or is it? (remember that 300-pound guy who played guard against you one day here many years ago?) one of those brothers. He was so fat I had a time finding a vein. I got there finally, a swell bunch of kids full of boloney and general hell. All we have to do now is "screen" them. It means having them stripped in a line; they walk up to the examiner who takes blood for a Wassermann, glances at them to see if they have both legs and passes them. Took me about ¾ hour to do the twenty. They say at the final army exam in Newark they tell them to separate their buttocks. If there are any tabs visible the examiner snips them off with his scissors and hands the guy a swab of cotton to stop the bleeding with. I told that to one of the nurses the other day. I told her they were doing the same for the W.A.A.C's. She was incredulous but scared. I don't think the army is going to get her. . . .

Ma has just come in to say that Darlan has just surrendered the French fleet to the Americans! Geezus, if that's true we're really on our way. Poor Frenchies, I suppose they're in a hell of a spot—somebody's going to be killed.

I don't mean to write a book and I've probably forgot half the things you want to know about—but maybe I'll think of something later.

Generally speaking it's been a beautiful fall season, no frost, as I have said, and flowers still in bloom, the zinnias in the third bed back of the two with roses in them are still doing their bit.

You'll be receiving your Christmas packages early unless I miss my guess. What are you going to do, keep them unopened?

Oh yeah, I quit smoking three weeks ago. I feel much better, saves wear and tear on my nerve and—my wife!

Lots of love,

DAD

1943

[*Babette Deutsch, poet and critic, was among the first to notice WCW's poetic talent outside the little magazine. In* This Modern Poetry *(1936) she established his position, and in* Poetry in Our Time *(1952) she was able to reinforce her earlier observations in terms of* Paterson *and the later poems of WCW.*]

137: To Babette Deutsch

Blockadefrei Tag, 1943

Dear Babette: Why you should feel so kindly toward me I do not know unless it is that we are both of the Old Guard—I have never forgotten that day at Princeton, ten or more years ago, when we were both set upon by the horde of little instructors who would gladly have destroyed us if they could have done so. You were a great pal that day!

You know as well as I that what others say or show touching what we have written adds a third dimension to it, one way or the other. Either we see our work in horrible perspective through antagonistic eyes or it flames up to us magnificently when one whom we love and respect admires it. Your perception of the particular set of phrases enhances it for me too in a way which, alone, I could not have perceived. So that it has become yours, actually a creative act, when you praise it and I appreciate it, even tho I wrote it, through you.

Yes, I'd like to have you hear me read some day. I'll try again. And thanks for writing as you did to *Poetry*.

Best,
Bill

January 18, 1943

Dear Babette Deutsch: Wish I could have heard you read my stuff, you probably do it better than I do. I've never heard anybody read anything of mine—so far as I can remember.

Pound never attended Columbia University. He was at the University of Pennsylvania in 1902, '03, '04 and in 1905 was banished by his father to the sticks for general insubordination of what quality I don't know, probably nothing more than refusing to do anything but what he pleased to do in his classes, perhaps spending more cash than the old man could give him. He certainly was a most gingerly and temperate young man in everything that I had an occasion to observe. If he ever got under a gal's skirts it must have been mainly with his imagination. He did not drink. I don't know what the hell else he did that was censorable. I never at least, as I say, saw any evidence of it. He liked to talk and bluster about, played a little lacrosse, very little, and fenced less —never could make the team. But to hear him, you'd think he was at least D'Artagnan. He almost poked my eye out once with a walking stick through his awkwardness and stupidity.

From Penn. he went to Hamilton College, where, as I say, his father had sent him to cool off. At Hamilton he was the laughing-stock of the place with a continuous impersonation of Ronsard, I think it was Ronsard, carried on throughout the year. Not that I despise that, he put that on no doubt to shield himself from too close approach by the yokels. He could work when he wanted to, thought nothing of getting up in class and putting the profs in their places. He was all right though and I admired his abilities with words.

He knew of Yeats slightly while in America but to my knowledge did not become thoroughly acquainted with Yeats' work until he went to London in 1910 [*sic*]. There a strange thing took place. He gave Yeats a hell of a bawling out for some of his inversions and other archaisims of style and, incredibly, Yeats turned over all his scripts of the moment to Pound that Pound might correct them. That is not imagination but fact. Yeats learned tremendously from Pound's comments. I happened to be out with Pound and some others in London one night when we stopped in at Yeats' lodgings and heard him read several pieces of verse—at the end Yeats asked Pound to stay. They were just becoming acquainted at that time. Oh well, I wish I could find a stenog who would listen to me talk for a week about all those things.

Yours,
WILLIAMS

139: TO ROBERT McALMON

January 19, 1943

Dear Bob: Thanks for the stamps which we're putting aside for Bill and for your occasional letters. Letters are damned important in my life. I love to get them and to write them—when I have anything to say. I don't seem to have much recently. With four of the younger medicos in the services, the rest of us in the community have had to double up on the work with the result that it's seven days a week of it and from twelve to sixteen hours on many days. Doesn't leave room for much else. We never even go to the movies any more—not, by God, that we want to. But I like the work, as you know. It keeps me from thinking these days or perhaps not thinking so much as mumbling to myself over the state of things generally and my own position in particular. Boy! and is there work to do.

I ain't letting myself get too excited though, there's no sense to that. I just want to help the war effort in every way. It's strange but I've noticed that I don't get as tired as I used to when I had much less to do than now. I suppose I used to fret over the stupidity of the thing, treating useless bastards for the effects of their own stupidity whereas I wanted beyond everything else to be writing. But now everyone is important in some sense and so I can forget myself and plow through. It really rests me sometimes to have more than I can accomplish.

I know I'm on my way to old age but that doesn't stop me planning work in the literary field far ahead. Why not? There's plenty I want to work at. I don't mean that I want to hurry up and finish this or that before I croak, not that. I mean only that I want to push on into improved work and make myself a better writer. I can see many profitable leads, some of them I'm already working at. Hope to get out another small book of poems this year perhaps in the "Poets of the Year" series—this is the new name for Laughlin's series.

They say Djuna Barnes has painted a really good picture recently, a portrait of some female named Annie—in a red dress. The story is that it's pretty good. I wish I could see it. I'm going to try to get into the city some day soon but it's not easy now. I have too much to do here.

And what do you think about Pound? The inside dope is that he didn't want to leave his daughter in Italy since he couldn't get clearance papers for her and so refused to leave without her. But why the hell couldn't Olga have taken the child somewhere, she's a Swede isn't she? Maybe Ezra didn't want that. Anyhow, there he is and the State Department is talking of indicting him as a traitor along with several others who are broadcasting against the U.S. from Italy, France and Germany. I suppose he'll defend himself on high legalistic grounds—but a hell of a lot of good it would do us if we had to accept defeat by those guys whom Ezra came to admire, no matter how lofty the arguments should be supporting our defeat. I try to defend Ezra in my own mind and sometimes I almost succeed. A man has a right to say what he believes—BUT that's exactly what Ezra denies. Oh well, I suppose he's just a poor defeated son-of-a-bitch with certain virtues, to be sure, in his favor but not enough to save him. In some ways he's so marvelously stupid, just thick-headed, that I really pity him. Most people around here speak of him as poor Ezra.

However, he's getting himself talked about, the gov't. of the U.S. is concerned about him and there you have it. He's always wanted to be officially noticed and now he's being noticed. I wonder if he'll have the nerve to stand up and be shot if it comes to that; it's possible. Poor guy. He's never really faced the job of putting his talents on a contemporary basis—for years I never realized that all his best early work was translation from early masters. Not that that wasn't important. It puzzles me.

In a sense I know he's right. If a man doesn't live in this life, if he's always to be just a slave to his contemporaries, always merely trying to improve the general level, to work out a means to exist under uncongenial circumstances (as in or about New York, as I have done), if that's all there is to it, then it's a shitty job. Ezra wanted to live, live fully, exquisitely at the peak of feeling, and to feel that he was leading the others into a beautiful world of which he was the disciple. But Jesus, what did it lead him to? To an attempt to condone Hitler, to a completely un-feeling attitude toward the Spanish rebels, to real joy at the thought of Russians slaughtered by the millions at the time of Hitler's first successes. If that's the end of his grand schemes then he's a plain dupe of his own vanity. I suspect him more and more.

Heaven knows I'm not satisfied with my life or my work. I have always been too subdued, too uncertain and too shrinking from the punch in the nose I could see aimed my way if I persisted— unassisted—from going ahead. I had to protect myself to survive. And don't think Ezra hasn't taken plenty of assistance from sources he'd hate to acknowledge which alone made it possible for him to continue. But he was a friend, never quite under-standing what I was after, but a real friend for all that. I feel sick over him at times.

I'm working a little at odd moments on various things I'm interested in. It's always at the peak of my mind to write. I'm sure the thing I can do is more urgently important today than it has ever been. I don't mean any "message," but the way of writing, a short-cut through the pleasant shit which passes for the world of letters. Is that what Ezra wanted to lead? . . .

BILL

140: To James Laughlin

January 24, 1943

Dear Jim: Don't fuss about it, the idea of the new book was born in my mind while I was trying to squeeze up enough stuff for a

possible new appearance in your poets' series. It came of a difficulty I had to select a small collection of unpublished poems,
while a whole mass of scattered things, some already published
here and there, needed assembling.

My plan is to use a few of the very early things that did not get
into the *Collected Poems*. From there I'd go to a script you never
saw, I believe, called "A Folded Skyscraper." There is a series
of improvisations there, some of which appeared in *transition*,
This Quarter and *The Little Review*. In this script also several
notes, auditory scraps from the language, are piled up among
these, for my plan was not to follow a strict chronological order;
this time I'd put in various small bits, poems from this or another
magazine that have escaped general notice, use at least half the
things from *The Broken Span*, the complete short verse scene from
the 2nd Act of *Many Loves*, all the worthwhile pieces from the
original script from which *The Broken Span* was selected, and
finally the new things, eight or ten of them to bring me once
more up to date. This would be a useful book for anyone interested in me and would at the same time have sufficient bulk of
diversified interest for the general reader. It would show in
retrospect far better than any chapbook of carefully selected new
work could possibly manage just what I have always been trying
to do.

"Paterson," I know, is crying to be written; the time demands
it; it has to do just with all the peace movements, the plans for
international infiltration into the dry mass of those principles of
knowledge and culture which the universities and their cripples
have cloistered and made a cult. It is the debasing, the keg-crack-
ing assault upon the cults and the kind of thought that destroyed
Pound and made what it has made of Eliot. To let it into "the
city," culture, the benefits of culture, into the mass as an "act,"
as a thing. "Paterson" is coming along—this book is a personal
finger-practicing to assist me in that: but that isn't all it is.

If Stevens speaks of *Parts of a World*, this is definitely Parts of
a Greater World—a looser, wider world where "order" is a
servant not a master. Order is what is discovered after the fact,
not a little piss pot for us all to urinate into—and call ourselves
satisfied. They don't know what they're talking about.

Would you want me to try the general market? I say this with full knowledge of the consequences. I know any number of reasons you might give for saying you'd rather not have me do this and I know that I don't want to do it. At the same time you've got to be asked. Maybe no one would have the book. You'd be in a much stronger position to me then. And if they accept it, I know it will only be to tie me up with some later work. I'd rather stick to you for both friendly and also selfish reasons but I myself feel too cloistered with you. I get restless; I want to break out and take my beating if I must. I know the venality of the general publisher. In other words, I wish you'd do the book.

After trying you out thus, I'll do just what you want me to. If this is an impossible time for such a book to appear, I'll be glad to wait for further developments and your advice. If you are definitely not interested and want to turn me loose, say the word. I merely want to get your impression and to talk the thing over with you in complete confidence.

Sincerely,

BILL

141: TO ROBERT MCALMON

August 8, 1943

Dear Bob: I've had it in mind to write you a long letter for the past week but it hasn't come off. Nerves mostly, the war, this, that, and the other. But there is one thing I wanted to tell you. Paul announced over the phone Monday morning . . . that I'm a grandfather. A boy. Jinny came through it all right so there starts another generation. . . .

We get letters from Bill on his isolated island fairly regularly; he has apparently not much to do as yet. May it continue. He spends most of his time when not busy wandering out on an old coral reef enjoying the things he finds there. Most interesting is that as a physician he has become father confessor to his battalion, censor and general protector of the men. Strange for one so young. It has turned him to thoughts of the arts—poetry in a vague way.

It's a strange world made up of disappointments for the most part.

I keep writing largely because I seem to get a satisfaction from it which can't be duplicated elsewhere. It fills the moments which otherwise are either terrifying or depressed. Not that I live that way, work too quiets me. My chief dissatisfaction with myself at the moment is that I don't seem to be able to lose myself in what I have to do as I should like to. I wish I could omit the news from my days entirely. I can't help more than I am doing and I do castrate myself by the constant disillusion I feel before the news. Perhaps our leaders are smarter than we know. No doubt the things that get printed in the papers are put there for an effect. But sometimes the thought comes over a man that we may be in a far worse fix than they are telling us and our leaders may be infirm. I know I can't help, but when I see the smug faces of many in the street, I don't know, I don't know.

I've written a few poems, one or two, and a very short short story. I'm in process of writing a book, the book I have contemplated doing for many years—prose and verse mixed: "Paterson" —an account, a psychologic-social panorama of a city treated as if it were a man, the man Paterson. I want to work at it but I shy off whenever I sit down to work. It's maddening but I have the hardest time to make myself stick to it. In spite of which I have done a hundred pages or so—it ought to be nearly finished by now. I hope I can finish it soon.

Glad you're going to get a vacation. Wish I could be with you.

Bill

142: To Robert McAlmon

Sept. 4, 1943

Dear Bob: Floss always, for some reason, looks at the obituary notices in the N. Y. *Times* every morning. Yesterday she found the name of Marsden Hartley. The *Times* gave him ¾ of a column, a brief summary of his accomplishments. I was going to send you the notice, but what's the use. I went in to see his last show. There were some florid, formalized flower pieces, a mountain or two, some fish, a group portrait of a man kneeling on Fifth Ave. or thereabouts in front of the Rockefeller Church, a ten-foot man in overalls, scrawny, pathetic. So what? Why do we live? Most of us need the very thing we never ask for. We talk about revolution as if it was peanuts. What we need is some frank thinking and a few revolutions in our own guts; to hell with most of the sons of bitches that I know and myself along with them if I don't take hold of myself and turn about when I need to—or go ahead further if that's the game. I'm afraid Marsden was stuck—in his own mind, in his technique obsessed with fears—unwilling to use the good eyes he had and think. This is an ungracious and ungenerous attitude to take before the spectacle of a man dead. There it is.

Floss has just come in to tell me there are twenty or thirty young robins in the back yard, scrawny young birds flocking together for comfort and because they are too young to have mated yet, the gang stage. I've never seen so many birds in our yard as this fall, hundreds of them at times, starlings, purple grackle, robins, sparrows and an occasional blue jay. No very delicate spectacle but birds for all that. It's a gloomy, half overcast day with bright green grass and many late flowers.

We've been on a short vacation, first to the Connecticut shore for five days of delectable swimming, which is paradise to me when I'm overwrought and mentally fuzzy, and then a week at the Sheelers' at Irvington-on-the-Hudson where they live. Charles and his 38-year-old Russian ex-dancer wife Musya. They have an old gardener's cottage; a small graystone building that is all that remains of the buildings on an estate that the millionaire owner dismantled to get square on Roosevelt. . . . Chas. has made a beautiful thing of the little house, a really beautiful home for him among the hundred-and-seventy-five-year-old purple beeches, jonko trees, and oaks and maples of the estate. . . .

I've been trying everywhere to find a publisher for my next book[1] of verse, probably the best yet. They all say they're so sorry but that they have no paper. I've tried about all. Jim Laughlin, who promised me that he would print anything I wrote, merely

---

[1] *The Wedge.*

said he'd like to do the book but that he also could not get the paper for it. I've merely put the script aside. I'll get going on something else now. It seems I'm not really happy except when I'm writing. I was glad, by the way, to hear that you had got a start on something. Hope to see it someday.

Bill still writes from his South Sea hideout. It must be a small island and hard to get to, for he says they are drinking distilled seawater and that a replacement, a young officer of some sort, took two months to get there. Bill says the land crabs cart off your socks, the rats chew up anything they find, and so it goes—they get any water they can to wash in. Paul is at Naval Training School at Cornell. He's just finished his first month, equal to the first year at Annapolis. . . .

Floss and I go along doing repairs on the house, planning to have enough oil to heat with next winter and fighting the telephone as usual. We don't get to New York much, a show once in a while but that's all. No incentive to visit anyone there any more. Sally has written us about Bill Bird who is in Algiers or Cairo or some such place. I wrote him a letter at her request but have had no answer as yet. Started last night to read the *Encyclopaedia Britannica* on Poetry. Try it.

Got to go in to lunch. Then office hours. I used to hear something of the French gang in N.Y. a year ago but of late nothing, not interested. Peggy Guggenheim is putting her money at their disposal, I suppose through Max Ernst—I think it's Max Ernst. They say Hemingway is writing short stories from his hacienda in Cuba. Probably getting up some more of 100-calory stew. He sure is a money-maker. . . .

Hope you're keeping well.

BILL

1944

Jan. 14, 1944

Dear Jim: Maybe you're right. If you're able to and want to, then do—for the life to come may be an awful bust. And besides, who can say you were not driven to it, of a purpose? Those are things we may not decipher being only one, one at a time.

You know what? Poets are being pursued by the philosophers today out of the poverty of philosophy. God damn it, you might think a man had no business to be writing, to be a poet unless some philosophic stinker gave him permission. But the shabby little stinkers all want to write poetry themselves and try again and again. Let me not mention any names. I shan't quarrel with philosophy as such, let 'em have it. But there is a fallacy in always insisting that poetry shall "mean" what some little stinker thinks it should. Poets are becoming scared to death lest someone put up a little tennis net for them to hop over before being admitted to the game. It runs deep; I'm not stating it half forcibly enough here. But what is sorely needed is poetic construction, ability in among the words, to invent there, to make, to make well and new. When that is done let the scabby philosophers scramble to interpret—which is their field if any. But we're letting ourselves be gelded by them. To hell with them. I'm afaid the Freud's influence has been the trigger to all this. The Surrealists followed him. Everything must be tapped into the subconscious, the unconscious—as if poetry had ever been different. But poetry has also been a construction in the words—very strange news this is to the present day. Am I living too long? I wonder.

BILL

Do try to have *In the Grain* set up in a type of larger face this time if that is at all feasible; it will make all the difference in the world.

144: To Robert McAlmon

Feb. 23, 1944

Dear Bob: There are lots of things that you and I don't agree on, plenty, but Ezra Pound, generally speaking, isn't one of them. You may not like my way of handling the situation as it concerns me. That's my business. But you're dead right in combatting the bastards who pick on him when he's down, as an excuse for their own culpability in the mess to which the world has come. They brought it on, if it comes to that; he didn't—stupid as he is. There are several numb spots under his skull (such as his inability to distinguish between musical notes), that's why I call him stupid, because he won't acknowledge them. It amounts to genius. . . . I say these things because I want you to know that when I say Pound is stupid I'm not talking out of personal resentment or even momentary anger, I say it because I can't in any other way account for some of his actions. I have come to believe with the years that he simply doesn't know certain things that comprise human consciousness and never has been able to know them for the simple reason that the apparatus is missing. I think this is the truth. He is actually like those child marvels who go through college before they are twelve years old —and are forever afterward complete failures. He's not that, of course.

Having said that, I think without question that Ezra is a genius in his use of words. It is true, his best poems are rekindled translations, but that's no drawback to their genius.

I hope he'll be remembered as he most surely will be. I have made up my mind to defend him if I am ever called as a witness in his trial—for I may be. I have already been warned. He's a one-sided bastard if there ever was one, who has borrowed from everybody, including myself in the old days, but he's done a good job, surpassingly good. And I've borrowed from him much more than I've given. Everyone has who has followed him. Yeats especially.

Each of us is born with a certain authority at his command

which is innate. You have it. Pound has it. I suppose it's a sexual component in the Freudian sense. Not that that makes a damned bit of difference. The main thing is that it's there. I acknowledge it and always have in Ezra. I still do. Your definition of it as an evocative power over the word is good. I think you hit it on the nose. Good criticism; it's the authority behind it that gives the word power. Something that is in the man himself, really great— and unaccountable.

I'd like to possess Ezra's powers, sure I would, but that sort of thing is innate, as I say, and belongs to the man himself. Or, as the old people used to say, to God. I don't care about such things. I feel elevated and warmed when I read the best Ezra has written. There's a finality and a continuity about his work, continuity with the past, that is both generous and farseeing. It's really an illumination in the sense that Apollinaire might have best understood. But that doesn't include all that Ez would wish it to include or exclude.

What, in thinking of Ezra, one should call to mind is not, as he would have one think, what he has read (which may be plenty), but what he has not read and what he should have read and understood if he had wanted to be the universal man he blandly thinks himself to be. He's an infant. One should remember what he has been unable to read and is to this day unable to grasp when he has attempted to read it. He can't do it.

I agree with you again, we got to keep using our heads even when we follow loyally in the step of our leaders—leaders, let's say, like Ezra in literature. But I just dragged that in to illustrate a point. You mean and I mean political leaders. . . .
(1 day's interval)

It astonishes me to observe how irritated moderns become, not so much at the thought as at the mention of death. That's one thing they don't quite know how to take. I don't mean that we should be "brave." That stinks. But it is equally asinine to pretend to ignore it. I don't think there has been evolved a modern equivalent to the old religious certainty that by death we will be justified in our thoughts and deeds. In other words that the good we do will triumph and the bad we do be punished. That's "out" as far as thinking people are concerned and only effective as a whip used to keep the various hierarchies of church corporations in power. But there is nothing to take its place. The end result of the modern attitude being to taboo death as a topic of thought or conversation.

However, many critics tacitly assume the old opinions in what they do—Eliot among them. And if they do not assume that viewpoint then much that they assume is void if their logic is followed through.

For instance, is it or is it not a bad thing to be killed young (we're not at the moment talking of being maimed)? Is it or is it not a crime for older men to send armies of the young to kill each other for "countries" or "principles" or even "freedom?" These things are never discussed, not even in the churches. But they've not only got to be discussed but a definite answer has to be given to them before some of the cruds can be told off in their shallow maneuvering for a position of advantage—which most theorizing and arguing is anyway—Ezra foremost like all the superman type being pressed only by those he hates and that's why he hates them.

If death is a wiping out and a finality then what the hell does anything matter at all? The man who gets what he wants is kind and we'd better all shut up fast. If there's anything to death apart from a simple canceling out, then it had better be stated (in a modern acknowledgment, a modern language—which it has never been) at once so we can know just how to evaluate self-seeking. (Two hours later)

Sorry the above has been so incoherent but it can't be helped— better so in fact. I've been going nuts trying to find a bed in one of the overcrowded hospitals for an acute appendix in a young mother of 28 or so. We're going to slice her open in about an hour.

What I wanted to say, of course, is that unless we have some moral code, based on our responsibility to our fellow-man to go by, based that is on the essential value of the individual, any individual—then we have no right to judge as between two sides in any contest and there can be no objection to war and slaughter to your heart's content and one side is like another once it wins.

Yours,

BILL

I know Ezra's objection to anything I'd say on these grounds, it is that he, being a surpassing individual, not only has a better right to survive than another but that it is immoral to think otherwise—and that's an impossible one to beat without an absolute faith in man's value from an absolute standpoint. I say there has been no modern statement of this in convincing words in our time and no attempt at it, the subject being taboo.

It brings up the subject of what gives a man authority in whatever he does. I knew a football player who used to play at Penn. He was a low bastard but he had that authority that held everyone at attention when he was on the field. His very voice jerked heads in his direction. And what was he? He flunked out of college, got gonorrhea, syphilis—ended up as a Y.M.C.A. secretary in France during the First World War.

Some Negroes have that authority in the way they wear their clothes. I know a colored porter on the Erie like that. He's a better man than another just by the way he walks up the street. Some women have it, others pack it. Pound has it in the evocative power he has over words. What is it? Damned if I know. Even some little children have it, even infants when they are born. To me it is an immoral quality. I suppose Napoleon and Alexander had it to perfection. It makes a man think he is better than anyone else. But unless he uses it for others, to make himself a servant in some sense for humanity, to man, to those about him who need him—he turns out to be a selfish bastard like Pound, like Napoleon—like the Negro porter, like the infant as soon as he grows up.

I don't know the final answer but I do know that Ezra is just a self-destroyer when he talks as he has done to me of the Russians and the Spaniards and now of the Americans. Make what you can of this and to hell with you.

BILL

145: TO HORACE GREGORY

May 5, 1944

Dear Horace: Eliot's article in the new *PR* [*Partisan Review*]
should be answered by me direct but, strange as it may seem, the
feeling there is antagonistic to me, unfriendly and offensive. It is
characteristic of them, for instance, that Eliot should be the one
given I haven't counted how many pages of space to say something thoroughly known, long since digested by the best minds
and really nothing more than a talking to one's self at inordinate
length—whereas a direct application of an American culture is
never mentioned.

The ideas come so fast I cannot keep up with them and in the
crowding I confess that I become incoherent—I need a friendly
audience.

In a discussion of local and general culture Eliot is a maimed
man. He fled the rigors of an American application, embracing
the Church largely to cover up that. But of recent years I have
noticed he is trying to get down to the local again, trying to find
his own youth. I have no objection, but he wants to do that not
by an ACT of reconversion but by endless talk about the philosophy
of literature. He has steadfastly ignored the application of the
principles which he affects now to discover, the essential nature
of local culture, while spouting at length upon its necessity.

I have written guardedly and very briefly to *PR,* stating that
the mere definition of the natures of cultures, local and general,
is valuable in its way but that the essential thing is that there be
an interchanging flow between them. There has to be a recognition by the intellectual heads (Eliot among them) of the work-a-
day local culture of the United States. In fact, there can be no
general culture unless it is bedded, as he says, in a locality—something I have been saying for a generation: that there is no universal except in the local. I myself took it from Dewey. So it is not
new.

But Eliot has been more than offensive in his escape from that
which now he prates about—and ties to his Christianity, which

somehow makes a man ill to contemplate. I don't know what it is, if I have not defined it, about Eliot that is so slimy. It is the affectation of authority, an offensive leaking from above so that the water is polluted wherever he appears in print. *PR* loves it. They act as do so many of New York literary journalists, as if they had learned our history and morals in Odessa—which would be all right if they had not brought their spurious pride out of the same container.

The flow between the man of intellect and the formally trained intelligence is what we are after, a direct interchange which perhaps the homosexuals have presaged in their pathetic manner. The interchange from the local toward the general, and the refreshing of the general from the local (which Eliot at last recognizes—as if it were new!), is what we are after: freely, warmly, with mutual acknowledgment and even eagerness. The homos at least know what it is all about, even if they distort it in the familiar fashion. But they have the particular in mind, they apply their understanding in a broad symbolism. The symbolism of the homologus in their lives can be taken and enlarged from that to enhance the world: Siegmund and Sieglinde were brother and sister, they produced Siegfried—tho I do not particularly want to stress that.

Besides, just as the city depends, literally, both for its men and its materials on the country, so general ideas, if they are to be living and valid, to some extent depend (at least for their testing) on local cultures. It is in the wide range of the local only that the general can be tested for its one unique quality, its universality. The flow must originate from the local to the general as a river to the sea and then back to the local from the sea in rain. But more particularly, since we are speaking of the arts (as they represent culture), and still more particularly of the poet, since Eliot is speaking as a poet—it is the poet, locally situated, and only the poet who is the active agent in their interchange.

It is the poet who lives locally, and whose senses are applied no way else than locally to particulars, who is the agent and the maker of all culture. It is the poet's job and the poet lives on the job, on the location. But if the head, the intellect, on which he rightfully calls for direction, contemns him, fails to leave a friendly channel open for him but blocks him off—then dynamite is the only thing that will open that channel again. And it has been my chief objection to Eliot that being an expatriate American, being a gifted mind, being what he is, he has no reason to be followed as—he should be branded for the worst possible influence in American letters—simply because he more than anyone I know has blocked the interchange of fertilizing ideas between American and English letters. But add to that his tedious talk, his mock seriousness while hiding behind it, timidly afraid to come out with one bold critical statement on local values here . . . I find him not only misleading but offensive.

I yell for someone to take his place. Take his place. Do it with the authority of informed learning, with a feeling for a culture which is one of the most outstanding of the world. America is a culture of unique value; she needs you—or if I am growing too offensive myself—she needs someone to act the critic but in a enlightened and most particular sense and not with the sick, defeated sense that this man hides in his pathetic spoutings.

BILL

146: TO HORACE GREGORY

May 9, 1944

Dear Horace: If, as I believe and keep always before my eyes, if art is a transference—for psychic relief—from the actual to the formal, and if this can only be achieved by invention, by rediscovery, by reassertion by the intelligence and the emotions in any and every age—and if the grand aspect of this living drive is, when it occurs, a culture, then, I say, our chief occupation as artists, singly and jointly, should be the clarification of form, new alignments, in our own language and culture.

This should be for us a foremost topic of conversation and of interest—and investigation: to make clearer what we want and must have and to give whatever new form we can find IN our culture (if any) the greatest possible distinction.

I have maintained from the first that Eliot and Pound by virtue

of their hypersensitivty (which is their greatness) were too quick
to find a culture (the English continental) ready made for their
assertions. They ran from something else, something cruder but,
at the same time, newer, more dangerous but heavy with rewards
for the sensibility that could reap them. They couldn't. Or didn't.
But they both ended by avoiding not only the possibilities offered
but, at the same time, the deeper implications intellectually
which our nascent culture accented.

That is by avoiding the difficult formal problems presented they
found themselves stripped of the philosophical and psychic under-
pinnings which make up the very rock upon which any new and
more highly developed cultural necessities rest for us today. So
that both Pound and Eliot have slipped back, intellectually, from
their early promise. Which is to say that the *form* and the gist, the
very meat, of a new cultural understanding are interlinked in-
separably.

That is why the question of FORM is so important and merits
such devotion and the keenest of wits, because it is the very matter
itself of a culture. We cannot go back because then the form becomes empty, we must move into the field of action and go into
combat there on the new ground.

We here about New York are most fortunate in having such a
difficult ground and such a history, so beset by the enemy. I think
you and I should institute a research into the form of our culture
—rather the forms—anyhow, we should discuss the correctness or
falsity of what I am saying. Let's not project a "book"; that would
be to place the emphasis in the wrong place—but it gives me a
talking point, an investigation as to what we have and how it is
distinguished, let us say, from the conventional in English.

This should be done as (*eine Arbeit?*) not by thinking so much
as looking, reading, keeping in mind what we think we are after.
It is this approach that should be practiced on the work of Poe,
Whitman and whatever of the moderns we care to look at—to
discover high-lights, the formal distinction which may be there.

[YVOR] Winters denies all this. He went back to the conventional stanza and in his best work has done some fine things, but
how empty they seem to me when taken with the view I have of
our culture as a whole. His poems are tight, hopeless, sterile.

Maybe our culture is the same. In that case I'm a fool—but I don't believe it.

That, so far as I can present it (badly) is the concept that haunts me. Between us progress might be facilitated by the complementary qualities we may wish to bring to bear on it: a study of the formal resources of a new cultural concept (not to be narrowly designated American though perhaps first adequately perceived here).

Be seeing you.

BILL

147: To William Eric Williams

Wednesday, July 12, 1944

Dearest Bill: Read the enclosed and if you have no further use for it return it. Don't destroy it, please, in any case.

Proud of you, Bill, real proud of you. A father follows the course of his son's life and notes many things of which he has not the privilege to speak. He sees, of course, his own past life unfolding—with many variations, naturally. Sees moments when he'd like to speak a word of warning or commendation, places where he himself went wrong or made a difficult decision that was profitable later. And all the time he can't say much.

He can't say anything largely because he realizes that in the present case, the case of his son's life, a new and radically different individual is facing life, that the life he faces is different from the life the older man knew when he was young. But mostly he can't speak because—he can't. It would do no good. Likewise he can't praise, much as he'd like to.

Queer how easy it is to go wrong. I'll never forget one day at Camp Roosevelt in Maine. There was some sort of a boat race going on, I think it was a canoe race in which you boys had to paddle the boats with your hands, and you were ahead, it looked as though you might win but some one cut you off and in your anger and disappointment you burst out crying. I laughed. You looked at me and said, with bitter reproach in your voice, "It was the only chance I've had to win anything!" Boy, did that hurt! I could have sunk into the ground to think that I should have ridiculed you at that moment in front of that gang of your fellow campers.

Well, all that's past now. You've won and won in a most important way, you've won the affection and approval of your fellows under conditions of severe physical and mental trial. You're no hero, I'm not saying that. All I'm saying is that you have shown qualities of a man such as I admire. And I have the right to speak this time because what I feel did not arise in me but came to me through others, who were with you and who know.

Best of luck. I hope you enjoyed a good week-end with Buzz and Nancy. I'd like Dotty to see Barlow's letter and unless you disapprove I'd like to send it to her.

Mother joins me in sending love,

DAD

Home on Sunday! It has to end sometime, perfect as it still is.

[*Wallace Stevens, Marianne Moore, and WCW have been linked together for many years as the acknowledged leaders of the* avant garde *of American poetry. Stevens and WCW had met in New York whither Stevens journeyed regularly from his work in Hartford, during the* Others *days. WCW wrote* on *Stevens and Stevens* on *WCW, but they seldom wrote to each other.*]

148: TO WALLACE STEVENS

July 21, 1944

Dear Stevens: With a little more practice you'll really be able to write. I refer to your delightful prologue to Morse's interesting poems.

You know, it makes me think that we do begin to have an elder group who are, in fact, in themselves, a critique and a *vade mecum* of an art that is slowly acquiring reality here in our God-forsaken territory.

It will later generate an assembler who will make the history.

Yours,
WILLIAMS

149: To Wallace Stevens

July 24, 1944

Dear Wally: Yes, New York is pretty sad, I practically never go there any more—not for anything. Perhaps after the war, well after the war, if I am still able to toddle. Hadrian lived in Tivoli.

But you should really have got into a bus at 43d east of Broadway and come out to this sun-parched suburb, the drinks here are at least authentic and I think reasonably good. Call us up and we'll cook you up something nice.

My vacation for this year is past and I passed through Hartford (standing) about a month ago on my way to Bennington College to talk to the girls there who laughed so hard I could hardly finish the poem. But they were nice. Maybe later in the season I'll be in Connecticut again. If ever I am there again I will look you up for I'd like very much to see you.

Horace Gregory is finishing a book on the last four decades of American poetry. I enjoyed Gregory's, *The Shield of Achilles.* This book he is doing now should be worth watching for.

I have a small book of verse being brought out by the boys at Cummington. I had never met Duncan so stopped off there on my way to Bennington. He is very earnest and makes very attractive books. Have you ever been there? If not, go—when you want to get away from things—you'll enjoy the people and the place: the birthplace of William Cullen Bryant, completely off the earth. A hell of a place to get to. Train to Northampton then bus from there to Cummington, then walk up the mountain. I took a taxi rather than wait four hours for the bus—and drew a very nice girl driver in a black dress. Ask her if she remembers me.

Your short note gave me, as my mother still says, "a little moment of happiness." I'm working at my trade, of course, harder than ever, but also gradually maneuvering a mass of material I have been collecting for years into the Introduction (all there will be of it) to the impossible poem *Paterson.*

Then I'll do the biography of Mother, then either break loose to play for the rest of my days or die in the interim.

I'm glad you wrote.

Sincerely,

BILL

150: TO MARIANNE MOORE

November 7, 1944

Dear Marianne: It's hard to focus the mind on praise, one thinks too much of the holes in the cheese or the slice of cheese, of the emptiness that goes with all good. As you yourself said once, in substance, so well: what good is all this stuff? It doesn't work, it doesn't split any rocks after all—except to enter the heart (and mind) of some friend whose heart (and mind) were only pseudo-rock after all. We convince only those who were of themselves disposed to be convinced—or so it seems.

Say what we will, I believe we all expect our verses and our pictures and our music to do work, to make a better world of it. But they are so weak, they travel such a small distance. When they get there they take a small, cheap room and go and visit the "great studios" where the "stars" earn their millions and feel very small. One wishes one could be president so that one could make new rules and bring new aspects to life and to the eyes of—the tenant farmers!!

But there is no more civilized pleasure I know of than for writers to exchange their books. It *should* be a pleasure, that is. I remember that Robert Frost once offered to exchange books with me. I was delighted and said that as soon as I had received his book which he promised to send me the next day, I'd send him one of mine. I never received another word from him. So that was a pleasure missed. Later I discovered that he thought very little of me and what I was about.

I enjoyed the poems in *Nevertheless,* but I especially enjoyed the first one, the title poem. I liked least the "A Carriage from Sweden" perhaps because Flossie is Norwegian in sympathy and blood and dislikes the Swedes! A silly reason—and one that holds little weight of course with me, just weight enough to make me suspicious. The "Elephants" are like flies in amber, there they stand permanently: this is something you do like no one else— with that modesty which is the hallmark of the artist—a modesty that cannot be broken down by any statement about it since it is made fixed by the poem itself and so cannot be altered by anything that anyone says.

That's the release we get from writing, we may retreat there ourselves, into our own work (if you can call it work) from praise and censure—or contempt. Our poems are to us the mouse nest in the grass where we actually live and about which we feel, the less said the better. All artists are secretive and fly from a style which has been found out. You have never been found out and so you go on making these constructions.

Whether or not my book has caught anything (much) that I wish to present, it is hard for me to say. I enjoy looking over some of the poems—others rather abash me with their rather too obvious a putting together, more like a blob of muddy statement which should be or should have been a dandelion seed floating. There is too often no convincing form or no form convincing or promising enough to hold me over or take me over to some more satisfying invention.

Well, better talk about something else. Let me speak about Kenneth Rexroth and Byron Vazakas. There are two poets who are as far apart as the Metropolitan Museum of Art (Rexroth) and the girls' dormitory at Barnard. Have you read Rexroth's *The Phoenix and the Tortoise?* It's a love poem or a series of love poems celebrating marriage. Who would believe it? It is not very subtly made as far as the phrasing, the words, the godliness of words is concerned, but its impelling reason is surprisingly refreshing if one has the hardihood to go on reading—and is not thrown over the horse's head by the exhuberance (is that the way to spell it?) of the beast. Rexroth is no writer in the sense of the word-man. For him words are sticks and stones to build a house— but it's a good house.

Vazakas interests me because I think him an inventor—a form inventor (maybe only accidentally so). I like the way he forms his stanzas in his latest poems. They offer much room for improvisation while retaining regularity—an American mode which has possibilities. Aside from that he has a Lamb-like urban talent which used to appear in some of the work of Wally Gould. Do you remember? Wallace Stevens used to have more of it but he has lost all that now. A metropolitan softness of tone, a social poetry that Chaucer had long ago to such perfection. You remember how Chaucer had Cressida sign her letters to the man she left behind her in Troy? *"La votre C."* Marvellous! Vazakas may possibly develop that opportunity if he is able. We have no one now who can do that—except the blacksmiths who mar the pages of the *New Yorker* and such swine.

I am having a group of poems in the winter issue of the Chapel Hill *Quarterly Review of Literature*. It will be the largest group I have ever had published at one showing—imagine that in my OWN country at the age of 61! You see how far praise goes? I'll see that you get the issue. A man named T. Weiss, the *Quarterly* editor, is an excellent critic, don't forget him, he is doing a good job. Send him something some time.

My best to your mother. My mother is still alive and in spite of her handicaps wants to live and still feels happy when we talk to her or let her hold her new great-grandchildren (the latest is Paul's Suzanne—3 mos.—who lives with her mother, her brother and Floss and me here for the duration). Our Bill is as yet unmarried, a Lt.M.D. in a camp in Maryland. So there it is.

Yours,
BILL

Paul jr. is at sea—a destroyer.

1945

January 1, 1945

Dear Horace: Here it is the first of January (the two-faced) and I have already delivered two babies, both boys, since midnight. The warm rain is pouring down over us from heaven; I heard two of Beethoven's later Sonatas beautifully played in private last evening, and friends have showered me for some unknown reason with the best of liquor ever since Christmas day. Were it not for the tragic news from the war front (contrasted with the intellectual front and many another), we might look at the approaching last years of our lives (I speak of my own generation) with real anticipation—for this has grown to be a sober period—and I refuse to start again after this bad beginning.

I appreciated what you said of *The Wedge* in *The Saturday Review of Lit*. It particularly interested me that you chose that one about "the ugly woman" for comment. How lost a book of poems can seem to its author! This one of mine is as though it had been dropped down a rat hole.

All this fall I have wanted to get to the "Paterson" poem again and as before I always find a dozen reasons for doing nothing about it. I see the mass of material I have collected and that is enough. I shy away and write something else. The thing is the problems involved require too much work for the time I have at my disposal. I am timid about beginning what I know will surely exhaust me if I permit myself to become involved. I know it is a cowardly attitude of mind but I get knocked out every time I begin. Too much is involved. Just yesterday I learned one of the causes of my inability to proceed: I MUST BEGIN COMPOSING again. I thought all I had to do was to arrange the material but that's ridiculous. Much that I have collected is antique now. The old approach is outdated, and I shall have to work like a fiend to

234

make myself new again. But there is no escape. Either I remake myself or I am done. I can't escape the dilemma longer. THAT is what has stopped me. I must go on or quit once and for all. Here's hoping. Your confidence and favorable words help me inestimably to grab myself together for the final onslaught. . . .

Happy New Year to you and yours. We go on working and reading—of the confusion of others.

Yours,
BILL

Winter issue of *The Quarterly Review of Literature* (T. Weiss) will contain a short "anthology" of new work, poems, I have done in the past year.

I don't know Weiss, but he's been friendly to me, so that I am for him (not of course for that alone—he's a shrewd critic). He owns the quarterly outright & is its sole editor—I think. Owning the quarterly, when he moved from Chapel Hill to New Haven (Yale) (English Dep't) he brought the Q with him. Look his quarterly & him up when you get the chance. I like him.

BILL

152: TO HORACE GREGORY

Feb. 8, 1945

Dear Horace: It was a cold night, but I enjoyed seeing you again and talking with your wife and seeing the others also and talking with them all. You have taken a somewhat elusive critical position for me in American letters, as I have tried to make clear at various times. I can't define it, quite, other than by my sensual reactions to it—a very unreliable approach. Yet since it is all that I have to speak of, for the moment or until I can be more intelligently lucid, I have to say that I feel strangely reassured by something in your attitude toward our poetry today.

I'm trying to dig out a meaning. I get an impression of a rocky projection from a plain. I don't quite understand myself. I find in it a sanctuary—a cave perhaps to which I run. I don't want to overemphasize or overvalue. I'm trying to describe something which I can't quite grasp. It seems to me important—not only to myself. I suppose what I lack most is scholarship. I won't have it because what has been available to me is tainted, even permeated by something which I won't have, that stinks to me. Like a piece of meat set out by a trapper to decoy a coyote. You got to put on gloves to put that kind of bait out for a coyote and I've got a hell of a good nose.

But you seem to offer me what I want and it ain't tainted. At least I am perfectly willing to eat it. It's a scholarly fare, sometimes I think it's too staid. But I seem to react immediately from that attitude toward something which, as I have said, calms me but makes me eager to work. What more can a man want from another man? Yet I am not sure it's good for me.

Sometimes a chance hint, such as that about avoiding footnotes in the "Paterson" thing, completely resolves my nerves, and I do docilely what you have suggested with absolute assurance that it is the correct answer—such things as that. It doesn't seem much but—it is in fact everything in the relationship between composition and criticism.

One thing only a writer must beware of, he must accept nothing that lulls him to sleep. He needs assurance but more than that he needs daring, etc., etc.

Had my dear friend Kitty Hoagland (who wants to meet you and your wife) type out the first finished draft of the 1st quarter of the "Paterson" thing two days ago—she and Flossie were both curiously impressed and agreed that I should have my pants kicked—a good sign.

BILL

153: To James Laughlin

Feb. 4, 1945

Dear Jim: When I finish the "Paterson" thing (sometime before St. Patrick's Day) where do I send it? New York or Utah? It frightens me a bit and, as always, I don't think it's real; I wonder if it's really there—among those pages of words. It doesn't seem likely. And if so, WHAT is there—gravel for critics? I hope it cuts their hearts out. It won't; they're too grooved in their protected tracks ever to turn aside to see the dulled world close about them —always whistling into the distance.

It was, as you say, a good evening: I liked the feel of the little girl nestling (among her dachshunds) against me on the couch. She said she didn't feel very well and no doubt appreciated the physician in me—poor, deluded soul.

Yes, the Joyce is of the essence. In Ireland they call such men "spoiled priests," a horrid epithet—it reveals the place. Yet Joyce could never go far from it—in his mind. He might have gone further if he had been a continental instead of an islander. His island choked him in the end, made him clutch his throat, out of which the garbled speech flowed, whereas he might have spoken in magnificent measures—if there had been such measures in his day. We have the opportunity he perhaps made for us. This early work shows him speaking with a personal voice, as a man—later he became seraphim or cherubim or cousin to God—but here he was a man. It is warming, brilliant stuff. I am glad you brought it out and I am very happy to have it to enjoy. I haven't even finished the book as yet, in the midst of my pleasure with it. Good, very good work—in spite of what he calls it.

Let me know where to send my contribution to the meal of the gods, perhaps a radish—they call this the Garden State, you know. I want to get this away from me so that I shall be able to start the second part. As I told you, all four parts are sketched and partly written. All I need now is time, time, time. If I could only permit myself to take six months off!

Yours,
BILL

I hope you like the thing, that's always the danger—that you won't. I know you'll like parts of it.

[*Literarily and personally, Norman Macleod was perhaps closer to WCW than anyone except Robert McAlmon. He writes that "Williams had a great influence on me, teaching me the necessity of avoiding the blurred and irresponsible image." Macleod has been a constant contributor to or editor of innumerable little magazines. He started the Poetry Forum at the New York Y.M.H.A., where WCW made some of his first public readings.*]

154: To Norman Macleod

July 25, 1945

Dear Norman: A very generous offer, it might be a valuable gesture for us both if we can organize and manage it properly.[1] The first point is not to attempt too much; after all you can't include my entire life—unless that can be included in parentheses. What I'd most appreciate would be to have the whole coherent, if possible, lucid. For I know that whatever my life has been it has been single in purpose, simple in design and constantly directed to the one end of discovery, if possible, of some purpose in being alive, in being a thinking person and in being an active force. The purpose in my "composit" is never clear or has never been made clear. Oh well, that's to be found by the critic, not me. I know my own difficult answer and it is not to be put into words —but work.

Poetry, an art, is what answer I have. My poetry appears to most as formless, to the neo-orthodox as an offense to be safely ignored. The God-damned fools. That's why I despise the crew! I won't offend again by naming any. There are recruits to their regiment every day, famous figures. Why famous? Isn't it clear? As famous as Hemingway and for the same reasons. The thing that offends me most tho, is that they have crept before the public as artists! That's the offense, that's the real offense. So that when I say, and some well-meaning critic attacks my intelligence for saying it, that art has nothing to do with metaphysics—I am aim-

---

[1] Projected WCW issue of *Briarcliff Quarterly*.

ing at the very core of the whole matter. Art is some sort of an honest answer, the forms of art, the discovery of the new in art forms—but to mix that with metaphysics is the prime intellectual offense of my day. But who will understand that?

The first part of *Paterson* begins my detailed reply of which I want only to live to complete the full four parts—but already I have been informed that *Paterson* will not be accepted because of its formlessness, because I have not organized it into some neoclassic *recognizable* context. Christ! Are there no intelligent men left in the world? Dewey might do something for me, but I am not worth his notice. I say "I." What the hell difference do I make as I? I am satisfied, however, that what I have hold of is worth holding, if I can hold it. I need help to hold it and to tame it—a little. That's why I want, if I can get it, coherence in any agglomerate that you would publish touching me. I want a transfixing light through the whole. But not too blinding a glare, just a candle light—if I am worthy of that.

The stuff I read! good stuff too. But unaware of the full implications of what they are saying. The philosophers are trying to label the arts, to pigeonhole one's works without realizing that —they'll burn their fingers off in the end, if they are not careful— somewhere, in some piece of art resides a radioactive force beyond anything but their copying in their static spheres. I fight with Blackmur, I feel resentments against them all, and all I can do (growing old) is to compose. It is the only recourse, the only intellectual recourse for an artist, to make, to make, to make and to go on making—*never* to reply *in kind* to their strictures. It is his *doing,* I mean, his only doing to compose: in a sort of night, in a sort of dumb philosophic stupor—except to himself where, within, there burns a fiery light, too fiery for logical statement. It is not of the nature of logical statement . . . and he is in a prison before it—to break out only *one* way. . . .

Well, here it is 10 A.M. Wednesday and I've got to get the hell out of here.

I'm doing a practical, I hope, play. Don't let it bother you, it'll probably prove immoral or something before it is ready to be shat on by the shits.

CHRIST: In my house there are many mansions.

ELIOT: I'll take the corner room on the second floor over-looking the lawns and the river. And WHO is this rabble that follows you about?

CHRIST: Oh, some of the men I've met in my travels.

ELIOT: Well, if I am to follow you I'd like to know something more of your sleeping arrangements.

CHRIST: Yes sir.

Sincerely,
BILL

And I'd like to write something on the Surrealists, as *French* artists (knocked about by the Spaniards). "The Nude Descending a Stair-case," a misnamed picture: *Chute de la France, nu,* etc. Therefore an art *had* to be made to fit a misnomer. They are selling it. Pure thrifty French. Surrealism, the science of misnomers (a purely local and temporal phase) evading correct nomenclature, entirely a product of contemporary France. The immediate sequel of Dadaism and the First World War with the actual but diverted defeat of France.

Thus, "The Nude Descending a Staircase," is actually the Fall of France—which could not be stated—formally in any other way. The Surrealism that followed this early and isolated example, a continued misnaming of external events, an appearance had to be invented to fit the misapplication. Its general character is thus self-evident, both the subject and its treatment. Nothing to do with Freud. An interesting sidelight is the Spanish accretion (nothing in common with the French urgency and necessity) there-fore tending to fly off into still further irrationalities.

Surrealism being what it is it proves itself useful to other psychologic and aesthetic categories able to sublimate their in-securities into what the French discovered, etc.

1946

Wednesday—8:30 A.M. [1946]

Damn it Ken: This just HAD to happen. At 4:30 this morning a woman—age 26, Para I, whose last period occurred January 26, 1946, and whose Wassermann was negative 5-16-46, who weighs 137 lbs, whose urine is normal, whose blood pressure is 110 over 80 and the heart tones of whose belly-borne fetus are at 128 in the ROA position—called me on the phone to say she was having pains every ten minutes.

I sent her in leisurely fashion to the hospital whose delivery floor I called just now. They warned me away, saying it was a "madhouse" at the moment but that my patient was doing nothing in particular (except, I'll bet, getting an earful of shrieks, groans, lamentations and jazz from the doctors' rest room).

That means in all probability that I'll be sitting on my tail all day long waiting for this gal to come down where I can handle her. And the worst of it is that she was due on the 2nd of this month and should have left me in the clear long ago.

But there is a good side to it also, as there is always a good side (they say) even to death: that is that I haven't another maternity case on my schedule before the 20th of this month. THEREFORE I plan, rain or shine, snow or tornado, to drive out to Andover this coming Friday IN THE MORNING to stay and eat with you at midday and talk with you and yours for the daylight hours. Floss will be with me.

Which is all very American and infraideational and RIGHT. Our greatest leader was not an intelligence, all our greatest intelligences have always been marginal. Our two-party system which saves us from boredom yearly is a subintelligent maneuvering. THUS we are left to be based solidly on the unvarying emotional substratum of the midbrain area, therefore we are REPUBLICANS today and slaughtered in the field tomorrow. Bitter as it may be, it is in many ways what the world is in its seasonal fluctuations,

each season bringing emotional relief from the last by thus stim-
ulating the intelligence to every athletic exercise known to apes in
a cage—thus insuring the future of the race, I suppose. At least
it induces to books—which I like. We are now approaching
winter. Thank God, I don't live in the tropics.

Cheerio and chuck chuck (but the groundhogs have gone to
sleep long since, I imagine).

Best to you all,

BILL

156: To Parker Tyler

February 9, [*1946*]

Dear Parker: Yes, I wondered what had become of you, but presumed you had something else to do that interested you more—
which would, God knows, still leave you a large choice. I spoke of
Lorca with a very brief and general reference to the attempts of
Longfellow and Washington Irving to break away from the con-
fining British tradition and go to Spain for instruction and release. But they didn't get very far and scurried back to Mama
without accomplishing anything worthwhile. As far as I know,
neither one of them ever made mention of Góngora.

Then I took up something of the modern French—to show how
the recent men, in breaking down their fixations toward the
metrical traditions of yesterday, could be useful to us. They have
let almost everything go, structurally, in the expectation, perhaps,
that when you reach bottom you reach elementary lines (too many
interruptions for a consecutive story). Breton, Éluard and a poem
by Antonin Artaud in the recent *Transition* 3. The trouble with
the French at the moment is that they're so fixed on the first stage
of placing words on the page, the loose-jointed dredging up of
their precious guts, or whatever else a Frenchman has instead of
a soul (watch it) that they forget there is a second phase. It still
goes on existing and working; it is in fact *the* work of art. In
Breton's case, for instance, his poems are conventional and sentimental in spite of all his contortions. But to us Éluard, for instance, with his looseness can be very useful.

Finally, I had prepared to speak of examples of our own work here using your *Granite Butterfly*
(6 hours later, in all honesty)
and some other works, not my own. But you didn't appear. So I kept on with Éluard—drifting off into a general discussion, as usual, touching upon "verbal design." I had prepared to read "Portrait" (p. 22) of your poem and the Seventh Canto, Slow as—which is very useful in showing variations of metric all in one pattern.

Someone in the audience, I have seen him before, an older man, asked me if I thought I had given any evidence of the "new way of measuring" in anything I had read that night or in anything that I myself had written at any time. It was a fair question but one I shall have to postpone answering indefinitely. I always think of Mendelejeff's table of atomic weights in this connection. Years before an element was discovered, the element helium, for instance, its presence had been predicated by a blank in the table of atomic weights.

It may be that I am no genius in the use of the new measure I find inevitable; it may be that as a poet I have not had the genius to do the things I set up as essential if our verse is to blossom. I know, however, the innovation I predict must come to be. Someone, some infant now, will have to find the way we miss. Meanwhile I shall go on talking.

For one thing: what I see, the necessity which presents itself to me has already motivated and colored my critical opinions. I see many past writers in an entirely new light when I set them against the scale by which I am coming more and more to measure. And for myself, if I can write three lines—the day before I die, three lines inspired by the true principle by which I work—everything else, good or bad, in my life will have been justified.

Next time I'm going to speak of my own work only. As far as I am able I'm going to tear it apart in the light of my newer concepts. Either what I have done in the past has helped to clarify that or it has not. If it has not then it must be rejected and the reason for rejecting it shown lucidly. Or at least, so I argue.

Best,
BILL

157: To Parker Tyler

April 20, 1946

Dear Tyler: Thank you, sir. The pitiful thing of the world is its loneliness. No wonder they flock to Jesus and "his church": to escape what he taught.

The loneliest thing I have seen in months was, last night, a five-months-old fetus lying in the bottom of an enamel dishpan among its impedimenta of muck and afterbirth—its heart still beating lustily. I was sick to my stomach from a case of intestinal grippe at the time.

Am I a critic? If I am anything else it's a miracle. But the words have to be learned, and learned well (but first they must be invented). I saw Mark Van Doren at a cocktail party the other afternoon and told him I recognized him from pictures I had seen in the papers. The standard language he speaks makes him a critic also.

Keep writing and relaxing your spirit, it's that that gives value finally to everything.

Sincerely,
W. C. Williams

158: To Charles Abbott

June 26, 1946

Dear Charles: It is plain that I had no conception, no adequate conception, of the cunning of the Indians inhabiting the region of Beau Fleuve—I was taken completely by surprise. In fact, I was knocked out, that's why it has taken me three days to begin to reply to the letter of your chancellor offering to confer upon me the honorary title of Doctor of Laws.

All right, I accept—but with many misgivings. Why laws? Letters, yes, but laws? Not that letters as a title does not, in a sense, include laws, only, to confer a title of laws on me makes me feel pretty inadequate. The truth, no doubt, is that the conferring of such a degree is indeed honorary and is the degree conferred by the university in such a case as mine. Only it was a hell of a trick to play on a guest!

Did you say Auden had something to do with this? Now, I know he's really intent on becoming an American. If true, the situation as it concerns him would be really very touching. It does him also honor.

But listen to this:

September	28	Martha	A.	age 26	Para II
September	28	Lillian	B.	age 26	Para I
October	3	Mildred	C.	age 34	Para I
October	5	Alice	D.	age 23	Para II
October	5	Frances	E.	age 27	Para I
October	7	Florence	F.	age 29	Para II

Any one of these cases might fall due during the time I am expected to be at Buffalo; at least one of them I myself delivered (by the grace of God and with her mother's leg around my neck) a quarter of a century ago. I simply can't abandon them even though the man I entrust them to would be more skilled than I am. What am I to do?

I'll do something. Maybe I could fly up and fly back the same day or night. It wouldn't be much fun, but when the situation is desperate, desperate means have to be adopted to meet it.

So now I'll write to the chancellor (there is, by the way, no printed reproduction of his name on his stationery and his secretary did not spell it out under his signature) whose name I take to be Samuel? Capen—I'll check that.

Best luck and you'll hear from me again soon.

Sincerely,

BILL

[*Early in the 1920's WCW met Charles and Katherine Sheeler at Matthew Josephson's place in the Village. Sheeler, whose work as artist and photographer was beginning to get world recognition, found a kindred spirit. In 1939 WCW wrote an introduction to the Sheeler exhibition at the Museum of Modern Art and introduced him to a Russian emigrée, Musya, who was to become Sheeler's second wife.*]

159: To Charles Sheeler

10/12/46

Dear Charlie R.S.V.P.: I've been sitting out here in my office correcting the galleys of stuff of mine that is to appear in the "W.C.W. Number" of *Briarcliff Quarterly* next month. It's hot and stuffy tonight with a heavy wet wind blowing. I've been thinking of you ever since yesterday when, with the printed stuff, they sent me the reproductions of the illustrations, mostly snapshots and other photos of myself at various stages of my development which are to be shown in that same issue. Among others there will be two pictures taken of me by you.

It's strange to be sixty-three and to think of the honors that have recently come my way, this issue of a small magazine devoted to my history along with the rest. It's pleasant but that's about all. I appreciate what is being done and yet, aside from the effects it seems to have on those about me, it seems to have very little meaning for me. Why should it, of course? The celebration is for those who celebrate, the poor victim is merely incidental to their party. To tell the truth it's too much like a farewell for any joy there may be in it. Depending on how you look at it, it isn't even worth mentioning to anyone. It would be impossible to speak of it except jokingly to anyone other than to a friend who realizes there were other and better days before any recognition had reached us. Many a man has lived and died and could have lived and died twice over having succeeded in his achievements that are a thousand times more important than anything I ever accomplished.

I am more embarrassed than anything else. It won't last long when I hope I may be able to get going again on something new.

But it does bring some very beautiful looks into the faces of one's friends, in unexpected places sometimes. It's really amazing to read jealousy, fear, astonishment just from a little newsprint read. To tell the truth, indifference is the principal reaction noted by me in others—masked by an effusive effort to say something nice. But now and then some big fat thing will beam from ear to ear with pleasure at my "honors." Or some prosaic guy with a strong foreign accent will fairly jump out of his skin for joy that *"someone"* has broken out above the humdrum flatness of the hospital life, let us say. The Jews are always appreciative of fine things and know how to show it—not all Jews, naturally. Well it's been an experience.

One thing it has done for me is to give me more confidence, make me feel surer of my words. For if with what has already been written I have had some success, knowing inside myself how much better it might have been, I can go ahead and improve that.

At Buffalo on the platform and afterward I enjoyed seeing some of the big boys who received honors along with me. I was impressed by their records. For the most part they have been names in newspapers and periodicals for me; it is somewhat startling to realize that they are no more than extremely fallible men and women who, as a matter of fact, hold the world in their hands. It gives one a dramatic feeling of uncertainty in affairs but of courage also—and a great feeling of sympathy—almost a startling sense of realization of *what* makes the world of events move—for pathetic human beings. It is men who very literally and very uncertainly move the world. And they unconsciously perhaps but very really look to the artists and the thinkers to speak for them. The sense of the importance of the artists as a direct influence on men, men who actually carry the world in their hands, awoke in me on that platform.

Among the rest the man Bush, the head of the atomic bomb project, was the most interesting to me. I liked him at once. It is amazing what he and his associates have accomplished—looked at simply as work, as brains. He seemed curious about me and was astonished to know I was a physician. I told him that I was deeply impressed by the sheer accomplishments of the persons on the platform. He replied that it took a lot of energy also to write books. That was that. But then I said that the books might have been better if the writer had had a better opportunity to know the important men of his epoch—as the men of past ages, living in city groups such as Florence, Paris, London once lived, fertilizing each other's imagination, by daily conversation and other intimacies. He agreed that it was a great advantage the past possessed over us and that we ought to find some way to make up for it today.

Bill and Floss went up to Buffalo with me on the sleeper a week ago last Thursday. We arrived there Friday morning, went through with the ceremonies and took the train back that night. Two women whelped while I was gone! That's how close I live.

Geez! here it is eleven o'clock again and I've got to turn in to save my eyes. I'm glad you're finding it not too restricting where you are. That's the only thing that counts: to feel loosened in spirit. What the hell difference does it make where you are or what you're doing so long as you are stimulated to go on producing the thing you *can* do? Rembrandt went back to the slums and painted better than ever. Bush, now that the bomb has been discovered, is going back to his own little laboratory. I enjoy my practice of medicine—and the rest of it. Anything, so long as it loosens us up—makes us *go*. That's why idleness kills.

A magnificent Sunday morning! The garden's full of just opening chrysanthemums. Peep! Peep! Up to the hospital at 8:30 to look into the ears of week-old brats to try and discover why they are running high temperatures: a pseudo-hermaphrodite on one side and a premature on the other! But it's all right. I've been reading a very good textbook on the modern poets (just out) by Horace Gregory. I'll send you one within the week, I think it will be worth your reading. Floss is well, Bill is home for the week-end and the grandchildren are—exhausting!

Yours—I'd like to see your show which Floss insists is up where you are but I insist is in N.Y. I'll look again. Best to Musya and thank her for her card.

BILL

160: To Ezra Pound

Oct. 30, 1946

Dear Ez: Your predicament has at least done this, it has made the Rev. Eliot vaguely intelligent in his prose; his approach to actuality is only partial, of course, but he shows at least a few symptoms of what might have been a profitable establishment for him. It is strange at the same time how your present position shows him up; he is all but incapacitated by it—not at all smart, in nothing the brilliant mind—more the surprised student into whose study window someone has thrown a brick. The second part of *Faust* perhaps. Too bad there isn't a third part with a return to the beginning, the actual beginning when Faust was in fact young, not the dream. Nobody thinks of Faust actually young or that he was ever young—and mistaken. Goethe knew better or he'd never have written his lyrics, but the times made him "philosophic." Poor dead bastard regretting the past "beautifully."

This last letter of yours is the most coherent so far and the most informative concerning the best of you—or at least the best of you as you, aside from your words. I understand perfectly your adult concern for government, discipline and your courageous defiance of the spurious, lost in half measures. But you make an ass of yourself for all that—by misjudging the difficulties and successes of others: it was stupid of you to attack the President of the United States as you did—plain stupid. Stupid because you destroyed more good than what inevitable evil the man represented and because you sided with the most vicious and reactionary forces in the country in seeking to destroy him—by foul means, such as attacks on his wife and family—too contemptible to list.

Nevertheless, right or wrong, government is a major subject for the aging poet, and your work strikes along the path with some effect, if weak since you step outside the means of poetry very often to gain a point. You deal in political symbols instead of actual values, poetry. You talk about things (which you yourself have sufficiently damned in the past) instead of showing the things themselves in action. A magnificent opportunity still exists for you if you can ever bring yourself back from your excited state to the calm which true poetic achievement demands. I doubt that you'll be astute enough to do it—or indeed that you'll ever again have the opportunity due to your present position.

Yes, I read the *Harper's* article and understood it. There again you act like an infant. Did *you* understand it? I doubt it or you would not presume to question the ability of others who could twist you around a little finger where technical matters are concerned and show you to be the ignoramus you are in most things of which you boast. Will you never learn *that?* You make a fool of yourself to gain what? Perhaps self-esteem. You must be pretty low to want to gain that kind of self-esteem. . . .

I want to rescue you (for myself) because I need you—I being one of the few who would be benefited—but I want you whole, the good in you, not a hunk of bacon fried too crisp.

(I rushed out and found NOBODY in the front office for the moment, which is a blessing—I can go on writing.)

Except for the God-damned telephone in my right ear!

Eliot's article (in *Poetry*) is really very good but it contains warnings for you, the same which I have posted, to which you continue to pay no attention. Read it yourself—the part about Gesell: it will aid your effectiveness.

On the other hand, perhaps you cannot help yourself. In fact I am sure it is the defect of your qualities that annoys us—as Eliot very ably points out.

The great thing you have to say to us, as poets, is: READ! Read and learn, learn to hear. . . .

Your "Canto" in *Quarterly Review* is the best of the recent ones as far as I can tell.

WCW

1947

Feb. 25, 1947

Dear Ken: At last we are in perfect agreement—or almost. I don't want to have to call you the philosopher of Andover, but that aside, nothing remains as an obstruction between us.

You see, the moment you drop logic, as an incentive, at least, to action, you become convincing. Instinctively you sent me the summary of Vergil's plan (an instinctive plan, no doubt) for the composition of a long poem. I am delighted, not to say thrilled by both the summary as you copied it out and your thoughtfulness in doing so and sending it to me.

But when, logically I suppose, you think I will be furious over the matter, plan and action, you are absurd.

I do not believe you think Vergil formulated any such preliminary plan as this before beginning composition on the *Aeneid*. He was an alert and intelligent citizen of his times and a gifted poet besides; he saw a need (he also saw words) and must have felt a tremendous pleasure of anticipation. In composing the poem he felt an undoubted pleasure—of various sorts: sensual, sociological, historical identification, and so forth. He may, at an outside guess, have indulged in a bit of logical philandering—if he found the time for it in a dull moment! But that he set down a primary scheme and followed it I can't for a moment believe.

The thing is, Ken, and in this I am sure we perfectly agree, there are not many things we poor human bastards can do. Or shall I say there are not many approaches we have to our satisfactions and not one of them all is of any more worth than the other. We each of us do what we can. My approach, as a poet, is just as valid as your approach as a philosopher to whatever mass of material is presented to us to work with.

Now, Vergil having written a poem, someone comes along later (it could just as well be himself after the work is completed) and fools around in it like a squirrel in a box of birdseed for something he can use in his own economy. That's fine, granted the beast knows that the seed was not put there for him—or he might get shot—oh well, let that pass. I only object to the philosopher when he tries in the making of poems to insert his dictum before the poet composes and would reject the poem before it is a poem, of words. His function, to the poet, except in a very general way (important as it often is), comes after the poetic deed. For if the poet allows himself to fall into that trap (of listening too early to the philosopher) he will inevitably be of little use to the very philosopher himself as a field of investigation after he, as a poet, has completed his maneuvers.

The nascent instincts are the feelers into new territory—even Einstein has recently acknowledged or stated that. Deductive reasoning is in the main useless to us today or if not useless at least secondary in value.

Yes, words. I accept your differentiation between a fact and a book or train of reasoning about those facts. The book is only a defense or reasoning in support of the findings. I know all that, as you must realize (having lived in the age—of Gertrude Stein and Joyce), all that is primary to me also.

We, you and I, have nothing to quarrel about once we get by the simple beginnings of an understanding as equals in separate categories of composition (the universal activity of the mind—analysis is merely an adjunct to that). At that point we may begin to use each other at will—or perforce, if you prefer. My whole contention, so far, is that we keep separate in order to be of as much use to each other as possible—to penetrate separately into the jungle, each by his own modes, calling back and forth as we can in order to keep in touch for better uniting of our forces.

Do you know the story of the two French military officers conducting a column of infantry through the desert? It was a hell of a three-day march in the broiling heat, with rebellious troops and heavy work to be done. One of the two officers in charge asked the other at daybreak of the third day: "Are you going to march in the van today or the rear?" "Why?" said the other. "Because," answered the first, "I intend to take the opposite post or else I'll murder you."

Bill

Many thanks, really, for the bit you copied out for me. I may use it in the part of the *Paterson* I am working on now. Very helpful.

162: To Robert McAlmon

March 9, 1947

Dear Bob: I told Floss a moment ago that I was going to write to you and asked her if she had any message. She said, Nothing special. Tell him to reserve a room for us somewhere down there. No time specified.

If Bill gets through at the New York Hospital in July and finds himself ready or in a mood to take over my practice for a while, you may expect us sometime next winter—or as the luck may indicate. If they hire him there for another year then another year will have to bump by before I'm ready to leave. Oh well, there it is—for what it's worth.

Of late I've been plugging hard, every available moment, on *Paterson*. Book II. The whole of the four books has been roughly sketched out for several years. I've finished Book I. So now Book II is up. During January and February I worked on assembling the notes I had on this book and connecting them up in some sort of order. I'm no stenographer so that as I must do all the work myself, at odd moments, on what amounts to composition; I've been extremely busy. Yesterday I finally got the 90 odd pages of the "full" version—as I call it—down on paper. It's pretty loose stuff, but the thread, I think, is there. It's there, in other words—such as it is.

Now comes the job of cutting and clarifying. I dread the job of retyping the stuff and no one can help me. If I feel a bit optimistic things go well. You know the feeling. But if I hit a low spot and the whole business seems a redundant heap of garbage, the work stops short.

Having finished what I've finished, I started today to help Floss clean up the piles of second- and third-class mail that have piled up in every corner recently. We don't know what to do with it all. I get so many "little" magazines, so many books from this one and that one with letters sometimes asking me to comment on them that I just can't move. So, as I say, I began to gather up the stuff, some of it very fine but beyond my powers of reading it all, and carted most of it up to the attic where it will remain in a pile somewhere about until I'm dead, I suppose, when it will be dumped on some bookshop—it doesn't matter. I wish I could read more. There's a mountain of stuff together with books from all corners of the country.

With which I go down to my typewriter and proceed to add more to the mess. It isn't a happy picture. But while I was dumping the mags upstairs I luckily thought of you, that you would like to see some of Ezra's recent work. I found at least two of the recent Cantos which I am forwarding to you. Keep them if you like or hand them on or chuck them out, I don't want them. There are two other Cantos recently out, one in *Poetry,* a recent issue, and one in the winter issue of *Sewanee Review.* I have seen the former but not the latter. I don't think any of the Cantos, the recent Cantos, increase Pound's reputation or are likely to increase it. There are good passages here and there in everything he writes but, to me, it seems woefully repetitious—I can't find a new departure anywhere or any new lead in construction or enlightenment. I'd be interested to get your slant. Pretty sad stuff to me.

In fact there's a whole "enlightened" group, the self-elevated masters of our world of poetry today (in English) with whom (or is it, after all, whom) I grow wearier and wearier, since from them I get not a breath of anything new: St-J. Perse and all those world-weary souls—I dunno, I dunno—. If they are the great then I'm just a pig. It seems to me that that sort of judgment from above is horribly *passé*—finished—1925 or something worse. They know a lot, granted, and they are sensitive, granted, and skillful, granted. Well, one might ask, what more do you want? I'd answer:—they seem lethargic. An old story.

But I have to acknowledge that it takes more than one swallow to make a summer—after looking over the writing that has passed through my hands this afternoon I am very nearly crushed under its implied weight. It looks like everyone is writing and translating. We have translations from Gide on Valéry (magnificent by the way), etc., etc. They are even translating me into French and Italian—and Spanish! *White Mule* is out in Spanish via Argentina. The short stories are being done into French by one Jean Simon. *In The Am. Grain* also into French, etc.

But the mass of stuff in the modern little magazine is breathtaking. A person simply cannot read it all, and some of it looks good. I attacked a short novel last night by a Negro named Paul Bland, a Chicago product who begged me to do something for him. It's an excellently written book and a hot story. It's too good though, in a sense. Steinbeck or some of the other shrewd boys who do flashy caricatures or play the extreme type characters— you know who—to catch the public eye could make this chap look amateurish. You gotta have a touch of special genius to please the money today. Not that I would be so foolish as to ridicule or try to ridicule anyone who can write with the very near certainty of making half a million on the deal—but there *is* for all that a different sort of writer. I come finally to the conclusion that there are not many really good writers. But judgment is difficult if not impossible.

On the one hand, you have the university, world-weary boys; on the other, you have the brass knuckle gang. Both have their feelers out for the new—but in different ways, right and left. Those in between are all amateurs. At that I prefer Steinbeck and his pals. But it kind of comes up into your throat at times. The other sticks below. Maybe all writing is like that, one or the other. In the end, I suppose, I'm just like anybody else, I've got to write to relieve myself of my tensions. You ought to read some of the amorous descriptions in the colored boy's book, makes you go to bed and throw yourself about while your mind stews over infidelities and releases. A hell of a world. Especially when you see your own children growing up, and you wonder what in hell is to become of them. And your grandchildren with all their marvellous aptitudes that some sterile bitch of a schoolteacher is going to blast to hell for the next miraculous twenty years or more. I could puke. And there's no escape, no escape, but murder and revolution.

Where in hell can even I go after I quit my practice, if I ever do?

The snares that are built up, not consciously, by the power of cash are so strong and universal—that nothing even half-true ever gets into the news. Every attack is made plausible—you are forced to choose between "Russia" and "Democracy." Nothing could possibly be more false—or more vicious in preventing the truth from even coming up to be seen, much less acted on. They don't even begin to guess what an artist might be. Someone too at least might see the *possibility* of an art—a total basic invention in structure. They foul themselves top and bottom and show it by their intolerance (and I, I suppose, more intolerant than any).

They say there's a great literary renaissance going on in Italy. The concrete evidence I've had of it is the most recent issue of *Briarcliff Q.* I'm writing to Norman Macleod to send you a copy of it just as soon as I finish this to you. The bits translated in that issue are, to me, tremendously alive. They are *not* Steinbeck, *not* St.-J Perse, *not* Eliot, *not* Pound—but they are alive—if I should have to classify them I'd say, generally, that they are anti-university, anti-stodge, anti-fixation. Some of that stuff really breathes the air of the present-day world as if it wanted to be alive. They must be a swell crowd. All young, Looks good to me.

I confess I wish I could smash the hell out of where I am—but I've always felt that way and done nothing about it except write, which gives me a kind of escape. Not a Freudian escape—or if so not importantly that. It's mixed up with no free ducking, naturally, but that's only the skin of the snake, not the snake itself—not by a tenth part. Courage? No one is completely courageous except the fool who sticks his head into the machine. They want me to write something about Paul Rosenfeld, who died recently. I will if I can—I liked Paul.

One fine thing I've seen recently is the little book published by View Press (and perhaps more importantly in England by someone else) containing Edith Sitwell's most recent work—firm, convincing poetry. Very wonderful. "Green something or other," I've forgot the name of the book. Did you ever meet the woman?

Oh yes, I received a questionnaire from someone at Cambridge Univ., England, asking me certain questions upon the subject of the influence of present-day British poets on U.S. writers. Not too important but interesting. I told them I didn't think there was any influence at all as far as I could tell, that each of us had his own problems different from the other and was going his own way.

I'll be glad when this winter is over, it's been tough driving the streets. Maybe I'd better buy me a new car after all—tho I've been spending quite a bit on the old one keeping it rolling. Clear roads will make a big difference to me.

As far as I can tell my new play is pretty well buried. Laughlin will undoubtedly bring it out in his annual anthology but that will be all. I thought as much.

Best luck from us both.

BILL

163: TO KENNETH BURKE

St. Phatric's [*1947*]

Dear Ken: We seem to get on much better by the indirect rather than the direct approach. What you reveal in your letter over the Reich book[1] is to me thrilling in the extreme, it seems to state or does state what seems to be the basic reason for our interest, our sustained interest, in each other which has never been explicit—a desire on both our parts to find some basis for avoiding the tyranny of the symbolic without sacrificing fullness of imagery.

You know the dead-serious sort who know nothing of the symbolic. Or is there such a sort which does not postpone its heaven to another world—the deadliest symbolism of all?

My whole intent, in my life, has been, as with you, to find a basis (in poetry, in my case) for the actual. It isn't a difficult problem to solve theoretically. All one has to do is to discover new laws of the metric and use them. That's objective enough and little different from the practical deductions of an Edison. The difficulty lies in the practice.

For myself I reject almost all poetry as at present written, including my own. I see tendencies, nodes of activity, here and there but no clear synthesis. I am trying in *Paterson* to work out

---

[1] *Theory of the Orgasm.*

the problems of a new prosody—but I am doing it by writing poetry rather than "logic" which might castrate me, since I have no ability in that medium (of logic). There is no reason, besides, why I should do otherwise than I am doing. That is, if I succeed, the effect will be the same no matter what the approach.

Well, I'm glad you can use the Reich material. Best of luck to you—your letter was a revelation.

Sincerely,
BILL

164: TO BABETTE DEUTSCH

July 28, 1947

Dear Babette: Got home only last evening from Utah. I had never taken part in a formal "literary conference," so that it was a challenging experience for me to go on talking about modern verse, that was my assignment, for close to two weeks. It proved somewhat difficult at the start but in the end I found much to say to the hundred and ten "students" of all ages who paid their good money to hear us. They seemed satisfied that I had not cheated them.

There were six or eight of us, we "advisers," who with a few wives lived together in a vacant girls' house, a sorority house, on the campus: Allen Tate and his wife Carolyn Gordon, Ray West, Mark Schorer, Walter Van Tilburg Clark, Brewster Ghiselin and Eric Bentley. We really worked, what with lectures, workshop meetings and individual conferences, but we enjoyed the associations of literary tastes and ideas, the contrasts of personalities which such a meeting occasioned. It was valuable and amusing. We seemed to get along fine together. Too bad that such meetings do not occur oftener among writers.

In reply to your letters I must say that 1 have found little I wanted to say about the labor violence which has had Paterson as its scene during the last thirty or, perhaps, hundred years. You found "The Strike." Good. You will find more in the prose of *Life Along the Passaic River,* especially the first account contained therein. However, in *Paterson* the social unrest that occasions all strikes is strong—underscored, especially in the 3d part, but I must confess that the aesthetic shock occasioned by the rise of the masses upon the artist receives top notice.

In Part or Book II, soon to appear (this fall, I think), there will be much more in the same manner, that is, much more relating to the economic distress occasioned by human greed and blindness—aided, as always, by the church, all churches in the broadest sense of that designation—but still, there will be little treating directly of the rise of labor as a named force. I am not a Marxian.

Part or Book III may and probably will deal extensively with "the flame." We'll see.

Part IV will be something else again.

As to Jarrell's appreciation—I can only say that I was pleased by it. I invited him out to supper with his wife one night subsequent to his review's appearance and found him very pleasant. I haven't heard from him since that day. We had not been particularly friendly before that and can only presume that he had reverted to his old instinctive antagonism. I may be mistaken. What he said in his "interpretation" seemed to show an extraordinary perception of the elements which went into the composition of the piece. Did you see Lowell's comment on Jarrell's review of *Paterson I* in the *Sewanee Review?* If not, look it up; it is interesting.

[*Robert (Cal) Lowell, a distant cousin of Amy Lowell, wrote not only poetry but book reviews, one of which attracted WCW to him as critic.* Lord Weary's Castle *presented Mr. Lowell to WCW as a poet in his own right.*]

165: To Robert Lowell

August 6, 1947

My dear Lowell: Having just returned from Salt Lake City and the conference at Utah U. there, I find a copy of the *Sewanee*

Review containing your judgment of *Paterson,* Book I. Praise is always embarrassing, hard to take, but thank you for your observations, which will be of assistance to me in what more is to be done with the poem. I particularly appreciate your observation that, "It is a defect perhaps that human beings exist almost entirely in the prose passages." That's something to think about.

In any case it is a satisfaction to me when a person of distinction, particularly one who is skillful and accomplished in some craft which I myself employ, in the first place notices the work I have done and in the second place speaks out concerning it. The city cultures of the past had an advantage over us in that with men all living within a few rods of each other the immediate reactions over works produced were more immediate and probably more violent than the few and rare comebacks we ever get from the cognoscenti (the really informed) from what we put forth.

Anyhow, thanks. Best luck for future work.

Sincerely,
W. C. WILLIAMS

166: TO CHARLES ABBOTT

September 1, 1947

Dear Charles: This is Labor Day morning, a beautiful morning by the way, cool and full of sunshine, I've been wondering since awakening, getting up and moving about the quiet house, what I'd like to do with myself, if I had my choice, during the years to come. I'd like to live in a small garden house in my own back yard gradually developing it on a microscopic scale to suit my own diminishing physical needs. I think I could be as happy there as anywhere on earth, happier to my way of thinking and as little a nuisance to others as in any other place I can think of. You can well imagine that I'd have some books there and facilities of other simple sorts for study. Come and visit me sometime.

I suppose you've been more or less wondering what all happened to us this summer. I've been wondering about it myself at times. It seems that just now are we beginning to get ourselves to rights again after that shake-up. We really covered the ground. But I think our minds went faster than we did and perhaps further. We saw what we saw of the West with the greatest enthusiasm imaginable, though we did not go in for the big attractions. The two features of most importance to us, aside from the Conference itself and the common scenes along the roads, were a very brief visit to the cliff dweller ruins at Mesa Verde and our trip with Bob McAlmon to Taos.

Oh well, you know all about that. I am still in a daze and, strange to say, with no desire in me to write. I was the only nonuniversity person at Utah among those taking part in the teaching, which rather put me on my mettle, so that what I lacked in knowledge I made up for by emphasis. They seemed to like it, even my teaching pals took me in—we had a good time. The people of Salt Lake, largely through Laughlin's acquaintanceship there, his wife comes from there, were very kind to us, picnics, luncheons and all that. . . .

Yours,
BILL

167: To Robert Lowell

September 26, 1947

Dear Lowell: The week-end of October 18-19 looks like a possible date for our trip to Washington. If I can do my recording Saturday morning, the 18th, it would fit in well with my plans. That is to say I'd drive down to my friend's farm on Friday, stay over Saturday and so forth. I'm glad you found the recordings already made satisfactory, for myself I'd like to add one or two pieces from the *Collected Poems* which were overlooked at the first reading as well as read from *Paterson I*. A final selection would then be in order looking to the album. All this on condition that my friend will have me over that week-end.

By all means plan to spend a week-end in November here, we have plenty of room and should be delighted to see you. I suppose it had better be somewhere around the middle of the month, avoiding at least Thanksgiving, as early as you like.

No, Li Po cannot be imitated not with the synthetic moons we have about us nowadays. Mrs. Williams and I have been reading *Lord Weary's Castle,* it's interesting to me that you have found a way to mention local place names without that jumping out of context which so often occurs to make a work false sounding. It's very hard to treat of American things and name them specifically without a sense of bathos, of bad sentimental overlap resulting. Look at the John Brown thing. Look even at Thoreau. Something happens, something happened even to Henry Adams, even to Henry James when the United States was mentioned. It is very difficult and somewhat obscure what happens—but you have got by nicely I think. Maybe its because you anchored your data in ground common to Europe and to Christianity—if that has to be. Well, see you later.

Sincerely,
WILLIAMS

1948

3/10/48

Dear Tyler: I've been flat on my back for a month following an attack of angina pectoris (that's about all the Latin I know). I'll be here the good Lord knows how much longer—not too long I hope.

All the prose,[1] including the tail which would have liked to have wagged the dog, has primarily the purpose of giving a metrical meaning to or of emphasizing a metrical continuity between all word use. It is *not* an antipoetic device, the repeating of which piece of miscalculation makes me want to puke. It *is* that prose and verse are both *writing,* both a matter of the words and an interrelation between words for the purpose of exposition, or other better defined purpose of *the art.* Please do not stress other "meanings." I want to say that prose and verse are to me the same thing, that verse (as in Chaucer's tales) belongs *with* prose, as the poet belongs with "Mine host," who says in so many words to Chaucer, "Namoor, all that rhyming is not worth a toord." Poetry does not *have* to be kept away from prose as Mr. Eliot might insist, it goes *along with* prose and, companionably, by itself, without aid or excuse or need for separation or bolstering, shows itself by *itself* for what it is. *It belongs* there, in the gutter. Not anywhere else or wherever it is, it is the same: the poem.

Yours,
WILLIAMS

Thanks for the word about the lyric. You are very kind.

---

[1] In *Paterson.*

169: To Babette Deutsch

May 25, 1948

Dear Babette: Yes, let's hope the two later books will make what is said in the first two clearer. Have you read Auden's *The Age of Anxiety?* Read it if you have not already done so and tell me if that is the clarity you want. If so you won't get it from me. I have just finished reading the Auden; it is impressive in the ability with which it is thought out and performed, but it has over it, for me, an obscurity of purpose which I cannot fathom. Perhaps that is what is called "deep." It puzzles me and sounds singularly obscure—as the Christian dogma is obscure, leaning, as it does, on poetry and the imagination while deriding those props as frivolous, trivial even.

To me there is no escape—for me there is no escape from the necessity for invention and Auden's lines are dead—tho thoughtful. It is only the living that is truly obscure. Nor can I claim by that to be alive, I do not mean that.

I look at what I have done, with *Paterson* for instance, and tho at times I am impressed, at other times I find little to praise in my attempts. Laid beside the vigor of some of Pound's cantos, not only the vigor but the sensitiveness to the life in a thousand phases, I feel like a boor, a lout, a synthetic artist.

I am glad you came to the party. I did not feel equal to the trip upstairs where tho the refreshments beckoned—the crowd frightened me. I wish I had been able to say a few words to you.

Your letter was very welcome. I seem to be better and should, they say, be quite fit again by Fall.

Sincerely,

BILL

I suppose that green bottle piece[1] is a pure imagistic poem—if such a thing exists. It was, that piece, roasted by someone in England when the *Collected Poems* appeared, by which the whole book was thrown into the discard much to my delight. I always

---

[1] "On the Road to the Contagious Hospital."

enjoy seeing an ass set himself back twenty to forty years or more
by his insistences. There's nothing very subtle about the poem;
all it means, as far as I know, is that in a waste of cinders loveli-
ness, in the form of color, stands up alive. Epicurus meant something of the same. But your interpretation, tho not specifically
intended, fits perfectly and is quite "true." The cinders are a "lie"
as death is a lie contrasted with life. But I wasn't that clever, I
wish I could say that I had been.

Sincerely,
BILL

170: TO HORACE GREGORY

Tuesday [*1948*]

Dear Horace: Glad to hear from you. The purpose of the long
letter at the end[1] is partly ironic, partly "writing" to make it
plain that even poetry is writing and nothing else—so that there's
a logical continuity in the art, prose, verse: an identity.

Frankly I'm sick of the constant aping of the Stevens' dictum
that I resort to the antipoetic as a heightening device. That's plain
crap—and everyone copies it. Now Rodman. The truth is that
there's an *identity* between prose and verse, not an antithesis.
It all rests on the same time base, the same measure. Prose, as
Pound has always pointed out, came after verse, not before it—.
No use tho trying to break up an error of that sort when it begins
to roll. Nobody will attempt to think, once a convenient peg to
hang his critical opinion on without thinking is found.

But specifically, as you see, the long letter is definitely germane
to the rest of the text. It is psychologically related to the text—
just as the notes following the *Waste Land* are related to the text
of the poem. The difference being that in this case the "note" is
subtly relevant to the matter and not merely a load for the mule's
back. That it is *not* the same stuff as the poem but comes from
below 14th St. is precisely the key. It does not belong in the poem
itself any more than a note on—Dante would.

---

[1] Of *Paterson*, Bk. I.

Also, in Book IV, the poem does definitely break out to the world at large—the sea, the river to the sea. This begins it.

And, if you'll notice, dogs run all through the poem and will continue to do so from first to last. And there is no dog without a tail. Here the tail has tried to wag the dog. Does it? (God help me, it may yet, but I hope not!)

I'm going with Floss to Atlantic City for a short time to try to get on my feet.

My best to you,
BILL

[*David Ignatow was a young poet who, like so many other young poets, appealed to Williams for critical assistance. Williams gave of his opinion freely and forthrightly and contributed to the* Beloit Poetry Journal, *when it was edited by Mr. Ignatow.*]

171: TO DAVID IGNATOW

August 9, 1948

Dear David Ignatow: Many thanks to you and Milton Hindus for your *Poems*. It is an important book and one I'd like to say something about when I get the chance. I'll do a review of it for someone one of these days—I don't know when but I'll do it some day soon.

Strange that I should at the time of receiving your book have received a book of prose sketches interspersed with poems in French by Jacques Prévert, sent me by his publisher René Bertel. What you have written and what the Frenchman writes have many critical points in common. But the French book sold 50,000 copies, while yours will sell 350 if you're lucky.

One cause of that is this: we are a pack of artificial idiots who, not having suffered directly from the wars (except materially here and there), still persist in treasuring our fancy imbecilities of "beautiful writing," whereas the French, who have been through purple hell, appreciate writing that lets them down, breaks the artificial tide-barriers preserving "literature," and lets in common excellence.

There are, of course, dangers: when the house collapses even the earth on which it was built may be washed away also. We may forget in a relaxation that there ever was such a thing as a poem.

I wrote some things once called *Improvisations: Kora in Hell*. They were wild flights of the imagination. As I look at them now I see how "romantic" they were. I feel embarrassed. I was having "dreams" at that time; I was having "ideas." Both you and the Frenchman, Prévert, have escaped romanticism and ideas. I see how much more down to earth you both are compared with what I was 30 years ago, I like that. It is good medicine.

So thank you for the book: we are all caught in an era which has overtaken the world and which will "come out" into an unexpected shape fairly soon. We are all trying to get our hands and our arms *around* this total shape. No one has the answer to everything in the grand shape of the modern which we all look forward to. But there is enough which many of us have in common to begin to see that it will be an astonishingly new *thing* which is shaping itself, a newly designed appearance—to which each of us is contributing a part. I recognize one of the aspects in you.

Best luck,
WILLIAMS

172: To T. C. WILSON

Oct. [*1948*]

Dear Ted: Do me a favor. Joe Gould,[1] whom I occasionally help in one way or another, has asked me for a "contribution." But I have lost his last letter with whatever address may have been on it. Find him for me and hand him the enclosed envelope, it's no more than five bucks but he needs it. Many thanks.

---

[1] The noted Bowery and Greenwich Village character who was writing his endless "Oral History of the World."

If you can't find him about the Village send the enclosure back to me.

Reading the various "successful" modern literary mags and quarterlies I find them growing more and more academic, more and more scholarly, more and more learned and without the spirit of adventure among their pages. "Adventure" is a romantic word though and I'd like to retract that one. Say, more and more rational as opposed to the irrational as a thesis for the artist's occupation.

They abash me, make me feel my age, discourage me from sending them material for publication. But I must add that the Italian (American: Biddle) mag, *Botteghe Oscure* will be publishing a new 20-page poem by me in November (unless the old gal loses her nerve). *Paterson III* out the same month.

My stern, frivolous 93-year-old mother died Sunday evening.[2]

Best,

BILL

[*Jean Starr Untermeyer, singer and poet, attended one of WCW's readings in New York City. She tried to ask a question from the floor which confused WCW, so she wrote a letter clarifying her question.*]

173: To Jean Starr Untermeyer

Saturday [October, 1948]

Dear Jean Starr Untermeyer: I am distressed not to have recognized you. Please forgive me.

We can't have a new (or old) poem built on a no-good or worn-out framework or underbody. Everything else of the poem comes *after* a proper framework has been raised. You may take a block of stone and carve a figure of it without an *apparent* support but the frame is there tacitly before the start is made.

We've got to *begin* by stating that we speak (here) a distinct,

---

[2] Actually aged 102.

separate language in a present (new era) and that it is NOT English. For English connotes an historical background from which its prosody is derived, which can never be *real* for us. It is basic for us to know that the English prosody we imitate as a matter of course is not determined by the mere facts of the mechanical syllabic sequences but an accretion through the ages from English history and character. And that these are NOT *our* character.

We've got to know that we have to invent for ourselves as we are in the process of inventing, whether we like it or not, a new prosody based on a present-day world, and real in a present-day world which the English prosody can never be for us or the world. This is our destiny (toward English as well as toward the world) and our tremendous opportunity facing a world that cannot go on making poems unless we make good. For if we do not make good (the necessary invention) somebody else will do it and we shall be brushed aside. English can't do it because we are not so tied.

This must be first in our constructions. All you say in your letter about the poem comes after that. What you say is true, of course, when at last we shall have a framework to hang it on. You cannot have what you demand or require until you do, first, have a frame to hang it on. Until in fact you have a new frame, something consonant with our times demands an adjustment to liberate us all *in the poem.* Philosophy may and in fact must follow the poem. The poet is first.

In short, I agree with everything you say but I must insist that until the underlying mechanism is established you will never succeed in making it an organism. It must first be regrown from the ground up—from the skeleton out *before* the flesh, the muscles, the brain can be put upon it. I am speaking from much further back or deeper down in the organization of the poem than you are. It may be my scientific training that enforces it, if so it is a good thing.

It is amazing to me how the simple elements of the art are tacitly and erroneously assumed to be valid before they have been examined on their anatomic elements. Naturally you can't blame most students for accepting the surely adventitious phenomenon of English prosody (in a new language where it doesn't apply and never has been applied) when all our language departments in our supposedly American universities are called English departments where English is taught and not our own tongue.

When I say that specifically I am looked on by our teachers as though I were mad. They are threatened in their tenure of office. They literally want to kill me. I have seen it in their faces. I don't blame them. But the necessity is so much greater than they are and than I am that some one has to point out how basic the error is. Men have been befuddled in their thinking and their lives by just that basic error in our thinking. Whitman was an open but not clear-thinking rebel. He did not know what it was all about, that our primary conception of the prosody was at fault. Men like Eliot and Pound and many lesser examples have run away from the elementary necessity for differentiating the two prosodies. They never got to know the problem. They avoided it. And having made their great decision to abandon the problem naturally ignore any thorough attack on it which will unseat them and make their lives secondary.

Auden, on the other hand, came gropingly here looking for something that has not been defined. He has found nothing and gone back to old, respectable and accepted practices. I don't blame him. Today big audiences flock to hear Spender or any English, that is to say, accepted writer. They must do this until they learn better. They are afraid of novelty. They have been misled by all our schools. It's what you always find in the world facing innovation, necessary, liberating innovation or invention. People want to remain as they were, they do not want to get into new fields. They want to be assured, comforted.

After, *after,* AFTER all this has been recognized and the practice has begun, *then* everything you say will be true. But just so long as we lie half asleep in official teaching to the basic error and the necessity for a basic restatement of the problem we shall not be able to go ahead. Meanwhile there is little left for the poet to do than to write POEMS, and to hell with the bastards of false teachers and statists and religionists and all those who want the past to stay as it is for their benefit—mostly pecuniary.

W. C. WILLIAMS

1949

Jan. 12, 1949

Dear Bob: Well, practice being about nil today, I started to search for the books and mags you are interested in and turned up an astonishing lot of old stuff—including the diary of our trip to France 1924-25. Strange to read it now (tho God knows I didn't take the time to read it this afternoon). Among other things I found a copy of Carnevali's *A Hurried Man* and your *Companion Volume*—that I didn't think I had.

It's the damndest thing to be more or less idle today. It hasn't happened like this in years. Part of it is due to the lack of work everywhere in medicine this January (due, I suppose, to the April weather—63 degrees F at times), part is due to it being Wednesday when, people think, no doctor is on duty, and part to Bill being here to do what little work there is. My mood is affected also by the fact that I am now 65, which means that I have been retired from active work at the hospital, not even allowed to be on any committee. So that's that. So here I am whipping myself into action on *Paterson III*—but for the moment doing nothing. Floss and I intended to go to the city this evening to see a picture but—hell, rather stay home.

I found also two books Gertrude Stein has sent me after autographing them in very generous style. I wasn't able to talk or write to the old gal but in spite of that she seemed to want to be decent to me—as to how many others, perhaps, in her lonesomeness, if it was so. The books were *Americains d'Amerique* and—I've already forgot the name of the other (a small grey book).[1]

The trouble is I didn't find any more of the Samurai book. I know I have one copy (at the bottom of the trunk) but not another did I encounter. On the other hand I found my own two personal copies of the first two issues of *Contact* which I had care-

---

[1] The other was *Autobiography of Alice B. Toklas*.

fully put away in a drawer of my old attic desk. There they were in perfect condition but, Bob, I can't give up those. They are the only ones that I am *sure* I have. Later, if I find more I'll send you other copies—but not those.

I guess that sums it up.

I sat in a smoke-filled room last night at a County Medical meeting listening to two big boys talking about peripheral vascular disease until 11:30—and then a long drive home. I'm still groggy—but that's the way money is made by yapping, yapping, yapping, until someone pays attention to you—or you get noticed in the crowd.

Things aren't bad though, but I ain't making much cash these days. I guess I'll get by though. Floss says we'll exist. As long as necessary, perhaps.

Best,
BILL

[*John Crowe Ransom has edited the* Kenyon Review *since its start in 1939. His high standard of excellence in his contributors invited contributions from Williams but did not always guarantee their publication.*]

175: TO JOHN CROWE RANSOM

January 15, 1949

Dear Ransom: Jarrell's refreshing poem in your issue just arrived —rouses me to want to send you the enclosed. Not that they resemble his work or that I have any great confidence in them but— just want to keep the ball rolling. Congratulations on a good issue. I don't know that you ever use any tabs of literary opinion or data, small bits of observation (even if you think well of them) among your pages—oh well, here's this (inspired largely from your own pages in this issue).

The secret of all writing, all literature, is escape, true enough, but *not* in the Freudian sense. It is not, in other words, evasion.

But it *is* escape—from the herd. Old Ez "impervious to both patronage and criticism, suddenly rears back into the mist and we hear in his place the Voice." Hemingway assumes a cloak of vulgarity, let us say, to protect a Jamesian sensitivity to detail. Just when you think you have a good man, he's not there. Plato's exasperation when having saluted the sane man, the thinking man, the solid man—suddenly he recognizes that the poet, the unsound man, has twisted loose and, by a stroke, brings home the bacon. Is not Shakespeare, as hard as scholars (of a certain bent) try to nail him to learning, really the escaped man? He is a man who from indifference has escaped to the sun itself by the gift of words alone. For surely we can't call him an original thinker.

I regret to say that the complexities of the modern literary scene, between London, Paris, and, let us say, Berkeley, California (let me add Princeton) are strangely unrelated to "the light." I pick up sparkles of understanding now and again—whether from Lionel Trilling, Nicolas Calas, or some young Frenchman in the new *Transition,* but most words seem largely designed to be turned page by page. Perhaps it's my aging mood. Not that I don't enjoy reading, but there's too much of it. That's the true sign of an aging wit, I suppose.

Never bother to consider anything I send you as in any way "privileged." I am boiling mad at the moment with the tyrannical ukase I received in this morning's mail from the American Medical Association, which, in the name of "democracy" orders me to pay $25 into their treasury to fight "socialized medicine," like it or not. This represents what we are up against in our times. Our writing also affects it.

Sincerely,
WILLIAMS

[*Helen Russell, of Seattle Washington, was a member of WCW's short story seminar at the University of Washington in 1947. She continued her writing after her marriage, appealing to WCW for support, which he continually supplied.*]

176: To Helen Russell

Oct. 22, 1949

Dear Helen of the Little Round Straw Hat: Anyhow I'm still alive (that's the way I feel this morning). I only ache in three places at the moment. It must be the warm, damp wind from the Gulf of Mexico that's got me as it's got us all. I haven't the slightest idea why I'm telling you this. What are you going to do with that story? If it hasn't been published, let me keep it awhile, I'd like to send it to a couple of people who might be interested. It's good, straight writing, very well done. I'm proud of you. After all, when you've got that far all you need is a theme that engrosses you and a lot of paper and pencils—and to let fly. This story is obviously a short first chapter. . . . Why, from that start, can't you go on writing "short stories," that is to say chapters, so that in the end you'll have revealed a life as it becomes the key to other lives about you in their tragic or comic detail? The next starts with the guy leaving the house on his bender, what he sees, what he thinks, what he wants, regrets.

But the real story is people living the peculiar, if you can find it, character of that particular environment which becomes your material. This story rings true, and remember, as Proust once wrote to Gide, you can say anything so long as you do not say "I." You write to reveal, then call it John Henry but surreptitiously reveal yourself. Tell us how he was walking along the street at dusk watching a girl with straight legs and swinging a tennis racket in her hand, a blond girl, how he built up to it (in his mind), finally clipping her over the head, splitting her head open.

Imagine it! That's when you'll get away from bare realism into the imagination; that's when the feeling of creation will come over you with a thrill. All you are doing now of sheer good writing (like this story) will support you then. Keep hitting the trail on that writing. Some day you're going to click. Lord knows how it's going to happen, but I know quite well WHAT is going to happen: you're going to be shaken down by some disintegrating emotional quake that will send all your inhibitions to hell. The residuum will be what you have learned here and there to keep you in order.

My little mother died ten days ago or more. She just slept away, at almost 93. So there's that. When we, my brother and I, opened her big trunk in the attic, we found among other things three coin-shaped, bright red cases large enough to hold, say, a silver dollar. When we opened them we found in each a medal as bright as when it was first placed there, a prize in each case which she had won by her painting and drawing in Paris, at the School for Industrial Design, in 1877, '78 and '79. And in all these years she had kept those medals secret.

What the devil are we alive for? To hide ourselves? When I think of how little my own mother ever said to me of herself and her ambitions I grind my teeth in fury. There is no sense to it. It is one of the cardinal sins that we do not break bounds one way or another and come out of our prehistoric caves. It's indecent and silly besides. . . .

It's been fun talking with you. . . .

> Affectionately,
> why not?
> BILL

[*Selden Rodman, poet and anthologist, was apparently one of the first critics to notice the poetic qualities of Williams'* In the American Grain.]

177: TO SELDEN RODMAN

November 14, 1949

My dear Rodman: What a beautiful and thoughtful book![1] I haven't read a word of it as yet (except my own piece, God pity

---

[1] *One Hundred Modern Poems.*

me), but just to look at the titles has been an excitement. I shall
spend some time here and I have a foreknowledge that it will be
a happy sojourn and a profitable one too! I know that. For I have
already realized what a rich field you have set your plough into.
Many thanks for remembering me.

It was a startling and original thought of yours to include my
"Raleigh"[2] as a poem. Yes, I've known from the first that it was
exceptionally regular in its meter but I never looked at it as
anything but what it set out to be: an "imitation" of Raleigh,
Raleigh caught in the mesh of his own period's forms; to show
Raleigh according to my conception of how, by form only, we
must "make" our designs. Perhaps it is also an original poem. I
hope so. What you have done is precisely what I call criticism.
Merely to point the finger is criticism. A paragraph in the same
context is better than a book. To see clearly one must peek
through a pinhole.

You have done me a most generous service.

Gratefully yours,
W. C. WILLIAMS

178: To SELDEN RODMAN

Friday evening, Dec. 9, 1949

Dear Selden Rodman: I've been reading your *100 Modern Poems*
all evening—Flossie's head on my lap, she asleep after a visit to
the Van Gogh show—let's not go into that. I didn't finish the
book, though I went to the end of it, leaving many gaps. The
pleasure is there. It gave me what I so often miss in the work of
a single writer (my own stuff included), a sense of the great
sweep of the poem's meaning—whether it be Patchen, Fearing
or Auden. I got a warmth, a level of consciousness and of honesty
—a confession of beauty, an over-all seriousness that warmed and
comforted me—in what cannot be described otherwise than my
despair.

---

[2] From *In the American Grain.*

Somehow or other it is a sense of closeness, of opening the eyes above pettiness such as I got from an entirely different source today. My mother died a month ago at the age of 92. Among the objects that she left me was her Mass Book—for she had been a Catholic but renounced it years ago. In the book was a letter written in 1880 by a certain De Longueville. My cousin translated the letter and handed the translation to me this afternoon. It was a proposal of marriage from the young man, which apparently had been refused, for Mother married my father two years later. But she had not destroyed the letter—nor spoken of it to anyone, as far as I know, all her life. I wonder if she knew it was still in her Mass Book. If she did, she wanted me to see it, for the book was left specifically to me, her oldest child.

Well, that's the sort of continuation that the mind should have —it is the same continuation that I discovered in reading what you have gathered of the modern poets as inheritors of the poets who have lived in the past. We are all a brotherhood—or are so if we write well, that is if we deserve it. It's a delightful book to me.

Some will notice that you have not included this poem or that excellent poem. I could do the same. But that's precisely NOT the point. The point is that you were able to choose such a series, marked by your own choice, from the richness of the general field. It bespeaks what lies there neglected in great measure by the unable where you are able—and others might be as able if they would. You have wished to do it and so shown what amounts to love as well as acumen. It needs a little formality of statement to bring out what I'm after—but no pomposity—and I hope what I say doesn't sound that way. I say love and I mean just that— and that's what they all mean and what gives the poems meaning from first to last. . . .

Sincerely,
WILLIAMS

Perhaps the secret of your success is the consistency with which you rejected the dominance of the standard line—and found something as fine or finer to take its place.

Dylan Thomas' line, "And Death shall have no dominion," placed as you have placed it as an epilogue to the book is brilliant.

Rosalie Moore—comes off, as you have used her, in a way to show her as one of the best of our time.

Faulkner, placed as you have placed him, reveals not only his extraordinary sensitivity but a poet's use of the word in one of the most moving pieces in the book.

Kenneth Fearing's composition is for me just another revelation of his greatness. He is one of my greatest admirations.

Your translations are sometimes convincing, sometimes not, but I admire their insistence on putting what had to go in—*Le Cimetière marin*—the stanza of the girls carries over the meaning and the feeling: but it is an ungrateful task to translate verse. I admire you for doing it.

1950

1/29/50

Dear Charles: I'm having my picture took—to hell with it. But perhaps the angels will understand. If they care.

However I am helpless and expect to emerge without losing my hair or scalp or—as you may imagine. My hope is that I get some time for lunch before facing the angry horde in my office.
(10 hours later)
(12 hours later)

A photographer from *Time* Mag came out to take pictures of me and "some children" yesterday, Saturday. I was called up first at 8 A.M. (A man to do an article on me came out 2 days earlier.) I reluctantly assigned 11 A.M. as the time for the ordeal—for I had an excessively busy day ahead of me, lunch at noon, office hours at 1. And Bill would be busy in the office all morning.

So he arrived at 11:45!

He wanted a picture of me examining a baby, in the office that was jammed at the time. I had to be wearing a white coat—which I never wear. Oh hell. I borrowed a baby from among Bill's gang (with or without diaper?) Diapered.

etc etc etc

My gang had to wait until 1:30 (I finished at 5 P.M.) I had a sandwich for lunch.

And no doubt they'll never say thanks, never answer my letter asking for copies of at least one of the pictures, and the next crowd of thugs or thugesses will expect to do the same—always on short notice: We *have* to have it *today.*

I must be thrilled! Smile! Contort myself into favorable attitudes entirely strange to me and act the ass generally—for publicity's stake (which I am forced to treasure tho I despise it) and cash and leisure—out the window.

Sunday morning thought.

Best,
BILL

I had to be sitting "naturally" at my typewriter while a shot was being taken—so I began this letter to you.

[*Peter Viereck, American poet, political writer, and professor, is currently teaching at Mt. Holyoke.*]

180: To Peter Viereck

February 8, 1950

Dear Viereck: Thanks for your note and the enclosure. There are probably a good many points on which we radically differ, but there should be as many on which we agree. I see little use in attempting to coordinate opinions, one man with another. I am much more for each man driving ahead and letting happen what may. If there is good in what we have to present, let's go after it.

But I feel very strongly that there is a phase of the art, whatever art, that is cogent to its day. Everyone, more or less, strikes toward it. Some hit closer than others. Everyone takes his chances. It's a sort of microbiology of the word.

We talk of fair and unfair (I forget what I was saying as I had to go to breakfast—no matter)—most of it is beside the point—to hell with it. If you want to rhyme, go ahead and rhyme, maybe you'll be as good as Chaucer or Dante—with one fifth of the words they had, all smeared with the use of 500 "geniuses." I hope you like it. There are more important things to do and damned little time to do them in. Maybe you got something, I don't know.

Harvey Breit of *Times* "Books" has asked me to review your new book. I told him I wasn't much in sympathy with your viewpoint but that that shouldn't interfere with my speaking of your writing—even with enthusiasm; that I had admired at least one poem in your first book. So with this morning's mail I received the galleys of *Strike Through the Mask*—let's hope you do.

It's a tough battle to keep one's head above the ocean of print that inundates us these days. Good luck to you in your work.

Sincerely,

W. C. Williams

[*Srinivas Rayaprol was a young Anglo-Indian student of engineering in the United States, whose first love was poetry. He wrote to WCW, received encouragement, then based his poetic development upon Williams' advice. Somewhat lost in the U.S.A., "Seena" adopted WCW as substitute father. Upon his return to India, after Indian independence, M. Rayaprol founded the English-language-Indian-poetry journal,* East and West, *emphasizing the ties between India and the West.*]

181: To Srinivas Rayaprol

Wednesday morning, March 29, '50

Dear Seena: A really beautiful letter (I wish I knew how to keep it as fresh and pleasant and true as it is this minute), and the reading at the Museum did not go so well (I was disappointed), and I am not, surely not, a great man.

My wife, though, who is still asleep, seemed to like some of my reading (I know she also did not like some of it); she is a silent person and does not want to hurt my feelings. But she loves me and wants to correct me when I need it, so her position is difficult.

There is something wrong about reading poetry in public. Either the room is wrong or the people who come are the wrong sort—perhaps they only seem to be because of the mutual embarrassment that comes from trying to speak in public of a thing that by its very nature is intimately personal and needs to be warmed and loved to thrive as it should. You can't shout poems over the footlights, not at least all of them. Some can be read in a loud defiant voice but others, almost all, require close attention and preliminary arrangement of some sort. I can't imagine Homer reading in a hall. He must have read in villages or small circles. What happens is that we automatically select the obvious or pass quickly over a delicate, questionable passage. In a play we might do better with our verse, but I doubt it now; there is too great a temptation to exaggerate.

I am so very glad you did not throw your letter away before mailing it; it is the best you have ever sent me. In fact, your half desire to throw it away came from nothing but what I have been speaking in the above paragraph: that you felt you had revealed too much and might be boring me by its very triviality. But that is always the same with all of us. We are afraid, when we are at all as sensitive as you are, that we shall show ourselves to be shallow and trivial. So we roar—and shrink back disappointed in ourselves. Yet what else, often, can we do?

But your eyes are shrewd and good. You do see the American in one of his best aspects: his attitude toward his work. I thank you for speaking of that.

Last evening, after the reading, when a few people came up to speak to me—not many, there was among them a rather beautiful, not very young woman whose name I did not catch and whom I shall, no doubt, never see again. She said to me, I am an Italian (because I had spoken of the new Italian novelists in my talk). She didn't say much more except when I told her that one of the troubles with our modern world is that it consists mainly of names but that we remain too often strangers to each other—she replied, we do not wish to push ourselves on the privacy of others. I tell you I opened my eyes, her manner was so gracious. It opened up a vista—a rather sad world where we all go about in masks, or better than that, with our faces bent over a newspaper reading it on the subway or in our private houses. If only we could break into that world, that secret world —not to exploit it but to share and enjoy it, quietly—without intrusion or the sense of intruding.

Of your poems: You should be glad that people (the magazines) do not accept them (at your age); it is the first sign of worth—even of coming greatness (such as you imagine). Suppose they were accepted at once! what would that mean other than that they already exist in another? That would and should shock you and make you stop writing forever.

You want them to be uniquely you, you in the face (and the intimacy) of the world. They are an assertion that you, yourself, exist in every final delicacy of your being—without restraint and without fear of being crushed (by a bomb or other thing), for after all a bomb isn't unique and has existed in our wishes for centuries. There is nothing new in a bomb that would destroy "everything"—so we need not fear it. But the poem—under those circumstances cannot be accepted at once. It is you, therefore it is unknown.

It's something of the greatest significance that Shakespeare, the more or less ignorant person, didn't even bother to have his plays printed. He seemed to care nothing for them—at least he seemed to be of that mind. All he bothered were his "poems," his name, himself. Isn't that a natural reaction?

The Grandmother Poem is, I think, your best, your most felt—and you are uncertain! That too is, I suppose, inevitable—you want it too much.

Why man, "the thighs as the roof of the world" is the finest and clearest thing in the whole poem—anybody can see it instantly —it is a magnificent affirmation. Your trouble in that stanza is not there but in what follows about the wheat, which is too worn an image to serve. But you have the answer to your dilemma right in your hand: the belly is the apple tree. When you have developed that image—the summer and perhaps later the apple tree, you'll have your poem secure. But do not change that about the thighs, which is superb.

I hope you get your girl—or not. What's the difference?

Yours,

Bill

[*Dr. Henry Wells, Curator of the Brander Matthews Dramatic Museum at Columbia, has written widely on poetry, most recently on the poetry of Merrill Moore.*]

182: To Henry Wells

April 12, 1950

Dear Wells: Thank you for letting me see your two papers which, as soon as I have had a chance to study them a little further, I shall return to you. But you have certainly traduced my poor family. Let's get this for once straight.

My father's ancestry, whatever its virtues or defects, was pure English. His mother was Emily Dickinson of Cirencester. He himself was born in Birmingham and at the age of five, his father having disappeared, was taken by the old lady to the U.S. Here (in Brooklyn) she remarried and moved with her new husband—an itinerant photographer—to St. Thomas in the Danish West Indies where my father grew up. That's that.

My mother's mother was French, from Martinique. She was Meline Hurrard, which is a Basque name, along with Jurrard, Turrard and Urrard. Her ancestors originated in Bordeaux. They met their finish at St. Pierre, where they owned a liqueur business, when Mt. Pellé blew up. Her father (my great-grandfather) was Jewish and Spanish—a special Caribbean breed, as far as I know. This is very interesting to me.

The oldest Jewish cemetery in the New World is in St. Thomas, a Danish possession. (This is probably responsible for the rumor that I am partly Dutch!) My grandfather on my mother's side was Solomon Hoheb, he was an orphan whose mother remarried an Enriquez. He also had among his immediate relatives the Pereiras (whom I knew in Brooklyn) and the Monsantos who have made quite a name for themselves in our own Southwest (one of them, a Hubbard, has been President of the Woman's Industrial College at Denton, Texas, for the past quarter century). And there you are.

My brother might deny some of these details, which would be his right since many of them are hard to fix, but as far as I can tell this is the truth.

A strange additional detail on my father's side is that my grandmother, Emily Dickinson, an orphan also, was brought up in London by "the Godwins," a "wealthy" family, and that when she married this Williams she was quietly disowned—which is the origin of her wanderings. But who was this Williams? That, I have never been able to rightly ascertain.

Grandma obstinately refused to tell me about her childhood or her marriage—and you know the English when they want to be obstinate. I did my best but all I ever got was that the Godwins were uncle and aunt to her and that "she hadn't been done right by." Now there was a prominent family of Godwins in London at that time associated with some Shelleys and Williamses of considerable interest, etc., etc. You see where my thought is heading. I know nothing more.

I'll write again later.

Sincerely,
WILLIAMS

Paterson III came out in 1949 *not* 1950—just to be accurate.

183: TO HENRY WELLS

April 12/50

Dear Wells: Thank you for letting me see your two writings:[1] I read them with great interest and some embarrassment. I dread praise, even the thoughtful praise which you have granted me, nothing so upsets me.

As to the more general piece in which I am only incidentally concerned, I think your warning is a timely one and fairly delivered. But what are we to do about it? My feeling is that these "seasons" in the development of an art are ordained by circumstances over which no one has any control. What I would say is that the fact that certain writers, certain of our younger writers, are now college teachers of one sort or another comes about not so much because they have found a living in the schools as that the art itself has called for it.

In another generation you won't be able to get a poet within academic walls, but for the moment it is necessary for the man wanting to write to go to the academy because that's where the information lies closest to hand, the information without which the whole art could not develop.

We're an ignorant crew, we ex-British colonials. We are trying to stand on our feet, but the impedimenta are so great that we don't do it very well. At the moment a bit of book larnin' won't hurt us—if we know how to keep ourselves upon the great general theme of the poem throughout the ages as the great (often final) blossom of a triumphant culture.

---

[1] On *Paterson*.

The broad general theme is the one that has most impressed me in my life. The problem is to be both local (all art is local) and at the same time to surmount that restriction by climbing to the universal in all art. At the moment the wave washes backward to gather strength. These new boys are bound to add to our strength preparatory to the next lunge forward. But it is the forward surge to mastery which must be celebrated in their minds while they grub forward. Again I salute your sagacity and your ability as a teacher and a thoughtful person to look beyond the immediate field.

As to essay number two, the one concerning my own wild stabs into the ether—there too I think you fail sufficiently to take into consideration my role as a theorist. I think you need a word on that to pull your remarks together. For I think that only by an understanding of my "theory of the poem" will you be able to reconcile my patent failures with whatever I have done that seems worthwhile.

In a word I believe that all the old academic *values* hold today as always. Basically I am a most conventional person. But the TERMS in which we must parallel the past are entirely new and peculiar to ourselves.

The poem to me (until I go broke) is an attempt, an experiment, a failing experiment, toward assertion with broken means but an assertion, always, of a new and total culture, the lifting of an environment to expression. Thus it is social, the poem is a social instrument—accepted or not accepted seems to be of no material importance. It embraces everything we are.

The poem (for I never if possible speak of poetry) is the assertion that we are alive as ourselves—as much of the environment as it can grasp: exactly as Hellas lived in the *Iliad*. If I am faulty in knowledge or skill it is of small matter so long as I follow the ball.

Well, these are chance maunderings—all I am seeking to indicate is that, skill or no skill, obscurity or no obscurity—what I am trying to get over is that there is a theme which is greater than any poem or any poet worthy of following—or if not, there's not much use bothering about what a poem "means."

Whitman to me was an instrument, one thing: he started us

on the course of our researches into the nature of the line by breaking finally with English prosody. After him there has been for us no line. There will be none until we invent it. Almost everything I do is of no more interest to me than the technical addition it makes toward the discovery of a workable metric in the new mode.

It is useless to speak of Whitman's psychologic physiognomy, his this, his that. All of it is true and of no importance. As I say, he has (for me) only one meaning and that virtually a negative one. He cleaned decks, did very little else.

I'm driven off my feet by the consequences of having won some belated recognition—I almost wish they had left me alone. I was happy, my writing was hard won but I had what I wanted. This that it has brought on is a small hell. If it gets worse I'll disappear.

Best,
WILLIAMS

184: To Srinivas Rayaprol

May 24, 1950

Dear Seena: You write interesting prose, full of the keenest observation and shrewd wit. Someday you will write an account of your American experience that will be read and read for what it says, not a mere English book of contempts. When I think of what "style" has come to mean I want to puke. A clever, English "literary style," an Oxford accent in the writing, with proper disregard for everything commented upon (why do they comment at all?), an indirect puffing up their own contentments using the American background as a field to enhance the highlights of their own charm, is about as low as anyone can get as a writer.

But it sells! It sells to Americans!! They love it!! This too should delight us. It is for this reason that I have found it impossible to go to hear Dylan Thomas while he was here. Just the dreamy look that comes into the eyes of our partial writers and so-called competent critics—who control the publicity columns of the *avant garde* forums and publications, has been enough for me. They drool at the mouth. And I think I'd like Thomas if I could get him alone, but you can see that they are almost wetting their pants out of excitement over his voice and the wild colors of his imagery.

And I, as a consequence, must be jealous of him. They look at me out of the corners of their eyes as much as to say, Well, Williams, there's no one in this country who can read like that. So that if you speak slightingly of him we can only come to one conclusion: you'd read that way if you could, but since you haven't the voice or the manner or even his wonderful poems to give us—you try to belittle him. The result is that I haven't wanted to go to hear him. They pack the auditoriums. Poor guy.

What they cannot see is that American poems are of an entirely different sort from Thomas's Welsh-English poems. They use a different language and operate under a different compulsion. They are more authoritarian, more Druidic, more romantic— and they are, truly, more colorful. WE CAN'T AND MUST NOT WRITE THAT WAY. At the same time the audience appeal (and always take a careful look at all audiences during their affection by a reader) is much more intense than in any audience we can affect. They listen to me and shy away. They do not want me, they want what they have been used to, the old tradition, the virtuoso in an accepted mode. They want what I cannot and will not give.

Some of your depressions are native to you and cannot be avoided. But some of them are due only to your youth. Accept them and welcome them. Take everything that comes, for what you feel is at least an evidence that you are reacting intelligently and intensely—you to a world that is close about you. You are "being" when you feel, no matter how depressed you may be. But count on it. You have at your age no idea how you will feel ten years from now. What now you hate you may by then come to love, and what you now love—though not everything—you may in twenty years have so forgotten you can't even remember its name. But the basic love will remain, even though now you don't even name it (properly) to yourself. Only long trial will finally make us conscious of our true treasures.

About your feeling for India (I think your poem is well worth-while), no doubt some psychoanalyst could give you an answer—

and it would be the worst thing, in my opinion, that could happen to you. My own feeling is that, like all young men or women of intelligence coming from an environment which in its common aspect is dreadfully backward, you enjoy being away from it. The horrors of some of the phases of India must sicken you. You are young. You are glad to have escaped (temporarily) from the necessity for doing something about that country, your country, your father's and your ancestors' country, though in your heart you know you can never escape it.

In one sense your father represents all that is backward in India to your mind. You can't escape him. You want, like all the young, to live the thrilling intellectual and emotional life you crave. You don't want to be bothered to have to give that up and throw yourself into that ancient maelstrom. For it may very well be the end of you. Truly it may. For it is not at all certain that you will succeed in doing anything, even with the greatest wit and intelligence. You may not even be wanted. They may be better off without you. That's a hard thought.

Suppose you do what you want to and go to Paris. In other words, suppose you become as you wish, an international figure. If you have genius it is possible that may be the very best thing you can do. But if you want no more than the amusement of your appetites—well, you might, with money, still turn out to be at least a decorative person—and do no harm.

You are very young, praise the Lord for it and work. That's all I know. What you will end up by doing no one can say. But if I know you, I think you will, by understanding your father's position, come finally to accept him and understand him and become, curiously enough HIS father. Thus you'll learn to pity him and develop a final love and affection. Perhaps you had to leave your father and India to detach yourself from them in order to be able to love. You can't love at command. No one can. You went away to learn by detachment what you were. With your excellent mind and spirit you will, I am sure, not be the kind to waste yourself. Ulysses went out and returned intact. He was at first a liar: he deceived those who wanted to draft him for the wars, he did everything necessary to remain—or even to be himself, a one, an individual. You are going through something like that. But naturally today the conditions have to be differently understood. Today we give ourselves more easily than Ulysses did and are not destroyed by it: we cure syphilis in a week by penicillin!

Don't regret anything. For you are young, believe me. It doesn't make one damned bit of difference what you have done (except that you had to leave India and I think you did well to come here before Paris or Buenos Aires or London), you *can't* make any mistakes. It is all of a piece. Do anything you want to (so long as you keep your mind free). You can, if you must, throw away ten or twenty years (and provided you keep working hard at something or other and working intensely) and keep ears and eyes open. No one is going to capture you or maim you. Go!

Best,
BILL

[*Kathleen Hoagland and her husband, Clayton, live in Rutherford and are old friends of WCW. Kathleen Hoagland, who is also a writer, has often typed Dr. Williams' manuscripts and offered editorial suggestions.*]

185: TO KATHLEEN HOAGLAND

Saratoga Springs, N. Y.
July 26, 1950

Dear Kitty: My annual letter. You really ought to experience this place and I hope you will, some day soon for a month at least. Contrary to what you believe, it's very nearly a cloister and convent where work is the rule which everyone obeys. There is absolute silence here all day, from 9 to 4 in the afternoon.

Everyone closely confines himself, writer, painter or composer, and slaves his head off. I too work every day consuming reams of paper trying to complete a first draft of *Paterson IV* before I leave. In a week I've blocked out Part 1 of the 3 parts. I won't finish but without this period of concentration I don't know how I should have been able to complete the task for another year.

The only lost soul in the place is Floss; we are Guests of the Corporation, otherwise no wives or husbands are permitted on the ground except Sunday and before 9 P.M. They have to go into town for their hygiene! Floss has wandered the estate over, a bit chewed up by deer flies but on the whole contented—we did take one trip to Vermont to visit the grandson—who loves camp! which broke the monotony for her.

There are 24 people here—more men than women—and half the women deaf! It's very funny.

My favorites are Ted Roethke, Dick Eberhart, whom I have come to admire, Harvey Shapiro, and Nicholas Calas, whom I was amazed to find in residence. Let me not forget also a composer. A little beer-drinking guy named Weber—but everyone likes him. A woman named Jessamyn West, a short story writer, now doing a novel for Harcourt, Brace, I think is the chief of the women—and there are several others whose names I scarcely remember. One painter named Slocker (or Schacker) from Philly is one of Flossie's admirations and mine too—he owns a rickety bicycle on which he goes everywhere.

Now on to Buffalo—I wish I could hand you some of this pine-scented freedom. A wonderful place—

Love,
BILL

[*José García Villa is a well-known poet. When he came to this country almost thirty years ago, WCW was the first major American writer he called upon.*]

186: To José García Villa

Yaddo [*1950*]

Dear Villa: As far as I can remember, the story will run to 12 pages, double space, of typescript. It might be 14 pages but not more. It is called, simply, "Lena."

A cold east wind, today, that seems to blow from the other side of the world—seems at the same time to be blowing all poetry out of life. A man wonders why he bothers to continue to write. And yet it is precisely then that to write is most imperative for us. That, if I can do it, will be the end of *Paterson,* Book IV. The ocean of savage lusts in which the wounded shark gnashes at his own tail is not our home.

It is the seed that floats to shore, one word, one tiny, even microscopic word, is that which can alone save us.

Thank you for your understanding word.

Best,
BILL

1951

[*David McDowell met WCW in their New Directions days, and when McDowell became an editor at Random House, WCW went with him.*]

187: To David McDowell

January 14/51

Dear Dave: You ain't never gonna see none of it[1] until it's presented to you at Randam House, Thursday, March 1 1951, at 9 A.M., finished. After that, if it's acceptable to you all, you can hire it out as you see fit but not until then. I now have it at 1,008 pages longhand with 200 to go outside of the fifty original pages already printed. That ought to hold you. 1,000 pages in 6 weeks, longhand, no dictaphone phonies permitted, is a record anybody can shoot at as wants to. But if they equal it I'll do 2,000 pages next time if I have to give half my time to it.

My only worry now is the typing but I'll solve that too, right here in the suburbs.

Sorry I'll be in Washington the night of your birthday. Heil!

Had callers all yesterday afternoon. Ben Weber to talk about the libretto he's going to wrap in his music this coming summer, followed by Dallam Simpson, wife and 4-year-old daughter till after delicatessen and beer supper. To bed, both Floss and I exhausted. His wife holds his overcoat for him and hands him his cane at leave-taking! Kerist! I don't like that.

Am reading Faulkner's *Light in August* as I go along with my biography. It's a good American language traveling companion. That's important. How could I do ANYthing if I had to read British as I went along? Pound beginning to tell me that John Adams invented Americanese in his letters home from Spain. And that's supposed to put me in my place! When did HE wake up, you may ask?

---

[1] His *Autobiography*.

Do you realize that when I was in Paris in 1924 I retracted Hemingway's oldest boy's foreskin for him while the redoubtable lion hunter almost fainted? And remember that this is not for publication at this time. I count on you for this. Not to be told especially to "Back of the Book"—till later.

Love to little (big) Madeline.

Best,
BILL

What about McAlmon's work which lies close to my heart? Have you had time to look at it? If so, what about it? I have 3 manuscript additional volumes. I'm in this to push it to the limit, so let's hear.

BILL

188: To DAVID McDOWELL

March 13, 1951

Dear Dave: Best to Madeline, if it comes today you'd better call it Brutus (not Caesar), this being the Ides of March. But if it's a girl, Cinderella. No provision suggested for twins.

Provided you get here tomorrow won't you bring me two additional copies of *Make Light of It*—charge as usual.

Been working hard at Part II.[1] It needs it, as Part I needed it also—a close checking of all details. I was conscious of the defects but dumped it on you anyway to let you see what was going on. There's more to getting this script ready than meets the eye—but with patience we'll finally get it in order.

What I suggest is that we do not spend too much time on Part I tomorrow. I'll get your viewpoint, put down your specific suggestions and then keep the script here to be worked on further. You, then, will take Part II back with you. It is much further advanced in detailed corrections than Part I. Part III is coming along fine.

I'm looking up certain letters now, my own in some cases and a few others for inclusion in the text.

---

[1] Of *The Autobiography of William Carlos Williams.*

I think I have my title. It isn't spectacular but it describes the situation rather well:

ROOT, BRANCH & FLOWER:
The Autobiography
of
W.   C.   W.

Best,
BILL

189: TO WALLACE STEVENS

April 25, 1951

Dear Wally: I was delighted to hear from you, happy to know that you had written and happy, too, to be able to answer you as I am now doing. This is the first time I have used a typewriter again for a letter for a month. It's a major thrill. It's a month today since the damned thing hit—perhaps I shouldn't say "damned," as that might involve repercussions which I can't afford. Let me say the "sweet" thing kicked me in the slats. It was a great surprise to me, for although I know I am far from invulnerable, I didn't expect THAT! Quite a surprise. It seems to have resulted from trying to write a book in three months while carrying on a practice of medicine. Just couldn't bring it off. I almost had the book finished at that.

This morning working again, what else is there to do? I actually completed 5 pages of composition, maybe it was even 6 pages to fill in a gap which I had omitted when I originally wrote that section. Now the first third of the autobiography is ready to go to the publisher for the final overhauling, to be checked by the lawyers for possible libel and at last to the printer. The 2nd third is lying on my couch for me to begin my final check today and the third and last part, not quite finished, will go to my typist (after I have gone over it) the following week.

I agree with you, we're not old. We may croak at any moment but we're not old. I was all heated up to go to that party at Bard,

I counted on it, it looked like a good crowd. It was a major disappointment involved in the mass of disappointments to have to give that up. I had planned to do a daring thing, I was going to speak extempore, taking a chance on the result. I had never done that before for a whole hour. I was a little scared but that only whetted my appetite. Perhaps we'll try it another time.

I guess that's about my limit for today. I wish I could see you. Perhaps this summer or next fall; now that I have about given up medicine and will be freer to move around, a new way of life will begin, a longed-for time when I shall be able to hobnob with my few rare friends more as I wish to. Write again.

Sincerely yours,
BILL

190: To Frank L. Moore

May 21, 1951

Dear Frank: I'm a poor one to advise you on drama, for at heart I'm a nonbeliever; nothing makes any difference to me. Death is too real for me to want to become "dramatic" about it. It claps you between its hands like a flying moth, and you are done; only those who hope find that tragic. I find it simply leaden. The only effect of what I do is upon someone who is affected by my actions, so that drama becomes a very small and temporary thing. That, one might say, gives it a certain lightness. Agamemnon slaughtered by his wife, the most terrible scene from antiquity, was merely the final revelation in the education of the Athenian Republic. After that tragedy disappeared.

The myth wearies me. We never learn. We crave the often-repeated, to do over and over the same thing. Because an event happened in the past, we think that our lives too somehow partake of it; anything to give us a sense of reality. We think because it happened once upon a time, it must be so.

The Sacco-Vanzetti Case repeats itself in all our lives, every minute. Why else were they killed? We should make it into a comedy, with little angels to carry away their pure white souls at the end. You might as well eulogize Grieg's "Dance of the Gnomes." I see nothing dramatic about it. We live to see what hopeful men can do.

There is nothing to do with freedom once we get it but to enslave ourselves—under the name of love! We have no contentment otherwise. I have just finished reading the *Iliad* in a remarkable prose translation into colloquial English by some English schoolmaster.[1] Everything is predicted, every child or man or woman who heard the ancient bard recite knew what was going to happen before it happened—and they must have held their breaths, waiting for it to happen. And what happened? Death. That is all that happened: men deliberately approaching death in all the strength and pride while the "gods" sat aside and imitated their passions. I myself thrilled to the story.

Death dominates our world. I am amazed at the way my friends go about acting as if they were not doomed. They seem to want to ignore it, to entertain themselves with any play of wit, at the highest potential, some *South Pacific*. What is there else to do to keep from thinking of that other? There's nothing dramatic about that. Then you see what Merton did, became a half-assed monk. Or what Mr. Eliot did—went on writing books! Books! as if they had some hope of them.

We have a carved East Indian mask that was given to us by a sailor friend of one of my sons. We have it hanging in our front room. It's partly covered by a curtain at one of our front windows. I saw it last night while I was sitting listening to some music. It came to life, complacent before death, complete peace. It was a lesson to me—and no dogma to soften the blow. It had the peace before violent death that is in the *Iliad*, and the consciousness, the complete consciousness, before it that is in the heroes of Greek legend. . . .

To copy nature is a spineless activity; it gives us a sense of our mere existence but hardly more than that. But to imitate nature involves the verb: we then ourselves become nature, and so invent an object which is an extension of the process. The *Iliad* is a pure invention; the *Odyssey* is another. The *Divine Comedy* is another, though I reject it for the mist it invents to hide death from the

---

[1] W. H. D. Rouse.

eye which has bred that entire execrable horde of "the church."
In the *Iliad* the air is clear; there is no interested fog between the
words and the senses.

WILLIAMS

191: To Louis Martz

[*Prof. Louis Martz of Yale was at this time helping to edit* The
Yale Poetry Review.]

May 27, 1951

Dear Martz: I am astonished at and overhelmed by your kindness.
I had not anticipated such attention, such a reading of my slowly
developing viewpoint until after, at long last, I had myself been
able to bring myself into focus, not until perhaps I should long
have been dead. I cannot enough thank you for having made the
effort to gather up a meaning from my piecemeal and often rambling work. I realize fully that I have not been able to state
clearly enough, articulately enough, what I have to say and that
it is a duty which everyone (who reads me) has a right to expect
of me. I feel inadequate in that I have not done better. But you
have gone to some pains (I hope you have been justified) in dig-
ging up the meaning from the impedimenta. That is why I speak
of what you have done as a kindness. I do not imply any humility.

I have been ill, as you perhaps have heard. This is the second
time I have been knocked out. But this time I seem to have come
out of it with a clearer head. Perhaps it derived from a feeling
that I might have died or, worse, have been left with a mind
permanently incapacitated. That it has not happened is a piece
of pure good fortune. As a result of the enforced idleness and
opportunity for thought, it may be, I have brought hard down
on the facts of a situation which can no longer be delayed in the
bringing of it to a final summary. I must now, in other words,
make myself clear. I must gather together the stray ends of what
I have been thinking and make my full statement as to their meaning or quit.

Fortunately for me, there are men (and women) like yourself of good will whose statements give me a pattern to follow. You give me confidence. The first effect is in the writing itself. I begin to see what I have been after, by evidence of the sense of smell mostly, but which now is coming more and more into view. Verse form, the actual shape of the line itself, must be as it is the first visible thing. I'm finally getting to understand what I want to do. Such writing as yours supports me. There is also my recent reading (at all angles, from a prose translation of the *Iliad* by W. H. D. Rouse, to articles in the *New Mexico Quarterly* and elsewhere). I have been able to "place" the new in its relation to the past much more accurately. We have been looking for too big, too spectacular a divergence from the old. The "new measure" is much more particular, much more related to the remote past than I, for one, believed. It was a natural blunder from the excess of our own feelings, but one that must now be corrected. I see clearer now. I cannot tell you how much the encouragement of a man writing with your deep feeling for the rightness of my attempts means to me.

For there is not only a rightness in what must be done toward a new understanding (and practice) of the metric, but there is a new sensitivity that is required. We are through with the crude "fight" we have had to wage. Our position is now established, the approach must be more an inversion upon ourselves, we must now forget the external enemy, we must more question ourselves— a thing we didn't have time for formerly. Here is where your own delicacy of understanding and wit comes into play. You have thought it worth your while to take pains to study my texts. No one has done that. Most have put me down for a rough sort of blindman, who out of resentment against certain practices of the accepted schools of thought has gone wild with resentment and nothing more. At least I survived. You have been studious enough, attentive enough to see under that the real drive—something I myself have often lost sight of—and brought it into the light.

This is the true function of the critic. I applaud you for it and not solely for the reason that I have profited by the exercise of your talents. . . .

What will come of my "idleness," which has been forced on me by my illness, it is hard to say. Will I be able to maintain it? I should passionately like to use it for the further development of my reading and my thinking and my doing if I can. I don't want to go back to the practice of medicine. The opportunity to complete my task as a poet has never seemed so hopeful and attractive as now. I hope the next few months can convince me that I can survive and do nothing but think, read and write.

On June 18 I shall read a new 17-page poem[1] at Harvard for the Phi Beta Kappa ceremonial at the Sanders Theatre. It is an important event for me. Since my illness I have been working on it. It has taken up most of my spare time. I wish you were going to be there to hear it, but if you can't make it I will send it to you later. Whether rightly or wrongly, I feel that many of my culminating ideas as to form have entered into this poem. We shall see. Thank you for the spiritual assistance you have been to me in this work.

Sincerely yours,
WILLIAMS

My typing is as you see atrocious.

192: To NORMAN MACLEOD

June 11, 1951

Dear Norm: . . . My own autobiography is now being set up. I'll see galleys in a week or so—the lawyers have been holding us up a little in their search for possible libel. I don't think they'll find anything. I appreciate what you say, Norm, about my writing; I hope this script will prove worth reading. I told it in the only way I could tell it, in a series of incidents as I lived them. I didn't say much of the lives of others except as they briefly knocked against mine. Thus many names have been left out. It isn't a story of the times during which I lived. It is as though I were a trout living in the water of my own stream, shut away in its waters, only rarely breaking the surface. I hope it will interest someone. I have no confidence that many will follow me into that world. But it

---

[1] *The Desert Music.*

was a good experience to put it down. I am most interested in the 3d part. I have not philosophized. Trivial incidents may seem just trivial. . . .

You can see by my typing that I'm not too sure of myself as yet. I'm not practicing medicine, just sitting around at home, seeing a very limited number of people (I can't talk much without tiring) and going nowhere. I pound away at the writing, I'd go crazy otherwise. I try to keep up previous commitments. For instance, I am going to Harvard at the invitation of Phi Beta Kappa to read a "15-minute" poem at their Annual Literary Celebration on June 18. It has taken me a month or more to write it, transcribe it, have it typed, correct it and polish it. That took about all the drive I had. In addition I did an 11-page review of Carl Sandburg's *Complete Poems* for *Poetry Magazine*. Just the last few days I'm again in the clear. I'm going to stay that way for a while thinking up a novel which Random House has ordered.[1] I have to do a lot of thinking about that. It's going to be a job for me. . . .

Sincerely,
BILL

193: To Robert Lowell

1951

Dear Cal: You are very kind. But at any rate it is cheering to me to hear that you enjoyed the fourth book of *Paterson* and that you didn't think I had let the reader down. I couldn't stop to think of the reader, I don't mean that, but at least it's good to know that you found that the theme had not petered out.

That first incident, the charming old Lesbian and the little nurse (the female Paterson) got me into trouble. First, a year ago, Princess Marguerite Caetani turned it down flat when I offered the piece to her for publication in *Botteghe Oscure*. Her comment was merely that it was not my best work. I accepted that with the wry smile that was called for under the circumstances.

---

[1] *The Build-Up*.

But when Marianne Moore went berserk over it, taking me to task in no uncertain terms, I began to smell a rat. The ladies don't like that sort of talk.

Especially the ladies don't like to hear one of their sex mentioned in any but a genteel light; it infuriates them to be told that the Lesbian exists and has a perfect right to exist without their feeling that they, as women, have been denigrated. They don't have to rush to the defense of their sex because a type made famous by one of their greatest participants, Sappho, has been treated as a normal phenomenon. I like the old gal of whom I spoke, she was at least cultured and not without feeling of a distinguished sort. I don't mind telling you that I started writing of her in a satiric mood—but she won me quite over. I ended by feeling admiration for her and real regret at her defeat.

I did not have another heart attack; that member of my anatomical assembly seems to be carrying on as well as can be expected for a man of my years, but this time it was the coco which went off: I had a mild apoplectic stroke. It disabled my right side and knocked out my speech—for a time. I am still affected but not very much. I even gave the Phi Beta Kappa poem at Harvard on June 11. Quite an experience taken all in all. From the faces of some (not all) of the faces of those on the platform I think they must have fumigated Memorial Hall after I left. The student body was, on the other hand, delighted and showed it by their tumultuous applause after I had finished my "15 minute" poem. The Princess is going to print it in *Botteghe Oscure* but only against her better judgment, I feel sure; she has asked me to change "waggled her bare can" to "waggled her buttocks." I consented.

I hope you are having a profitable experience in Europe. I know that you are, you must be profiting, it can't be otherwise. I envy you your opportunity, it is another Odyssey from which, not like some earlier American writers, I hope to see you return to your Penelope (American) much enriched in your mind and ready to join your fellows here in pushing forward the craft. You can bring great riches to us or you can ignore us; it's your choice. But I wouldn't be myself if I didn't say that I look forward to your return. I think you are keeping your original frame of reference and not junking it. That, at least, is how I look at you and what I crave from you. Come back enriched in experience but come back; do not allow yourself to be coaxed away from us. I say this not for myself, after all, but for you. No one else has done that since John Adams voyaged in Spain—the trend has always been toward denial of origins, assertion of origins is the more fertile basis for thought—and technique. Greece should have been a revealing experience. The new world witnessed from the stones of the Theatre of Dionysius should have been a profitable experience.

I spoke at Bread Loaf this week. Robert Frost who lives on the premises did NOT come to hear me.

Norman Pearson has his summer place near our little shack on the shore at West Haven. Or rather he had his place on the other side of New Haven from this shabbier suburb of Yale. We went to visit him there a week ago. I have been here with Flossie, may I add, for a little rest at the shore (my God how it's raining today!) —it is a very small harbor made by huge knobs of granite, sculptural and bare jutting into the waters of the Sound. An isolated, primitive piece of original America such as you would not expect to find so near one of our eastern coastal cities. There we found the children of English relatives of his wife, spending the summer in the States: descendants of the Darwins, the Huxleys and, a generation further back, of Trevelyans, all engrossed over the possession of a huge white rabbit—and looking at this American, who had appeared so suddenly among them, as some strange monster!

Oh well and oh well, it will be fun to talk with you when you return.

Sincerely. Best luck.

BILL

194: To Marianne Moore

June 19, 1951

Dear Marianne: It is inevitable that, in the end, individuals, brothers though they be and closely allied as they have lived, will finally arrive at the place where their separate individualities are revealed and they will find themselves strangers. That will be the moment when their love and their faith is most tested. Let it be so with us.

To me the normal world is something which to you must seem foreign. I won't defend my world. I live in it. Those I find there have all the qualities which inform those about them who are luckier. I rather like my old gal who appears in the first pages of *Paterson* IV (if she's one of the things you object to); she has a hard part to play, and to my mind plays it rather well.

As far as the story goes, she represents the "great world" against the more or less primitive world of the provincial city. She is informed, no sluggard, uses her talents as she can. There has to be that world against which the other tests itself.

If the vaunted purpose of my poem seems to fall apart at the end—it's rather frequent that one has to admit an essential failure. At times there is no other way to assert the truth than by stating our failure to achieve it. If I did not achieve a language I at least stated what I would not say. I would not melt myself into the great universal sea (of love) with all its shapes and colors.

But, if I did not succeed on one level, I did cling to a living language on another. The poem, as opposed to what was accomplished in the story, came to life at moments—even when my failure was most vocal and went above that to a different sort of achievement. Or so I believe.

But maybe there's still another level on which I failed. If so, instruct me.

Take care of yourself, there are not many who care about those things that interest you and me beyond our very lives.

Best,

BILL

195: To Marianne Moore

June 23, 1951

Dear Marianne: Yes, when we are overactive, we suffer. I am glad you have learned that lesson even if it cost you a bad time. It

was from overwork on my *Autobiography* that I went under. I
might have died. Poets seem to be tough (though they are left,
sometimes, with the inability to hit the correct keys of their
machines).

I was looking for an image to typefy the impact of "Paterson" in
his young female phase with a world beyond his own, limited in
the primitive, provincial environment. It was the 4th book, the
end was approaching. I didn't want him to "disappear" before
this fulfillment.

It happens that I knew in my personal experience of an instance which contained all the elements that I needed. A distinguished woman, a prominent figure in the New York and international world . . . existed in my consciousness. I had written the
passage a long time before. It seemed to fit perfectly into the poem.

In writing out the passage, this woman, who was at first a mere
symbol, came to life for herself and I forgave her. I even realized
that she has as much reason for being as the cruder counterfoil
that the young nurse provided. All the background for the incident of the fishing concession on Anticosti has existed in my
mind for at least 15 years.

The form, an idyl of Theocritus, a perverted but still recognizable "happy" picture of the past, is there. It is a sad picture today.
It shows a desire to achieve all that we most hope for in the
world. We all share the world together, we none of us possess
it to ourselves. We WANT to share it. Only because we are thwarted
do we fail to achieve our release. But as poets all we can do is
to say what we see and let the rest speak for itself.

I think the technical parts are not limited to the first parts.
I say even that the language is even more sensuous, more convenient to the line, more fits the line in the last book than in
the first. It at least does not deny what was first captured.

The leisure that I have achieved through illness is a precious
thing in that it permits me to talk to my friends, whom I love,
more than I have ever in my life been able to do heretofore.

I have not been able to follow Stevens latterly as well as I
followed him in the past.

Affectionately,

BILL

196: To David McDowell

Wednesday [summer, 1951]

Dear Dave: Floss is sick in bed—getting better. Go up and talk nice to her a minute.

I'm in hospital delivering a baby—her 4th.

The unfinished (alas) script is on the bed in my studio, the "other" room.

Look around and make yourselves comfortable. Go up and see Kitty Hoagland—if you want to.

I'll be back as soon as—shdn't be long, possibly by 10:30. I'll keep in touch by phone.

Lucy will show you the rye, Scotch—water in the tap. Turkey in the straw.

Yrs.
Bill

Whyn't you visit Paterson Falls? 1 hr trip/
(Left for McD. while WCW was absent.)

197: To Kathleen Hoagland

201 Ocean Ave. West Haven, Conn.
July 23, 1951

Dear Kitty: I had better luck than you did; in the cottage next to us I noticed a fairly young woman rather attractive in appearance and with a definitely cultivated speaking voice. Naturally I had to find out who she was, her infant son is all over the place walking along the top of our sea wall which gave me a good excuse. Hearing her call the little man, Florence had already decided that she was a schoolteacher.

She is Irish Catholic, the wife of a professor at the University of Chicago, Livio C. Stecchini, who lectures on Greek and Roman Civilization, a dark-skinned, balding man, but tall and very sure of himself, who was away at the time. He returned later in the week. He speaks with a strong foreign accent but he is a remarkably well-informed, thoroughly well-informed, thoroughly well-read and unrestrainedly straight-thinking person, who has already given me one of his only poems to read and correct (for language). He also gave me the 4-page synopsis of his next project, a treatise on the origins of Greek culture in the change from an original matriarchy to the patriarchy which underlay the development of the intellectual achievements. I read it twice to myself and once aloud to Floss. He has got hold of the productive theme of major importance. I wish him luck. After we return from Bread Loaf we're going to have a reading in their cottage before I return home. Intellectuals have come out of their hiding places all along this portion of the shore like crabs from under the rocks that Bill Wellcome turns over in clearing the bathing beach in front of the cottage.

Our first week was a great one for little Suzanne. She was in the water every moment that it was possible for her to be there. We took turns watching her. Floss calls her Butter Ball and I am sure it's a good name for she never seems to feel cold. I have never had a small female in my immediate care; they are little different, in one way, from any other undifferentiated brat whose purpose in life it is to have his own way—and she is stubborn and resourceful as any other mule, but in another way the female sticks out all over. She'd go naked as willingly as not, stands in the open doorway to change into her bathing suit and only when we supply the caution that she is not to undress before the boys shows any modesty. How I hate to have to be the one to supply that contemptible artificial note.

I have read the *Odyssey*; I borrowed it from the Stecchinis—it is part of his material for study (I had read this translation of the *Iliad* in the hospital this spring) and part of Suetonius' *Lives of the Caesars.* Isn't it strange that I should now be so much interested in these classic books and then blindly run smack into a classic scholar at the shore in Connecticut?

On the other hand, I've done no writing myself. Floss and I did have one good talk last evening about her family life in preparation for what I intend to do in going on with the *White Mule* series but that is all.

Tomorrow we leave for Vermont for the talk at Bread Loaf on

Wednesday, then home on Thursday, visiting little Paul on the way, and home again on Monday the 30th. Dave McDowell, wife and bambino, were here last Sunday with the Kirgos. I had a note from him saying the Princess Caetani had accepted the Harvard poem for publication in *Botteghe Oscure* but she hasn't written to me about it so I'm not sure. We visited Norman Pearson at his summer home north or east of New Haven last week, a very beautiful spot on the coast, occupied by the houses of five sisters, one of them married to an Englishman, a relative of the Trevelyans, Darwins, Huxleys. Their children on the grounds, visiting American cousins for the summer, were interested in a white rabbit! We also visited Zukofsky and Patchen at Old Lyme and Ann Dull and her family at Essex.

I'm exhausted with all this one-finger typing, that's all the news anyway. Hope Clayton is able to get some peace for his sketching and that you may find some other amusement to get you some rest. Best to both of you from us both

Yours as ever,

Bill

[*Sister M. Bernetta Quinn, O.S.F., had written* "William Carlos Williams: A Testament of Perpetual Change," *the best study of* Paterson *in print, for* Publications of the Modern Language Association.]

198: To Sister Bernetta

August 23, 1951

My dear Sister Bernetta:

(1) leave a part for the irrational
(2) trim the concluding 8 pages—repetitious
(3) the rest has about it that rare element enthusiasm
(4) where are you going to publish it?

The above are notes I made while reading your thesis, which has about it something of second sight. For instance, your understanding of the use of "silly" in the first line of the first part of Book 4 is extraordinary. It is the same use Coleridge makes of it in *The Ancient Mariner* when he speaks of the "silly" buckets on the deck.

Your reference, at the end, to *The Wanderer* astonishes me. I had no idea that anyone would take the trouble to investigate my origins. You have gone to great pains to read your references. I congratulate you on your thoroughness and devotion. I am proud that you have thought it worthwhile to do such a piece of work on the poem. Certainly it frightens me to see, rather than how obscure it is to others' minds, how clear it is to you. It shows me that since someone has looked discerningly into its motivations then others *may* see as much. In other words, it is there to be seen.

Certainly I thank you.

You realize, of course, being a Catholic, that I am not a Catholic. Yet you have not once taken advantage of your position to lay imputations against me. I find that tremendously impressive. And don't think I do not see places where you could have done so and were perhaps tempted to do so. But you haven't done it. It is a great virtue.

Referring back to what I said at the beginning, one fault in modern compositions such as——(name it yourself) is that the irrational has no place. Yet in life (you show it by your tolerance of things which you feel no loss at not understanding) there is much that men exclude because they do not understand. The truly great heart *includes* what it does not at once grasp, just as the great artist includes things which go beyond him. Perhaps, if you understand what I mean, you and I share something bigger than ourselves when we are tolerant—each of the other—as I have seen you to be. The irrational enters the poem in those letters, included in the text, which do not seem to refer to anything in the "story" yet do belong somehow to the poem—how, it is not easy to say.

The last 8 pages need revision. Perhaps a severe cutting would be most useful. You repeat yourself several times. Cut, cut, cut, cut.

Go over that part over and over again. Cut it to the bone, it will improve all you have so well said in your exposition.

Best luck to you. I feel extremely grateful for your discernment. Even if the poem were now lost I should be satisfied: it CAN be understood.

Sincerely,
WILLIAM CARLOS WILLIAMS

199: To David McDowell

Oct. 17, 1951

Dear Dave: Here's this for the Chi. *Trib.* Hope you like it. Send it to them for me, please.

Finished 6 pages for Romano. It's being typed today. I'll give it to him as soon as it's finished. Hope he likes it.

That will leave only the 800 words for Sterling North to be done next week.

Then, be Jazes, I ain't gonna do any more special articles till after Christmas or until I can slap out some more chapters of the novel.

Letters take a hell of a lot of time.

Never did get to see the Scribner's window but I heard it looked good.

Now the full moon's past I'll be able to quiet down again, I always get stirred up when there's a new moon. Must be my ovaries.

Nice weather,
BILL

1952

Jan. 23, 1952

Dear Ken:

> Your iambs are wasted on me
> redundant, excessive but still
> since you labor the point, I shall see
> if Floss will not send you a bill

I damned near DIED reading my 10 pages to the wolves.[1] I could hear them growling before I had got half way down the first page. I was nervous enough as it was, I had not taken a cocktail, thinking I'd keep my tongue free, I didn't eat what was on my plate, but as the pressure mounted my old heart began to torment itself until it was a painful lump in my chest. I had to grit my teeth and grind out the words from a parched throat.

They wanted to kill me. That Irishman, [Francis] Hackett, former editor of the *New Republic,* I think, was the only one who defended me at least vocally. It was a stand-off otherwise; half the guys went away scowling, the other grinning. I felt better as soon as I had finished the reading.

Ho hum,
BILL

March 11, 1952

Dear Cal: A very discerning and friendly letter. Thank you for it, it has changed my attitude toward Eliot more than anything I have ever read of him. I accept him now for what he is, I have

---

[1] The National Institute.

never been willing before to do that. He is a "strong man" of letters, unrelated to the scene. Surely he knocked us higher than a kite in the early days. But we shouldn't have resented him; no doubt, if he could, he would have joined us, at least in what we intended. But we were so weakly based, so uncertain of everything, that a mere breeze could capsize us—and did. The longer wave takes him in its rise, but we couldn't have known that while the battle was on.

I'm glad you recognized my affection for Pound and saw what I intended to make known of him. He too was an orchid in my forest, he had no interest, really, for my trees, no more than did Eliot. They both belonged to an alien world, a world perhaps more elevated than mine, more removed from my rigors. I have always felt as if I were sweating it out somewhere low, among the reptiles, hidden in the underbrush, hearing the monkeys overhead. Their defeats were my defeats, I belonged to them more than to a more mobile world. . . .

Holland is an extraordinary place for you to have written from. I am interested that you have connected it in your mind with our colonial period. New Jersey was particularly marked by those early settlers. I remember Holland as a place through which I passed in 1910. I remember the museums and the coffee (and chocolate) houses as well as the beach at Schlevingen (?) out of season and a little fishing village at one end of it. I also remember a girl with her "mother" who whistled to me from across a canal. What strange things we remember, they must have been important to us. That one was to me then.

Especially I'm glad you wrote, in that you wrote. So it's another year for you in Europe. I'm writing a novel;[1] it's a novel, as usual, about my local scene (the scene is merely what I know). I want to write some prose fiction and not to tell anyone anything about today. I want to write it so that when I speak of a chair it will stand upon four legs in a room. And of course it will stand upon a four-legged sentence on a page at the same time.

I haven't written a poem in a year. I've become interested in a young poet, Allen Ginsberg, of Paterson—who is coming to personify the place for me. Maybe there'll be a 5th book of

---

[1] *The Build-Up.*

Paterson embodying everything I've learned of "the line" to date. Eliot could have saved me many years with that had he been willing to remain here and put his weight behind the working of the thing out. Pound helped at the beginning and has, it must be said, not weakened. Both Pound and Eliot have been faithful artists, both have refused to weaken. When Eliot says that new work (he was referring to the poetic drama, I think) cannot be written in iambic pentameters, he is hewing to the line. They are both top men in the craft. But I must go beyond that.

I must make the new meter out of whole cloth, I've got to know the necessity back of it. I am not driven by the search for personal distinction, I don't want to appear in person. But I want to see the unknown shine, like a sunrise. I want to see that overpowering mastery that will inundate the whole scene penetrate to that last jungle. It can be detected in the remote province of a Paterson as well as elsewhere.

I wish I could go to Ischia next year. Auden offered me or us his villa there, but I did not take him up. I am a little afraid of it, but it would be marvellous if we could get ourselves to do it.

Have a successful summer at Salzburg, it is a beautiful place. I particularly remember the Schloss, the snails on the bushes as we climbed the ramp there, the fish in the river and all that. It was a superb May 1st.

It was a delight to hear from you.

Sincerely,
BILL

202: TO DAVID McDOWELL

May 5, 1952

Dear Dave: I'm happy that the novel[1] pleased you in the first part; let's hope the interest continues to rise, as it should to the end. The check was very welcome.

I'm coming on. Some days during the last three weeks (for some unknown reason) I felt as if I was about to cash in my chips—

---

[1] *The Build-Up.*

and there was nothing that would have pleased me more. But now I have moments when life seems worthwhile again and I feel ashamed of myself. When I shall be able to see normally again I'll be cured. It's hard for me to be patient, and it's now that I need it. One day it goes well but my eyes suddenly jump out of focus and with that my mind goes also. It's a slow readjustment of all my faculties which for some unknown reason said good-bye; the word that Floss gave me that the novel would do was great food to my spirit. Thank you.

It's hell to be hit where you least expect it and to go down so unexpectedly low. I was all washed up. What do you do with people like that, drown 'em?

Cheerio, the come-back is slow but—now YOU take care of yourself and get some rest, because as young as you are it can (they tell me) happen to anybody. Best to Madeline[2]—tell her it was a big boost to me to know that she liked the book, she first!

Best,
BILL

203: To DAVID MCDOWELL

June 24, 1952

Dear Dave: I've really interpreted your silence as deference to me. Hope I'm right. This has been one hell of an illness, this nervous instability. I hope you are spared it forever and a day. It saps your marrow, it really does. It's a terrific drain too on the forbearance of a devoted wife and friends. And God knows you need your friends. I need mine, all of them. A man fears everything in the world and out of it, in heaven and in hell. I tell you the poets are not dreamers; they know what they are and what they are talking about is a living hell.

I'm coming out of it now, little by little, but there's no question I hurdled a few of the fences. I drove to Boston and saw Merrill Moore there (as psychiatrist). He was of considerable help to me, quite a guy. I delivered a talk at Brandeis and have since been

---

[2] Mrs. McDowell.

crowned with a Litt. D. at the University of Pennsylvania (last Wednesday). So I have not been idle. Now I have to complete arrangements for going to Washington the middle of September to be the consultant in poetry at the Library of Congress. Conrad Aiken was here for a conference yesterday for breakfast and I see Luther Evans, the Librarian, sometime during the week.

I'd love to see you again to hear what's happening to the book.[1] Perhaps the day I see Evans in the city I could run over with Floss (my constant companion these days) and have a talk with you. Well, Dave, let's hear a word from the horse's mouth—I ain't used to this neglect.

Love and kisses,
BILL

[*John Holmes, professor of English at Tufts College, is one of the many university teachers and creators who changed WCW's opinion about the deadening influence of the academies. Mr. Holmes met WCW first at the home of Charles Abbott.*]

204: To JOHN HOLMES

May 27, 1952

Dear John: I was genuinely glad to see you at Trinity, for if ever a man was in a position to understand another who finds himself unstable and unsure of his world, I am now in that position. It is only by persistent effort that I go on.

Your poem pleases me. It is, as with all you write, sensitively balanced. The perception and the statement of the feeling of rain with its vaguely felt mood of depression reaches one effectively. It is too near me right now for me to say I enjoy it; I do not. But my acknowledgement that the poem is well done is enough.

What shall we say more of the verse that is to be left behind by the age we live in if it does not have some of the marks the age has made upon us, its poets? The traumas of today, God knows,

---

[1] *The Build-Up.*

are plain enough upon our minds. Then how shall our poems escape? They should be horrible things, those poems. To the classic muse their bodies should appear to be covered with sores. They should be hunchbacked, limping. And yet our poems must show how we have struggled with them to measure and control them. And we must SUCCEED even while we succumb. . . .

Good luck to you, John, your mind is an able but impressionable one. I hope you survive to wrestle through to whatever victory a man can get over the world.

Sincerely,
BILL

(Enclosure in letter to John Holmes)
Here's something I woke up reciting one of the mornings I was at the Abbotts. This is the first time I've released it, at whose peril? (My typing brain is getting more and more uncertain as I grow older.) Is it a new paresis?

A TRIPLE TOAST

Here's to the baby
May it thrive
And here's to the labiae
That rive

To give it place
In a stubborn world
And here's to the peak
From which the seed was hurled

I think the woggling of the tenses and from the general to the specific can be absorbed without injury to the structure.

BILL

1953

[*Richard Eberhart, poet, professor, and business man, has had a distinguished career, gaining several awards for poetry, and teaching at leading colleges.*]

205: To Richard Eberhart

5/14/53

Dear Dick: I have before me your letter of last March, enclosing two poems upon which you ask me to comment. But first I want to be sure that you know all that has happened to me in recent months. Oh well, now that I come to tell it there seems not much to tell except that I was in a hospital which the less I speak of the more I am pleased. But I'm home again now and though I'm not yet cured I'm much better. When the old bean goes wrong it apparently takes time to put it to rights again. Meanwhile I've done quite a bit of writing, prose and verse, and for some of it I've even on occasion got a publisher. I am very limited as to what I can do, but as long as I can do something I must be content.

As to the verses which you sent me my feelings are somewhat mixed. I like very much the poem "To Evan," which with its use of refrain is very moving. It has about it the sense of recurrence, as much as to say, this has happened before and it will happen again and such is the fate of man and how beautiful and inevitable and sad it is. This is in the spirit of the Greek epitaph, a spirit which is wholly resigned and so at peace. The beauty of the verse is its only excuse for being so that you make it as sensuously beautiful as you can make it. The catch in the voice should not be too apparent.

Of the other poem I am not so sure. I am, as you know, a stickler for the normal contour of phrase which is characteristic of the language as we speak it. It gives to a poem a distinction which it can get in no other way. For the most part you respect that rule

317

but sometimes you appear to forget it, and it is easy to forget it with results which are not good.

It is hard to say what makes a poem good, but if it is not in the detail of its construction it is in nothing. If the detail of the construction is not to the smallest particular distinguished, the whole poem might as well be thrown out. And when you invert a phrase, even such an innocuous phrase as "great are" or "quietly I" or "violated is," the effect is for me disastrous. The thought that you CAN do such a thing makes me look for it to occur in other places. The exercise which comes to you in fighting the phrase to make it obey your orders always pays off.

The second half of the long second poem is verbose in any case, there are few telling images in it anyway, and the pace of it is not varied enough. You asked for it, and I thought I might as well give it to you straight. But that doesn't mean a thing except that it is not one of your good poems.

Time flies! Best love to Betty and the kids. Take care of yourself.

BILL

[*Oswald LeWinter was another of the multitude of young poets who appealed to WCW for assistance. Retired from the practice of medicine, WCW experienced no falling off in interest in literature. In the* Autobiography, *WCW noted that he had tried to answer every letter written him: after his stroke he still accomplishes this, writing on an electric typewriter, the gift of his former colleagues on the staff of the Passaic General Hospital.*]

206: TO OSWALD LEWINTER

10/10/53

Dear Oswald: Thanks for letting me see the poems, I like them, I like some of them very much indeed. It is hard to say why I like some of them less than the others, but since it is a critic's business to know what he is talking about, I shall try to make myself clear.

I like the one entitled "In a Lost Year: Mayan Ruins" the best, but not "I Caught a Boy," both because of its title which is unfortunate and a tinge of sentimentality which seems to be inherent in it. The handling of the material annoys me; it would have been enough to describe with gusto how "the boy" was lost without any regrets or moralizing. "A short life and a merry one" should have been your theme.

This latter poem must have been written some time ago, and the first one I spoke of shows more technical adroitness, it is more objective; it doesn't fall into the machine, in other words. Do you know what I mean by "it doesn't fall into the machine?" I mean that you do not become involved, too intimately involved, in your subject but hold it away from you as an artist should always do. An artist should always speak in symbols even when he speaks most passionately; otherwise his vision becomes blurred. He has to hold his objects away from him to be able to see them clearly. There is a story about the great French actor, Coquelin, in point. Once he was asked about a famous part that he had just played. The one who was speaking to him was full of praise. "No," said Coquelin, "I didn't do so well tonight, I felt the part too much and became lost in it." An artist, even at his most impassioned, has to hold himself aloof. The reason is that his brain must remain clear to look all around his subject, emotion must be kept always under control.

Now, if I have made myself clear on that point, we can go ahead. The more casually you speak, using a conversational tone, the better. When the language becomes rhetorical you are lost. Describe objects in your poems as if you are looking at them, not as if you are merely thinking of them—unless you are using metaphor, and then you have to make it plain what is meant. "The Mayan Ruins" represents one extended metaphor freely handled which gives you SPACE, within the metaphor, to maneuver to go about at will. It's a good poem, well handled. Has it been printed? If not try *Imagi* in Baltimore or the *New Mexico Quarterly*, John Husband is the Poetry Editor, tell him I like the poem. The magazine *Poetry* is also a good bet. Karl Shapiro is the editor. . . .

"An Inner Monologue of Dmitri Karamazov" is not especially my meat but I can see that it means much to you. It is good too. You might, if you think it worthwhile, try recasting it more formally as loose quatrains. Just write it out that way on the page and see what happens, the same lines and the same division of the lines divided into units of four. It may give you a new slant on the metric of the thing, make it more of a COMPOSITION, make it less *felt* and more a matter of the sound of the thing. I warn you not to get rhetorical, keep the conversational tone.

I can't always go into a group of poems in this way but I found that you appealed to me, your life and the way you have not let it influence what you think and decide to do. More power to you. That I am apprehensive for you goes without saying, you will not let that influence you which is as it should be.

Too bad you can't get a job on the docks; that would be temporary relief at least. Troubles all through life you will find never come singly.

I am glad I met you and hope to see you soon again. Joe is lucky in finding something to keep her busy. I hope you find something in the enclosed screed to interest you.

Sincerely yours,
WILLIAMS

207: To Richard Eberhart

Oct. 23, 1953

Dear Dick: I remember when Ezra Pound first went to London and met Yeats, Yeats asked him what he, Ezra, thought of his, Yeats' poems. Ezra was forced to say that he admired them greatly, as was the truth, but that they were marred by a deforming inversion of the phrase which was deplorable. Yeats at once set about correcting the defect and worked diligently at it for several years. The evidence of it appears in many of his finest pieces.

But the style of the older man had been set long and if, as you say, he reverted to the use of inversions in an abnormal contour of the phrase in his last work you can put it down to a dominance of a measure to which he had become accustomed and which he did not find it easy to escape.

What Pound did not realize, nor Yeats either, is that a new order had dawned in the make-up of the poem. The measure, the actual measure, of the lines is no longer what Yeats was familiar with. Or Pound either, except instinctively. Hopkins, in a constipated way with his "sprung" measures, half realized it but not freely enough. To escape the prosiness of the lines or the threat of prosiness in the line, the foot has to be expanded to make a freer handling of the measure possible. That's what Yeats was up against without realizing it. It had him restless under the restrictions of criticism. It makes you restless under the same restrictions. You, as Yeats was, are dominated by a concept of the line which comes from an old (pre-Whitman) prosody which stems from traditional English (and French, German, Scandinavian, Russian, Chinese and perhaps Greek) verse. Only in the present day are we beginning to realize how it restricts us. It restricts our lives as well to be measured after the standard and so, unless we become aware of it, our poems rather than freeing, as they should do, throw us back on old modes of behavior.

Whitman with his so-called free verse was wrong: there can be no absolute freedom in verse. You must have a measure but a relatively expanded measure to exclude what has to be excluded and to include what has to be included. It is a technical point but a point of vast importance. The question of the inversion or refusal to invert our poetic phrases is locked up in that. . . .

With all the love in the world,

BILL

208: TO SRINIVAS RAYAPROL

10/26/53

Dear Seena: The poem which I enclose is one of my recent ones. I expect to have a book of them published in February.[1] All will be made after the same fashion, an assembly of three-line groups arranged after a pattern which offers the artist, with much freedom of movement, a certain regularity. I hope you see the advantages which it offers. Do you know the work of René Char? I am impressed with his completely relaxed address to the words, the luxuriance of his imagination, yet the sobriety of his intelligence

---

[1] *The Desert Music.*

and mood. He is a man who adopts any form or no form at all with perfect indifference, writing regularly lines which scan perfectly or not according to the occasion, whatever it is. I envy and at the same time salute and love him. I wish I were more like him, but how he has survived the bruising existence he has been through and come out from it sweet in disposition with his love for humanity undimmed is more than I can say. It is the best of France itself that has survived. He has no doubt found it necessary to write to keep his mind undimmed. The forms his verse take do not satisfy but then I understand how important to him is escape from any form at all; a man has to be well anchored to occupy that position.

Mrs. Williams sends your wife and you her best wishes. It is inconceivable for us to imagine your life in India, the only thing that presents us with any conception of the place is that wonderful picture on the screen, *The River,* which I saw twice a year or two ago. The address, 9 Ridge Road, still exists, although last winter was so warm that we had almost no snow and it looks as if this winter will be the same. Recently we have had quite a drought, so that the reservoirs are almost dry and hunters have been forbidden to go into the woods for fear of starting forest fires. The whooping crane, a large bird, almost extinct, is expected in his winter feeding grounds in Arkansas any day this week. Don't be so concerned with your fate.

Good luck with the Grove Press Conference. If you have something to say either in the short story or a poem send it along but don't try to please a newspaper. Your soul should go to sleep and hope, when you wake up, to be refreshed. It is the country for it. I'll look for a photo of myself and one also from Charles Sheeler (correctly spelt!) as soon as I can find them.

Take care of yourself. Your passionate desire to enjoy once again on Broadway a good helping of spaghetti and meatballs almost made me weep for you; there was enough to wring the heart at so poignant a memory of anchovy pizzas. Cheer up, cheer up, cheer up! A week-end in the great city by plane would cure that in quick fashion—all you need—you know what you need. Mr. Laughlin can supply it very readily. Best Luck.

BILL

1954

[*Ralph Nash was an editor of* Perspective *of Washington University when he wrote "The Use of Prose in* Paterson," *(Autumn, 1953), which so pleased WCW.*]

209: To Ralph Nash

January 20, 1954

My dear Ralph Nash: When I read, or had read to me, your article on my use of prose in my poem, *Paterson,* I was left speechless. It has taken me until now to re-establish my equilibrium so that I feel only now in a trustworthy mood to write to you. You have penetrated to a secret source of whatever power I possess and it has frightened me. Fright was my first impression and that also stopped me cold because one does not like to be laid bare that anyone that runs may read! I felt that my very hairs were moving on my head, actually I felt my scalp move.

For no one to the present moment has so looked within me, if anyone has been interested in me enough to make the attempt, to discover why I have used prose as I have used it. But the point for me is that I have not myself gone sufficiently beyond instinct, very often, to discover the reasons. It is too deep-seated for that and goes to the very core of why I am a writer. You have laid me bare, as I say, for whatever I am worth, and at the same time re-inforced in me the feeling that I am worth something, a feeling which very often the world of my contemporaries tends to break down. It has been a revelation which, as I say, is frightening.

I shall have to study the distinction you make between your observation of what I have done, for it strikes me as on the whole so just and acute an observation of my style that I still can't believe it. You have got right down into the reasons which lie behind it. A man must, without relinquishing any of the reasons for the poetry with which he surrounds himself and with which the great of this world, at their most powerful, surround

323

him, fight his way to a world which breaks through to the actual. This has always been my most pressing concern, not always clearly envisioned but there nevertheless. It has always stood between me and Ezra Pound for instance. In my reference to Hipponax, the Greek in *Paterson,* you can again see it breaking out. You have spotted it in my insistence on the use of prose *within the poem itself* when I did not see the reasons so clearly and that's why I think it so remarkable.

What the secret reasons are for this I still do not see very clearly, but that it has a reason and an important one you have made or begun to make clear by your inspired and clinching analysis. This I know, that it goes deep. It has much to do with the whole of poetry, and what must be its place, its modern place, in our world, which is not its classic place, I have striven to emphasize as best I could; but something closer to us and more important to us besides, I have been much impressed by what you have put down.

Sincerely yours,

W. C. WILLIAMS

210: To EZRA POUND

April 12, 1954

Dear Ez: Ain't it enuf that you so deeply influenced my formative years without your wanting to influence also my later ones? A united front against the goons from the "academy" might be an attractive program but, frankly, interests me at the present time almost not at all. Cal Lowell is a man I respect and for whom I feel a strong bond of sympathy, but he don't need either you or me to further him in his career. In fact our presence would only hamper him in what he has to do. Leave him alone.

As far as advice is concerned relating to the present stage of your career I have almost none to give. You are a reader, a man who has looked into almost every book that exists, while I at best have been a very imperfect reader. Any book, any serious reading, that I could suggest wouldn't interest you and yet you might look into some treatise on modern medicine—the antibiotics for instance and something of the psychotherapeutic phases. The modern treatment of tuberculosis is also interesting.

We have just finished reading *Lelia,* Maurois' recently published biography of George Sand, and found it both interesting and amusing. It gives a slant to a complex life of a woman of the world which is really a triumph, a triumph of perception. It is humane too and well written. Books we have always kept in our library are two slight novels written many years ago called *High Wind in Jamaica* and—not a novel at all but an "account"—called *Viva Mexico*. Both of them are really amusing.

But I know that isn't what you want. What you want is something to help break down the barriers to ignorance. There's a Welsh poet named Jones to whom we have just given, by we I mean the National Institute of Arts and Letters, the Loines award. It's a poem. Believe me, if you want something tough but rewarding, tackle that. Some publishing firm in England publishes it or write to Felicia Geffen of the Institute mentioning my name and she can get it for you. I've forgotten the name of the work but it was too much for me.

Sorry not to be of more assistance to you in your quest of the Golden Fleece, but that is all at the moment I can offer. Best to Dorothy.

As always,
Bill

211: To Richard Eberhart

May 23, 1954

Dear Dick: Glad to hear from you. But sorry to hear about Betty's illness. The only thing I can add is that it is fortunate that the pneumonia occurred today and not when I was practicing. Today they have means of fighting it that we didn't possess. Glad she's well again.

I have never been one to write by rule, even by my own rules. Let's begin with the rule of counted syllables, in which all poems have been written hitherto. That has become tiresome to my ear.

Finally, the stated syllables, as in the best of present-day free verse, have become entirely divorced from the beat, that is the measure. The musical pace proceeds without them.

Therefore the measure, that is to say, the count, having got rid of the words, which held it down, is returned to the *music*.

The words, having been freed, have been allowed to run all over the map, "free," as we have mistakenly thought. This has amounted to no more (in Whitman and others) than no discipline at all.

But if we keep in mind the *tune* which the lines (not necessarily the words) make in our ears, we are ready to proceed.

By measure I mean musical pace. Now, with music in our ears the words need only be taught to keep as distinguished an order, as chosen a character, as regular, according to the music, as in the best of prose.

By its *music* shall the best of modern verse be known and the *resources* of the music. The refinement of the poem, its subtlety, is not to be known by the elevation of the words but—the words don't so much matter—by the resources of the *music*.

To give you an example from my own work—not that I know anything about what I have myself written:

(count):—not that I ever count when writing but, at best, the lines must be capable of being counted, that is to say, *measured*—(believe it or not).—At that I may, half consciously, even count the measure under my breath as I write.—

(approximate example)

   (1) The smell of the heat is boxwood
       (2) when rousing us
          (3) a movement of the air
  (4) stirs our thoughts
      (5) that had no life in them
        (6) to a life, a life in which

(or)

   (1) Mother of God! Our Lady!
      (2) the heart
        (3) is an unruly master:

(4) Forgive us our sins
    (5) as we
                  (6) forgive
(7) those who have sinned against

Count a single beat to each numeral. You may not agree with my ear, but that is the way I count the line. Over the whole poem it gives a pattern to the meter that can be felt as a new measure. It gives resources to the ear which result in a language which we hear spoken about us every day.

Hope I have been helpful and not confused the issues even more than they were formerly. Write again. Your plans for next year can't be more encouraging.

By the way, may I have a transcript of this letter, as I do not make use of carbon paper.

Best,
BILL

[*E. E. Cummings has known WCW for thirty years or so, but their association has been literarily casual. They share a mutual respect, but they seldom find anything to write about.*]

212: To E. E. CUMMINGS

Sept. 18/54

Dear Cummings: What the hell do I do about this? The *Art Digest* wrote me asking if I would do a review of your paintings and verse for them. I said that I would provided I could see the materials. This is their answer, not very helpful. If you have any suggestions I'd be glad to consider them. I offered, by the way, to go where the paintings were if it was not impossibly distant, but I can't go to Rochester for the view. Are there any reproductions? I did see your show years ago in N.Y., but although I remember a box of strawberries from it, that is not enough to write a detailed review upon.

I hear of you occasionally and read what I encounter of your

prose and verse with the same lively pleasure that I have encountered from you as always. I hope you are well and enjoying
yourself—not at any football games, I trust. If you find the time,
let me hear from you and, if you please, return the enclosed letter.

Sincerely yours,

BILL

[*John C. Thirlwall, editor of these letters, helped to change
WCW's mind about the animosity of professors of English.*]

213: To JOHN C. THIRLWALL

Nov. 30/54

Dear Jack: The fullness of the devastating discovery that my
native language was not English and the significance of that fact
to the mind was slow to dawn on me. For instance, the very transition of the step in the preceding sentence from "America" to
"the mind" has taken me a lifetime. My only excuse for this is
that of all men I have been the first to give it a practical bent—
and to take the consequences. I speak of *belles-lettres* only, but
that field of all fields comprising the scope of the written word is
of all fields the most far reaching and the most jealously guarded.
The violence of my reactions touching what I alone saw to be
the unintelligence of anyone who did not see as I did can be
ascribed only to that: I was shocked at his failure to follow me in
what I knew to be so important an enlightenment and could not
look upon his defection from my party (though there was no
no party at the time) as anything more than treachery.

It began for me as it must always do on the purely physical
plane; I was at the same time, besides being the product of a new
country, a child of a new era in the world, the era which was to
discover among other things the relativity of all knowledge. But
the world about me still clung to the old measurements.

I knew instinctively that it was wrong. My ears were keen; I
sensed it first through my ears, even as a babe in arms. My uncle,
who was a musician, noticed it and spoke of it to my mother:
Listen! he said and began to beat a drum. At a certain point in

the rhythm he would stop sharply and I, to complete the beat, would come in with my, tum tum. I did not have the subtlety of the best Negro drummers, but something fundamental had taken place in me of which I knew nothing. I began in my early twenties to realize that I was dissatisfied with my lot and with my relatives, neighbors and friends who seemed not to understand me when I spoke to them. I loved them and could not understand what it was that was keeping us apart.

The mind's a queer fish. It wants to live; when the air is denied it, it comes to the surface gasping for air, and when it is denied that, it turns on its side on the sand and soon expires. I did not intend to die but thought very often during my youth that my time was short; I was often depressed, for I was early convinced that I had in the compass of my head a great discovery that if I could only get it out would not only settle my own internal conflicts but be of transcendent use to the men and women around me. That it concerned something as evanescent as language I did not for a moment guess.

And yet I should have been more aware of it than I was. I did through my skin sense it, but for it to reach the level of consciousness should not have taken a lifetime. Convention or habit is a tyrannous master; all decency (and that's what makes men rebels) enforces it. Sex is one lead out of our dilemma, and that is why many men take it. That sex is intimately concerned with the rebellious mind is of vast significance, and that few men see its significance leads us to most of the torments of our early youth. It is another of the physical stages of my opening mind through which it had to pass before the flower. . . .

Sincerely yours,

BILL

P.S. I'm tired writing now, as it very much excites me to have the old noggin sound off and I am always interested in what it has to say, but it takes it out of me to have to be so slow in taking it down and as always the gates of my senses get crowded with the press of words and ideas: I have to say "Down Fido!" some time before I tire and run off into drivel. Why not now?

1955

Jan. 13, 1955

Dear Jack: Of recent years I have become more and more aware of a basic change that has come over the way in which our poems must be made. I say "must be made," because it is part of our present situation in the world that when we perceive an alternative to our actions which enlarges the field which they occupy, we feel inevitably impelled to give them the head to go where they are called. We cannot conceive of a world any more without the miracles which astronomy and physics have presented to us. And in aesthetics, the construction of a poem, we shall find ourselves equally bound.

There are leads, when we become aware of them, which point the way to the approaching changes, undoubtedly unwelcome, that have been latent for centuries. The tendency of the race is to resist change violently. At the same time the new presses to be recognized. Which is the most conservative? That which drives us to keep the old or that which seeks a place for us in some slowly, or at times, as in the present, some rapidly evolving new? Certain it is that we have no voice in the matter; we cannot refuse to go forward when the opportunity offers itself. Not to do so is the end of us.

Open to us is only a choice in aesthetic matters of what we prefer; the perfection of a Homeric line (which, by the way, we cannot any longer properly pronounce) or, say, a stanza from one of Villon's ballads. But that is not at all a choice, since all men are agreed that each in its own category is perfection. But when availability for human expression is broached, the structure of the poetic line itself enters the field. That is where aesthetics is mated with physics, to broaden the view.

What word will you employ to bring more meaning to your chosen text? That is the question which must open more avenues to your mind or fail to interest it.

The mind always tries to break out of confinement. It has tried every sort of interest which presents itself, even to a flight to the moon. But the only thing which will finally interest it must be its own intrinsic nature. In itself it must find devices which will permit it to survive—physical transportation to another planet will not help, for it will still be the same mind which has not been relieved by movement.

But in the arts, the art of the poem, lie resources which when we become aware of their existence make it possible for us to liberate ourselves, or so I believe and think, with reason I hope, can be made plain to anyone who will read. We are no longer children; it is in the mind, not on the moon, we must find our relief.

The first thing you learn when you begin to learn anything about this earth is that you are eternally barred save for the report of your senses from knowing anything about it. Measure serves for us as the key: we can measure between objects; therefore, we know that they exist. Poetry began with measure, it began with the dance, whose divisions we have all but forgotten but are still known as measures. Measures they were and we still speak of their minuter elements as feet.

If the measure by which the poem is to be recognized has at present been lost, it is only lost in the confusion which at present surrounds our lives. We don't, any more, know how to measure the lines and therefore have convinced ourselves that they can't be measured.

So what can we do but retreat to some "standard" which we have known in the past and say to ourselves, Beyond this standard you shall not go! That we do not know how to go beyond this standard practice or may not want to go beyond it for conservative reasons is humanly possible. Whole reaches of knowledge with the forms which attach to them, the academies and schools which are frozen into complex pattern, impress our minds and our emotions until we defend them even with our lives, fill the field.

We have our measures of English verse from Beowulf to the present and all the polite prejudices that stem from them but—in spite of their beauty none offers release from our dilemma. A new measure or way of measuring the line is beyond our thoughts.

The first thing that was necessary before we could look beyond the stalemate which had been created by the classic measure was to break it apart. That would be, under our ordinary understanding of the term, to destroy it. That was accomplished (I am speaking of the classically accepted measure,) by Walt Whitman. That he had no clear conception of what he had done is beside the point. A break had been made. He apparently thought that the break was toward some objective known as "freedom" and not, as was actually the case, toward a more *ample* measure.

If the measurement itself is confined, every dimension of the verse and all implications touching it suffer confinement and generate pressures within our lives which will blow it and us apart. It is no matter that we are dealing with a comparatively unnoticed part of the field of our experience, the field of poetics, the result to our minds will be drastic. You cannot break through old customs, in verse or social organization, without drastically changing the whole concept and also the structure of our lives all along the line.

That is merely and magnificently the birth of a new measure supplanting the old—something we hardly hoped to dare.

The realization of what can come about in any of the fields of human interest we must be ready to accept. It may seem presumptive to state that such an apparently minor activity as a movement in verse construction could be an indication of Einstein's discoveries in the relativity of our measurements of physical matter is drastic enough, but such is the fact.

Witlessly, but taking his cue out of the air, Whitman was in his so-called free verse only initiating a new measure. It is to the line, the ancient poetic line, that we have to look for what is to come next. The unit of which the line has in the past been constructed no longer in our minds is permitted to exist. That is the thing which makes poems as they still continue to be written obsolete. A new measure has supplanted the old!

That the foot can no longer be measured as it was formerly but only relatively makes a basic alteration necessary in our plans for it. But measure we must have, as long as we are impelled to know complexities of the world about our ears. The verse I can envisage, a measure infinitely truer and more subtle than that of the past, comes much closer in its construction to modern concepts of reality.

Sincerely yours,

BILL

215: To Henry Wells

1/18/55

Dear Wells: My instinct when Floss had finished reading what you had to say about *Paterson* was to start running, I wanted to put as much distance between myself and a prying world as if they were a pack of bloodhounds and I an escaped slave. I don't trust myself to say much at the present time, it is too close to me. I want very much to want to keep the writing and will return, do return the postage herewith. You have made me your debtor in the most moving and intelligent way that I can conceive. I'll write you again when I can cool down. It's a wonderful piece, I can't say more.

There is no question about it, a publisher must be found. I have no suggestions. *Kenyon* might be the place for it if they offer space enough. If I have any inspirations I'll tell you about them later.

I have never seen a piece like what you have written. I have to say only this: Many years ago I was impressed with the four-sided parallelogram, in short, with the cube. Shifting at once, to save time, the trinity always seemed unstable. It lacked a fourth member, the devil. I found myself always conceiving my abstract designs as possessing four sides. That was natural enough with spring, summer, autumn and winter always before me. To leave any one of them out would have been unthinkable.

I conceived the whole of *Paterson* at one stroke and wrote it down—as it appears at the beginning of the poem. All I had to do after that was to fill in the details as I went along, from day to day. My life in the district supplied the rest. I did not theorize directly when I was writing but went wherever the design forced me to go. Many of the things you say about what I "thought" are true, but I did not think of them in that way. They were there, and I did definitely think and plan them; I knew what I was doing, step by step, but I was so mixed up with the poetic imagination that I was scarcely conscious of what I was about—on a theoretical level. I knew most of the people with which I was in one way or another concerned, and that filled my eyes and my brain and allowed no room for anything else.

I did not have time to "think" and yet I knew that in the end someone would come along, you, would be able with infinite difficulty to follow and explain, and I counted on that and had enough confidence in myself and faith in "you" to be convinced that that effort would be worthwhile.

I couldn't in spite of myself stop myself from putting this much down.

Sincerely yours,
WILLIAMS

216: To JOHN C. THIRLWALL

June 13/55

Dear Jack: . . . The passage from *Paterson* which prompted my solution of the problem of modern verse (which I have long sought) is to be found in Book 2, p. 96, beginning with the line: "The descent beckons." That after having been written several years before, where the implications of the variable foot first struck me. I once mentioned to you privately that "one of the best lines I have ever written" was to be found in another part of *Paterson*. It may be, but the lines that have most influenced my life were those I have just mentioned. As my forthcoming book, *Journey to Love* (probably my last) [*will show*]—

(Written last evening, I had to quit for various reasons.)

As I was saying, the lines that influenced me most were those mentioned above. As far as I know, as my forthcoming book makes clear, I shall use no other form for the rest of my life, for it represents the culmination of all my striving after an escape from the restrictions of the verse of the past.

The rigid impositions imposed on us by the regularly measured foot (which Whitman felt but did not properly know what to do with) are to be understood only when we conceive of it as a fault in the foot itself. With the concept of more liberal interpretation there the difficulties disappear. New problems arise at once but they are at least not those by which we have been so long oppressed.

Gerard Manley Hopkins had a glimmer of what is to be done but he didn't go far enough. Our own Philip Freneau wrote a trenchant essay on verse forms which, due only to our stupid subjection to continental and particularly British models, should be standard reading in all our schools. The history of American prosody shows itself to have been troubled by a concern for something wrong with our acceptance of verse forms handed down to us. Emerson was another in that sequence. Poe was another American poet who was made uneasy by the structure of verses and wrote an essay about its mathematical implications. Most were content to imitate their betters, the asses, and as a consequence wrote slavishly.

The modernists who break their verses into convenient patterns of often incomprehensible jumbles of too abrupt transitions of the sense forget that in all they write the foot remains unaltered. They think to themselves that to be *advanced* in their thought (Freudian it may be or whatever) has nothing to do with the *poetry* of what is being presented. The *structure* of the verse alone is concerned.

As far as "verse" is concerned, it is no more than ineptitude if not an anachronism. The best of it is an instinctive approximation of the principle of the relativistic or variable foot which is at the base of all our striving.

It comes from a concern with a language which has not been taught to us in our schools, a language which has a rhythmical structure thoroughly separate from English. The English of Shakespeare is medieval in the structure of its poetic periods. It is magnificent but outmoded. Were we to submit to the implications of its structure we should, in our way of thinking, be pushed back to the 16th century.

We cannot afford this. We may not think that mere verse can have such an influence on our lives but we can't all be fools just to please the critics.

When Einstein promulgated the theory of relativity he could not have foreseen its moral and intellectual implication. He could not have foreseen for a certainty its influence on the writing of poetry.

All the problems have not as yet been solved, but [*we need*] some sort of measure, some sort of discipline *to free* from the vagaries of mere chance and to teach us to rule ourselves again.

BILL

1956

Jan. 21/56

Dear Sister Bernetta: My wife has just, last night, finished reading to me your *Metamorphic Tradition in Modern Poetry*. It was for us a very moving experience. Naturally, the chapter on myself, with which I was already familiar, came to me like an old friend, but in this setting among the others struck me with new force. The generosity of your treatment of the subject covers that particular and indeed the whole book with a heavenly glow. You reveal yourself to be a religious person by something not easy to isolate and of which you never speak; that, to me, is the book's outstanding characteristic and one which gives it its unique distinction.

You reveal yourself to be a phenomenal reader and not only of the books involved in your thesis but of others covering the whole field of learning. You frighten me that you have read so much and make me envious. But without an intelligence as keen as yours and as understanding a heart nothing would come of it. What has brought you to this small segment of knowledge that concerns the poets of which you write is what concerns me most. What is to happen to that mind and to that interest in the world from this time forward? For it is not to be believed that your judgments are absolute facing a world which in the main is antagonistic to us, for the world does not think we are as important as you think us or as we think ourselves. Are the underlying principles you speak or write of forward-looking enough and solid enough to stand the test of time? Will future generations think of us as good poets?

Your chapter on Jarrell is the most lyrical. It flows with a continuous movement from beginning to end. Both Flossie and I were taken up by it and carried on to its conclusion as if bodily lifted by its enthusiasm. I don't know, however, whether the body of the work quite justifies it—but let us be generous, as you are, and give Jarrell the doubt. Your Pound chapter is admirable, and as for the chapter on myself, I feel *hors de combat,* so that I will not comment on it further except to say that it is the most searching analysis of my purpose and style that I have ever encountered. I don't dare go further, but if I ever have the opportunity to go to that part of the country in which you live, pray give me the opportunity to get to know you better.

Sincerely yours,
WILLIAM CARLOS WILLIAMS

218: TO EZRA POUND

Nov. 21/56

Dear Assen Poop: Don't speak of apes and Roosevelt to me—you know as much of the IMPLEMENTATION of what you THINK you are proposing as one of the Wops I used to take care of on Guinea Hill. YOU DON'T EVEN BEGIN TO KNOW what the problem is. Learn to write an understandable letter before you begin to sound off. You don't even know the terms you're using and have never known them. At least you have found a man in ZWECK 2[1] who is conscious of the DIFFICULTIES and who, unlike you, has an intelligent understanding of those difficulties and how to present them. You're too damned thickheaded to know you're asleep—and have been from the beginning. You are incapable of recognizing what you mean to present and to hide your stupidity resort to namecalling and general obfuscation. Do you think you will get anywhere that way—but in jail or the insane asylum where you are now? Mussolini led you there, he was your adolescent hero—or was it Jefferson? You still don't know the difference.

Clear as mud—and for the same reason: too many insoluble particles suspended throughout the mass. Never mind, Ez, I hope we can still be friends. You have been of assistance to the world as a recorder of facts and I respect and really love you for it. Your letter says more than your enclosures otherwise.

It is comprehensible at least that we may have saved ourselves 2 or 3 billion dollars debt during the recent war with a valid

---

[1] A ward in St. Elizabeth's Hospital.

banking system—but in the rush of financing our money supply what could we have done other? We weren't governed by crooks, as you persist in saying, but by men who had to employ the instruments that were ready to hand; that they were not revolutionary geniuses may be true but they had a going country on their hands and many enemies such as you had to deal with. I "feel" that much that you say is right. I have tried to follow you as best I can and I am intelligent enough as I tried to follow the teachings of Major Douglass. But you don't come CLEAR enough, and the only result is further obfuscation: as fast as you open your mouths you put your feet in them.

But you personally do write poems that are at best supremely beautiful. I'm afraid that for the moment I'll have to let it go at that. I'll go on reading what I can and when a glimmer of brilliant exposition comes through the fog of your verbiage I hope I will still be alive to recognize it.

Greetings to Dorothy. Have been seeing more of Violer recently.

BILL

Index